Bahá'í Publishing, 401 Greenleaf Avenue, Wilmette, Illinois 60091-2844
Copyright © 2011 by Aaron Emmel and C. Aaron Kreader
All rights reserved. Published 2011
Printed in the United States of America on acid-free paper ∞

19 18 17 16   4 3 2

Library of Congress Cataloging-in-Publication Data
Emmel, Aaron.
    Zanjan / story by Aaron Emmel, art by C. Aaron Kreader.
        p. cm.
    ISBN 978-1-931847-88-9 (alk. paper)
    1. Young men—Fiction. 2. Bahai Faith—Fiction. 3. Zanjan (Iran)—
    Fiction. I. Kreader, C. Aaron. II. Title.

PS3605.M56Z36 2011
813'.6—dc22
                        2011025509

Book and cover design by C. Aaron Kreader
Illuminating Graphics by Bridgette Schnider
Arabic Caligraphy on page 104 by Tarek A. Ghanem

CONTENTS

PREFACE

This is a work of fiction based on actual events. Navid, Danesh, Cyrus, Iman, Mírzá Behrang, Mullá Karím, and their families are fictional characters. Hujjat, Zaynab, and the other characters are real.

The primary inspiration for the story that follows is *The Dawn-Breakers*, a history written by Nabíl-i-A'zam and translated by Shoghi Effendi. I encourage anyone whose imagination is fired by *Zanján* to return to the source by reading Nabíl-i-A'zam's narrative. I have also consulted the *Chronicle of 'Abdu'l-Ahad Zanjáni: Personal Reminiscences of the Insurrection at Zanján*, translated by E. G. Browne; John Walbridge's *Essays and Notes on Bábí and Bahá'í History*; and *The Bábí and Bahá'í Religions, 1844–1944: Some Contemporary Western Accounts*, edited by Moojan Momen.

Although the various accounts agree on the main events, some of their details differ. In these cases, I have favored those details that seem most consistent with the other available information. I have simplified, combined, and otherwise lightly edited some dialogue in order to be able to present the story in graphic novel format, particularly where points are repeated or where different sources disagree. The comments of fictional characters are invented, as are some brief comments of historical figures in places where what they actually said is not recorded, but without going beyond historical facts as known. Two additional liberties, which I did not base on any sources, are the name of Zaynab's village and Haji Sulayman Khan's presence in Zanjan. In all cases, I have tried to remain faithful to the facts as they are known: in other words, although not everything in this novel did happen, much of it did, and, to my knowledge, Navid's story could have occurred.

I am extremely grateful to Bijan Bayzaee for patiently answering what must have seemed a near-endless barrage of questions about the arcana of Persian culture and history; to Hoda Movagh for her insights and advice; and to Dr. Manuchehr Derakhshani for connecting me with invaluable reference materials, particularly his first edition, 1885 copy of S. G. W. Benjamin's *Persia and the Persians*. I am also indebted to Dr. Kavian Milani, Gloria Shahzadeh, and Dr. Wendi Momen for helping me to refine my understanding of a series of events that helped to signal a turning point in human history.

I also want to thank our editors, Ariana Brown and Terry Cassiday. Terry championed this book and never wavered in her support. She passed away before the art was completed, but she is a part of this project, and she is one of the main reasons that now you are holding it in your hands.

—Aaron Emmel

Dedicated to the Bahá'ís of Iran and
everyone who suffers because of their faith.

1: HERETIC

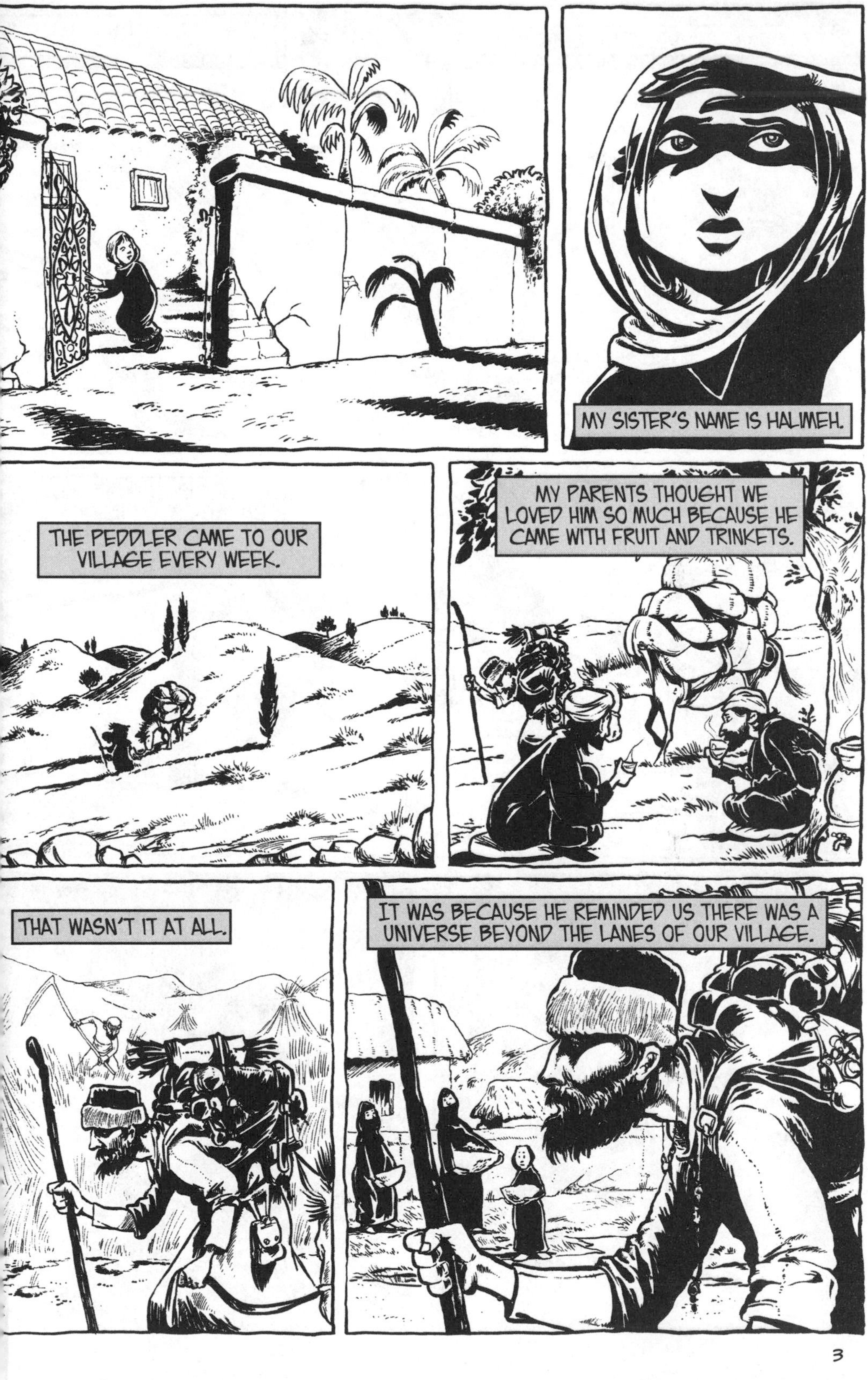
MY SISTER'S NAME IS HALIMEH.
THE PEDDLER CAME TO OUR VILLAGE EVERY WEEK.
MY PARENTS THOUGHT WE LOVED HIM SO MUCH BECAUSE HE CAME WITH FRUIT AND TRINKETS.
THAT WASN'T IT AT ALL.
IT WAS BECAUSE HE REMINDED US THERE WAS A UNIVERSE BEYOND THE LANES OF OUR VILLAGE.

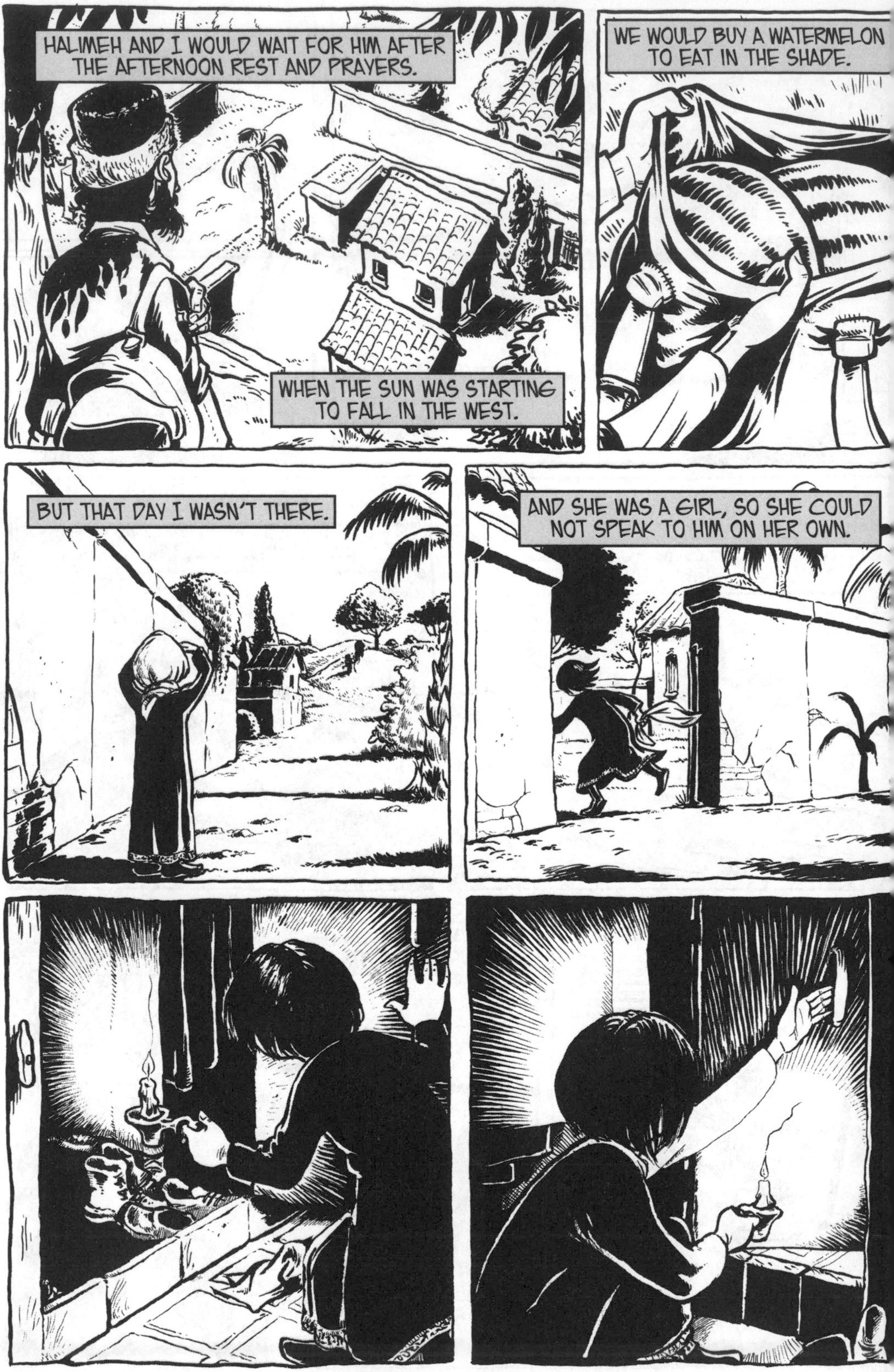

HALIMEH AND I WOULD WAIT FOR HIM AFTER THE AFTERNOON REST AND PRAYERS.
WHEN THE SUN WAS STARTING TO FALL IN THE WEST.
WE WOULD BUY A WATERMELON TO EAT IN THE SHADE.
BUT THAT DAY I WASN'T THERE.
AND SHE WAS A GIRL, SO SHE COULD NOT SPEAK TO HIM ON HER OWN.

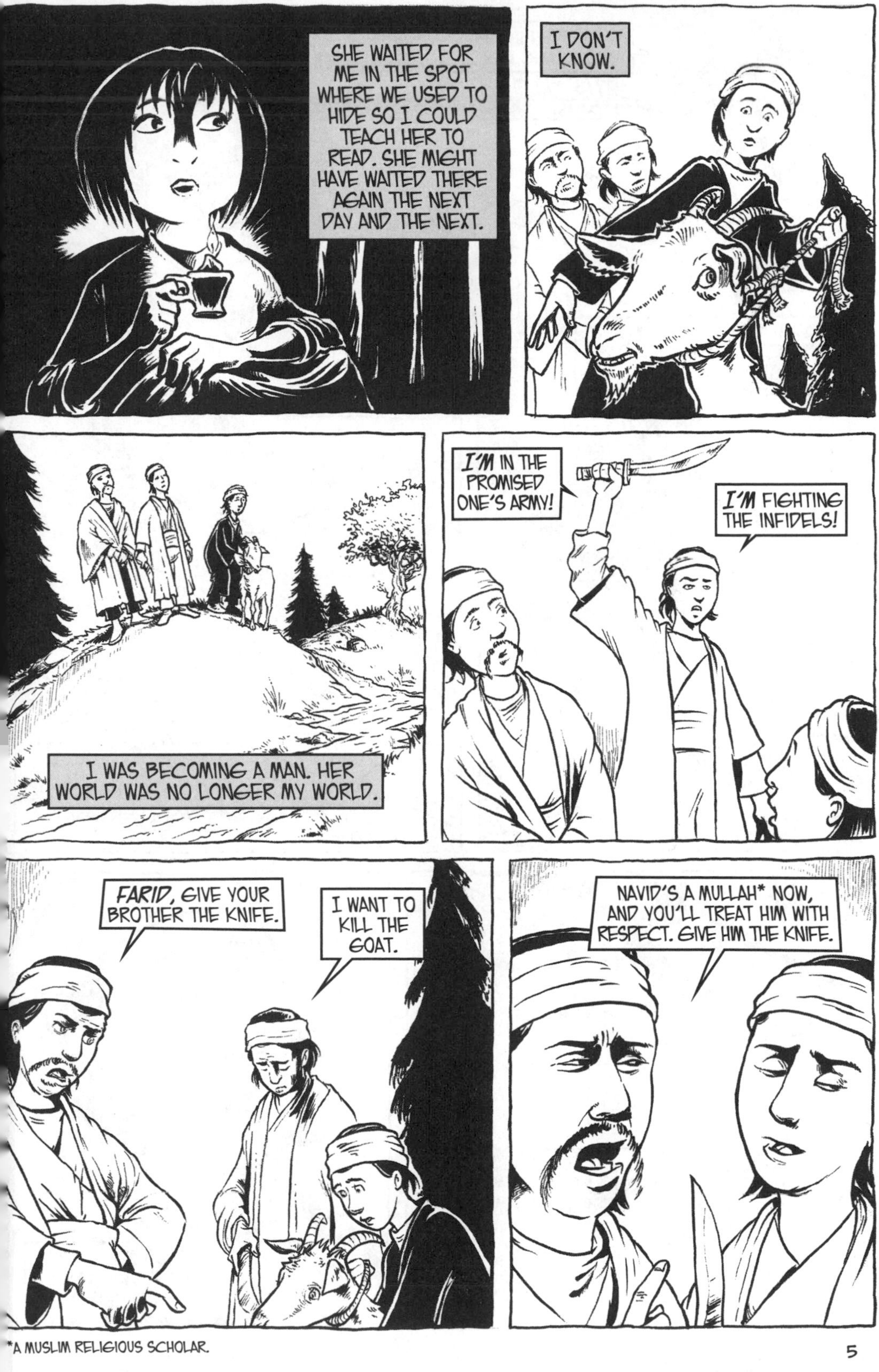
SHE WAITED FOR ME IN THE SPOT WHERE WE USED TO HIDE SO I COULD TEACH HER TO READ. SHE MIGHT HAVE WAITED THERE AGAIN THE NEXT DAY AND THE NEXT.
I DON'T KNOW.
I WAS BECOMING A MAN. HER WORLD WAS NO LONGER MY WORLD.
I'M IN THE PROMISED ONE'S ARMY!
I'M FIGHTING THE INFIDELS!
FARID, GIVE YOUR BROTHER THE KNIFE.
I WANT TO KILL THE GOAT.
NAVID'S A MULLAH* NOW, AND YOU'LL TREAT HIM WITH RESPECT. GIVE HIM THE KNIFE.

*A MUSLIM RELIGIOUS SCHOLAR.

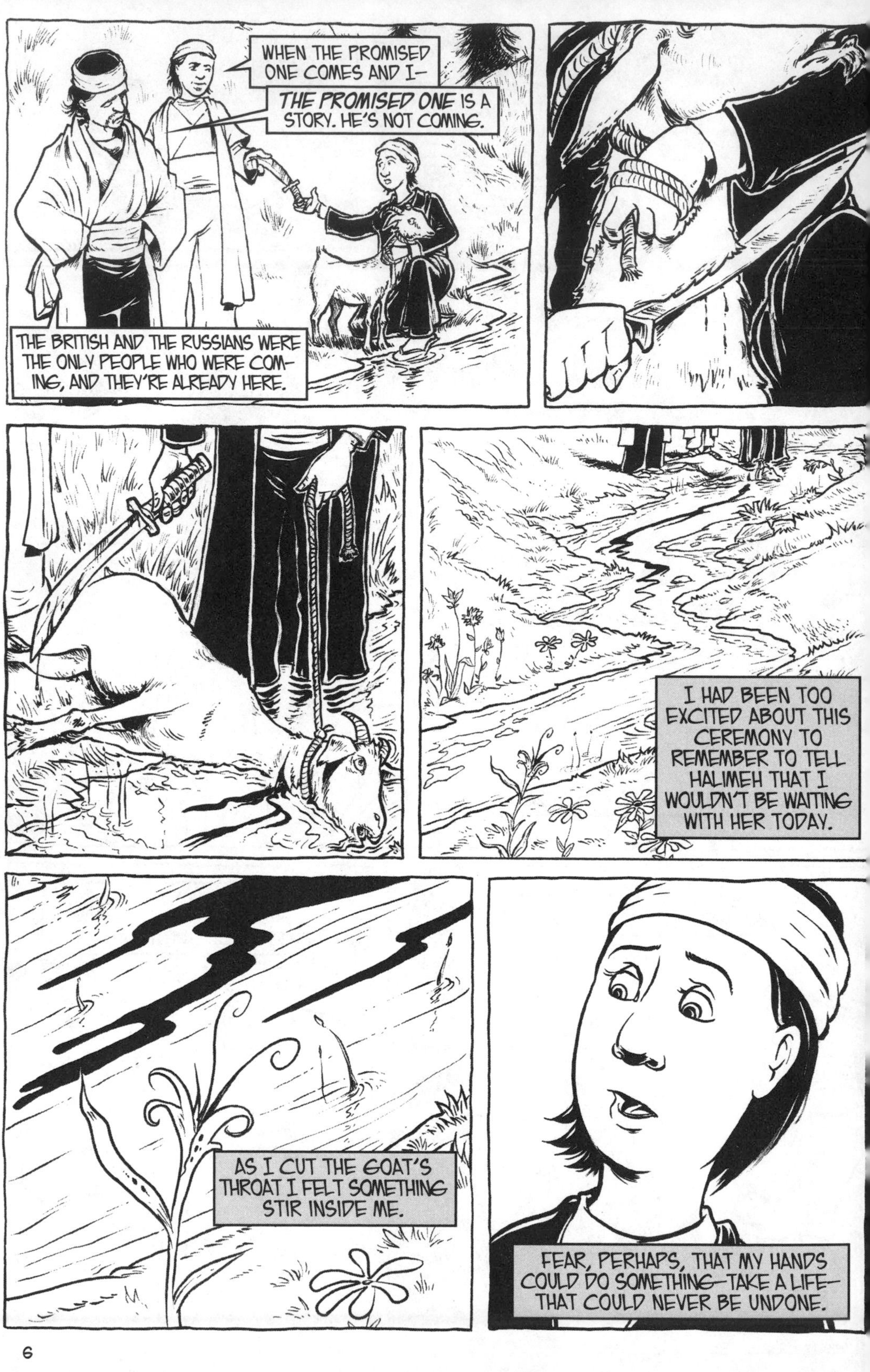
WHEN THE PROMISED ONE COMES AND I—
THE PROMISED ONE IS A STORY. HE'S NOT COMING.
THE BRITISH AND THE RUSSIANS WERE THE ONLY PEOPLE WHO WERE COMING, AND THEY'RE ALREADY HERE.
I HAD BEEN TOO EXCITED ABOUT THIS CEREMONY TO REMEMBER TO TELL HALIMEH THAT I WOULDN'T BE WAITING WITH HER TODAY.
AS I CUT THE GOAT'S THROAT I FELT SOMETHING STIR INSIDE ME.
FEAR, PERHAPS, THAT MY HANDS COULD DO SOMETHING—TAKE A LIFE—THAT COULD NEVER BE UNDONE.

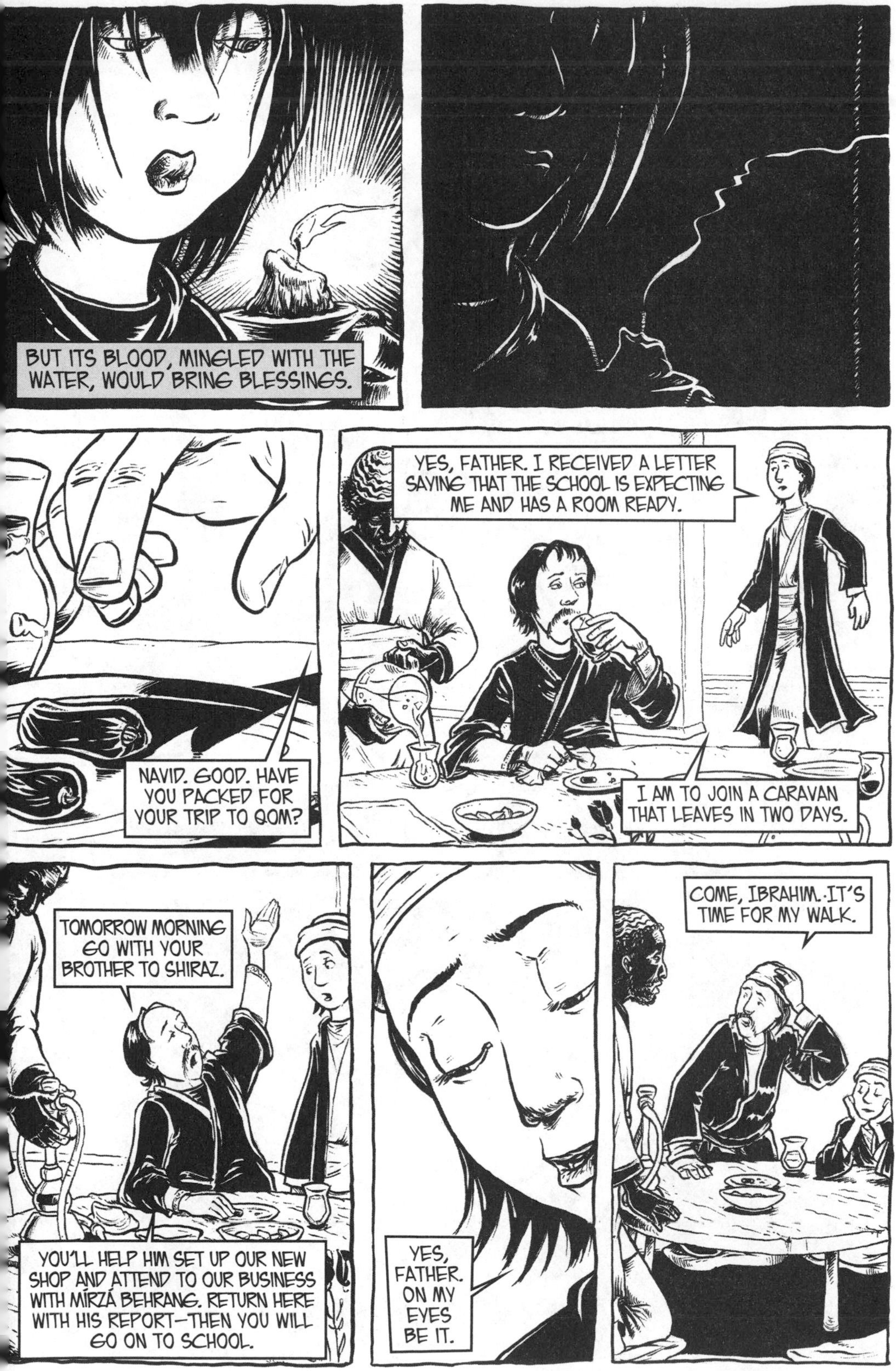
BUT ITS BLOOD, MINGLED WITH THE WATER, WOULD BRING BLESSINGS.
NAVID. GOOD. HAVE YOU PACKED FOR YOUR TRIP TO QOM?
YES, FATHER. I RECEIVED A LETTER SAYING THAT THE SCHOOL IS EXPECTING ME AND HAS A ROOM READY.
I AM TO JOIN A CARAVAN THAT LEAVES IN TWO DAYS.
TOMORROW MORNING GO WITH YOUR BROTHER TO SHIRAZ.
YOU'LL HELP HIM SET UP OUR NEW SHOP AND ATTEND TO OUR BUSINESS WITH MÍRZÁ BEHRANG. RETURN HERE WITH HIS REPORT—THEN YOU WILL GO ON TO SCHOOL.
YES, FATHER. ON MY EYES BE IT.
COME, IBRAHIM. IT'S TIME FOR MY WALK.

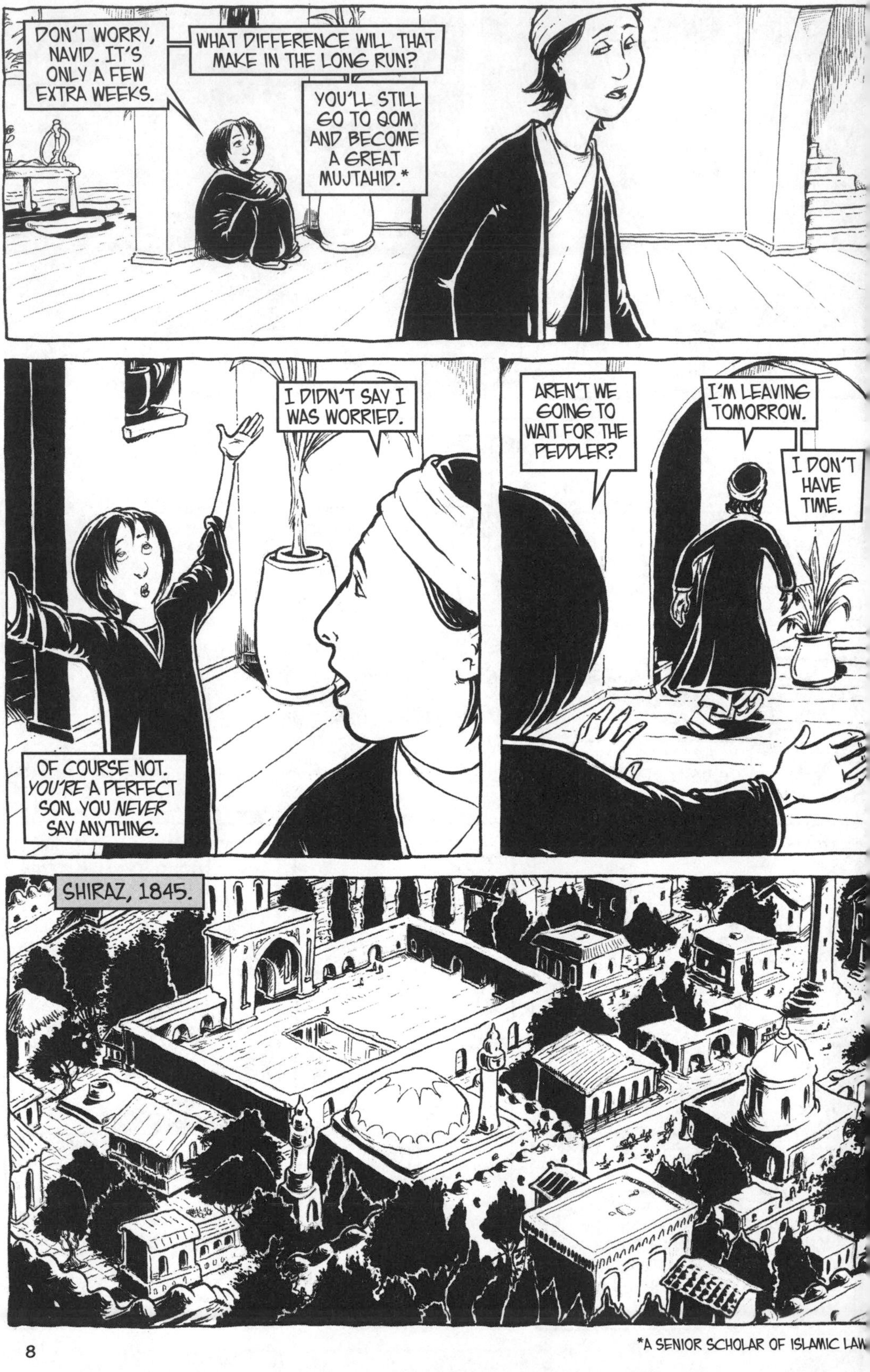
DON'T WORRY, NAVID. IT'S ONLY A FEW EXTRA WEEKS.
WHAT DIFFERENCE WILL THAT MAKE IN THE LONG RUN?
YOU'LL STILL GO TO QOM AND BECOME A GREAT MUJTAHID.*
I DIDN'T SAY I WAS WORRIED.
OF COURSE NOT. YOU'RE A PERFECT SON. YOU NEVER SAY ANYTHING.
AREN'T WE GOING TO WAIT FOR THE PEDDLER?
I'M LEAVING TOMORROW.
I DON'T HAVE TIME.
SHIRAZ, 1845.

*A SENIOR SCHOLAR OF ISLAMIC LAW

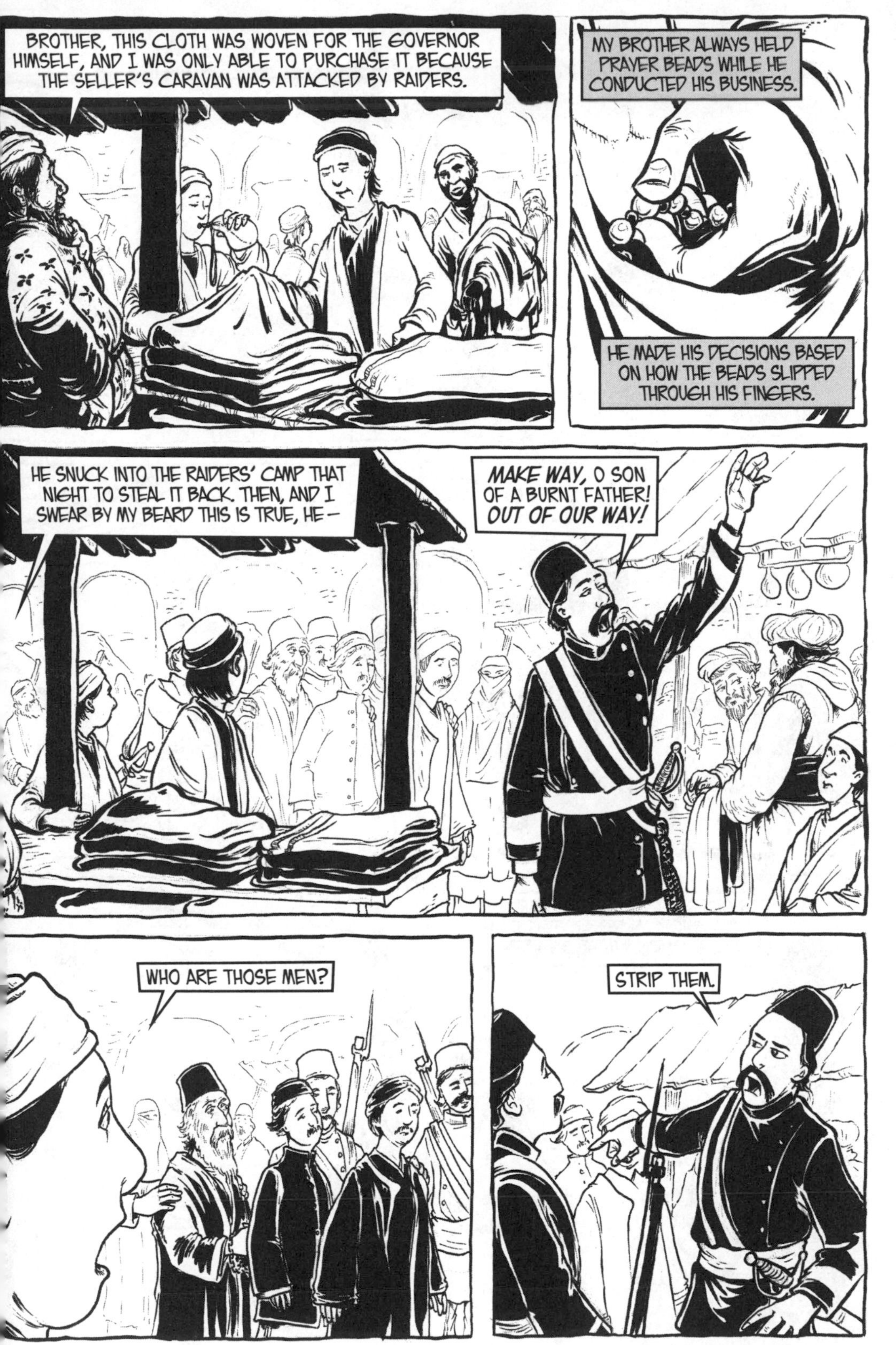
BROTHER, THIS CLOTH WAS WOVEN FOR THE GOVERNOR HIMSELF, AND I WAS ONLY ABLE TO PURCHASE IT BECAUSE THE SELLER'S CARAVAN WAS ATTACKED BY RAIDERS.
MY BROTHER ALWAYS HELD PRAYER BEADS WHILE HE CONDUCTED HIS BUSINESS.
HE MADE HIS DECISIONS BASED ON HOW THE BEADS SLIPPED THROUGH HIS FINGERS.
HE SNUCK INTO THE RAIDERS' CAMP THAT NIGHT TO STEAL IT BACK. THEN, AND I SWEAR BY MY BEARD THIS IS TRUE, HE—
MAKE WAY, O SON OF A BURNT FATHER! OUT OF OUR WAY!
WHO ARE THOSE MEN?
STRIP THEM.

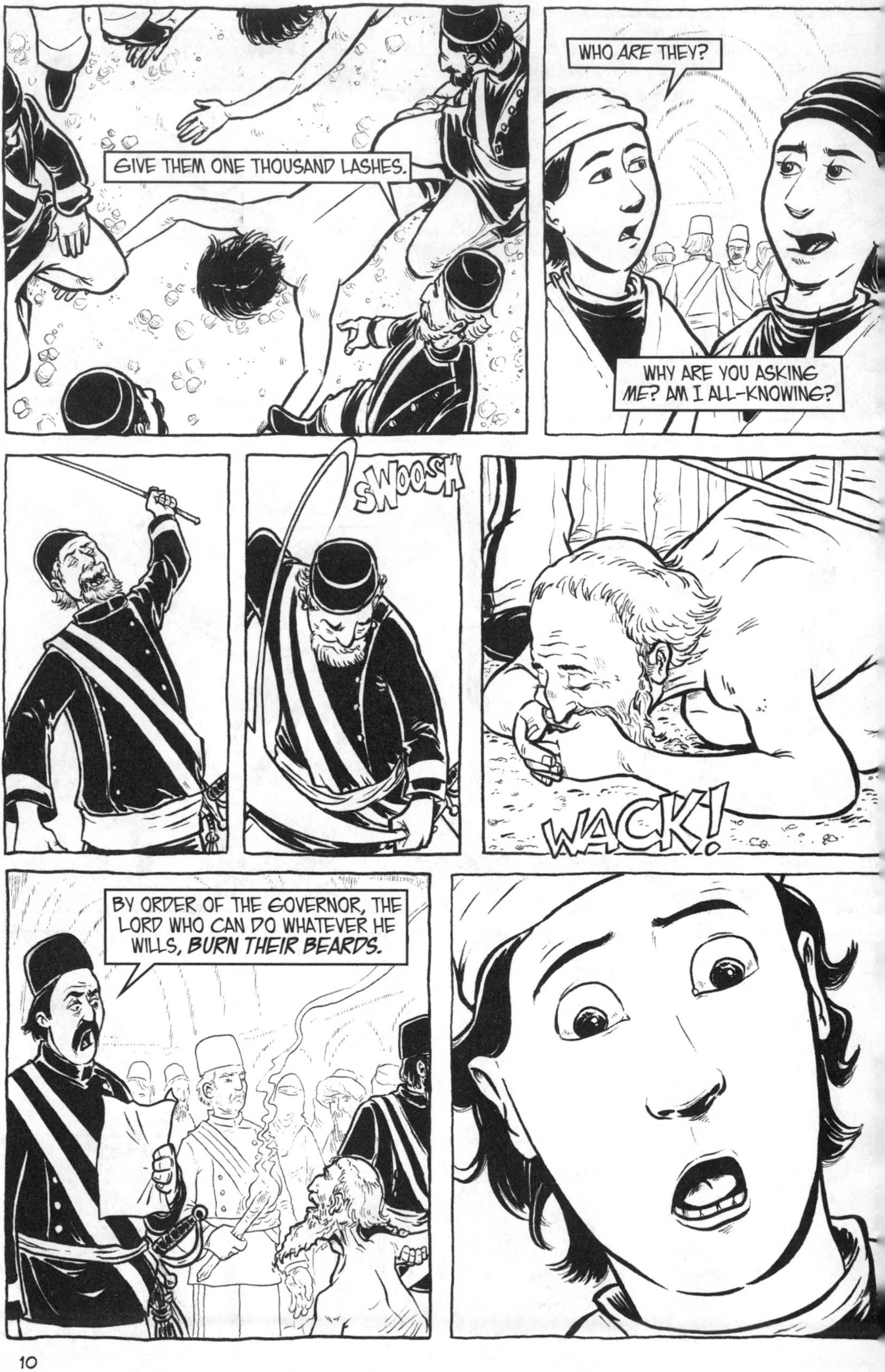
GIVE THEM ONE THOUSAND LASHES.
WHO ARE THEY?
WHY ARE YOU ASKING ME? AM I ALL-KNOWING?
SWOOSH
WACK!
BY ORDER OF THE GOVERNOR, THE LORD WHO CAN DO WHATEVER HE WILLS, BURN THEIR BEARDS.

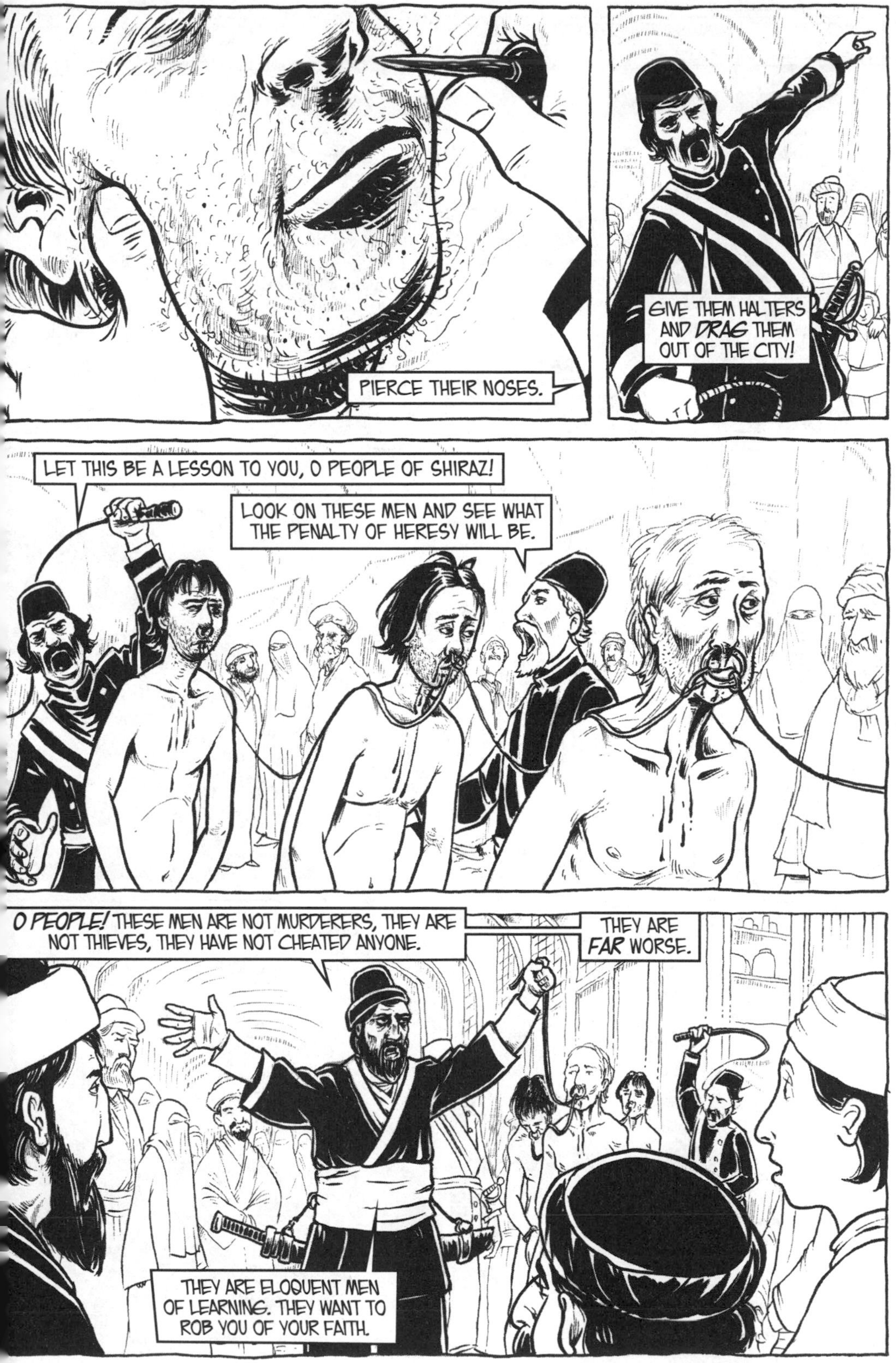
PIERCE THEIR NOSES.
GIVE THEM HALTERS AND DRAG THEM OUT OF THE CITY!
LET THIS BE A LESSON TO YOU, O PEOPLE OF SHIRAZ!
LOOK ON THESE MEN AND SEE WHAT THE PENALTY OF HERESY WILL BE.
O PEOPLE! THESE MEN ARE NOT MURDERERS, THEY ARE NOT THIEVES, THEY HAVE NOT CHEATED ANYONE.
THEY ARE FAR WORSE.
THEY ARE ELOQUENT MEN OF LEARNING. THEY WANT TO ROB YOU OF YOUR FAITH.

SINCE WE ARE PARADING THESE ENEMIES FOR YOU TO BEHOLD, YOU MUST BE GENEROUS WITH YOUR GIFTS TO US.

WHAT MANNER OF GIFT IS *THAT*—A SIMPLE POLE?

I TOO WANT A SHARE OF THIS RIGHTEOUS DEED.

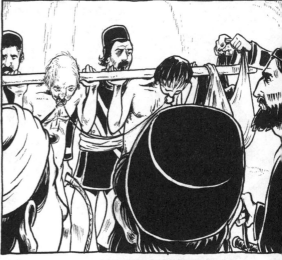

THERE *MUST* BE A WAY TO HELP THEM.

WHY? THEY'RE HERETICS. YOU'RE A MULLAH. ISN'T IT YOUR DUTY TO DEFEND THE FAITH AGAINST MEN LIKE THESE?

YOU HAVE OPINIONS THAT YOU WANT ME TO PASS ON TO THE GOVERNOR, BROTHERS?

12

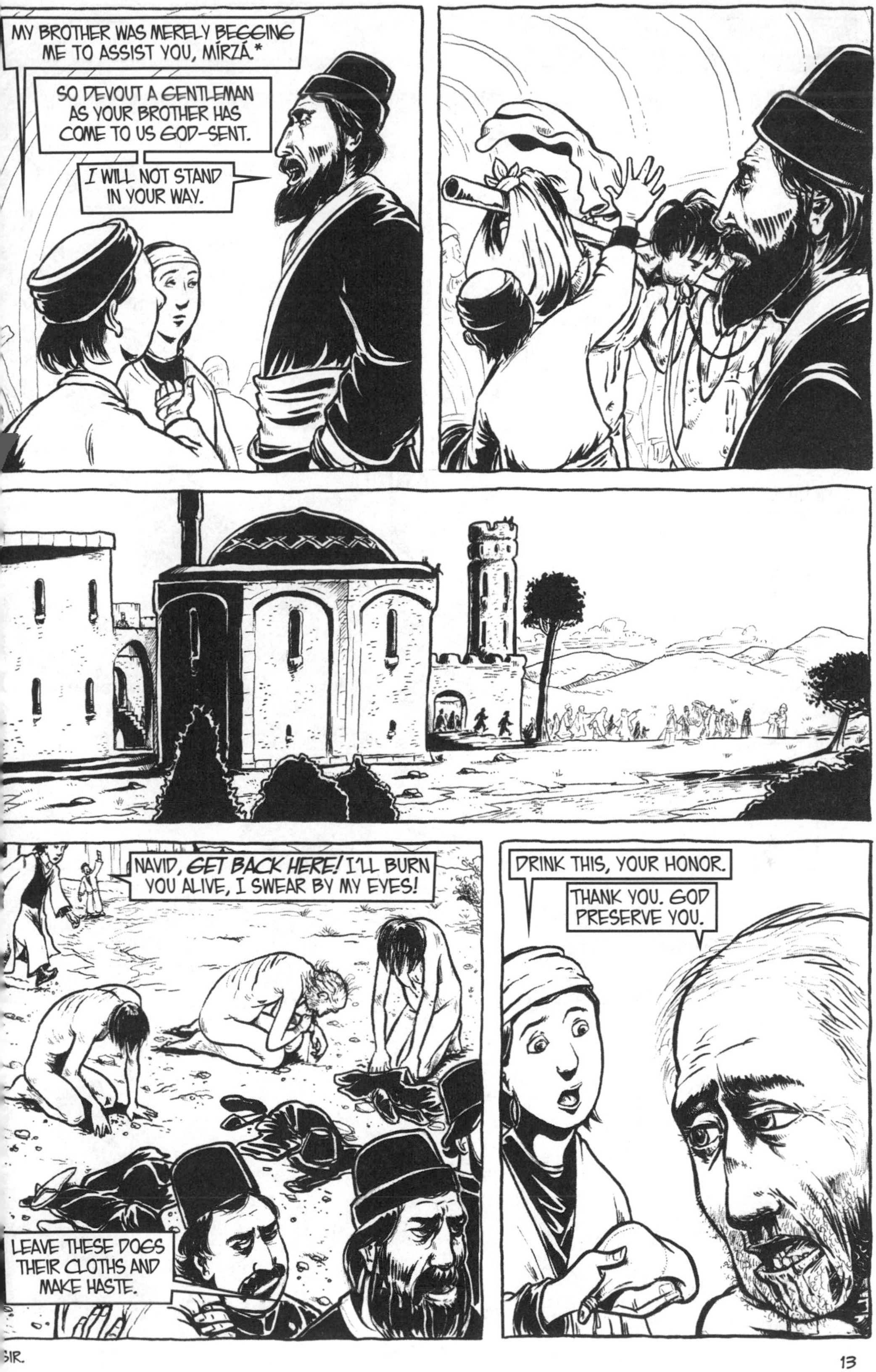
MY BROTHER WAS MERELY BEGGING ME TO ASSIST YOU, MÍRZÁ.*
SO DEVOUT A GENTLEMAN AS YOUR BROTHER HAS COME TO US GOD-SENT.
I WILL NOT STAND IN YOUR WAY.
NAVID, GET BACK HERE! I'LL BURN YOU ALIVE, I SWEAR BY MY EYES!
LEAVE THESE DOGS THEIR CLOTHS AND MAKE HASTE.
DRINK THIS, YOUR HONOR.
THANK YOU. GOD PRESERVE YOU.

SIR.

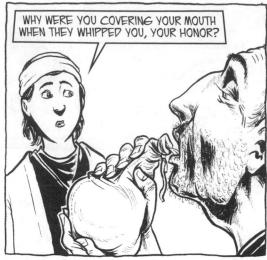

WHY WERE YOU COVERING YOUR MOUTH WHEN THEY WHIPPED YOU, YOUR HONOR?

THE FIRST SEVEN STROKES WERE SEVERELY PAINFUL.

TO THE REST I SEEMED TO GROW INDIFFERENT.

I WONDERED IF THE STROKES THAT FOLLOWED WERE ACTUALLY BEING APPLIED TO MY OWN BODY.

I CAN NOW REALIZE HOW THE ALMIGHTY DELIVERER IS ABLE TO TURN PAIN INTO EASE.

YOU SEE, A FEELING OF JOYOUS EXULTATION HAD INVADED MY SOUL.

NAVID! COME HERE!

I WAS TRYING TO RESTRAIN MY LAUGHTER.

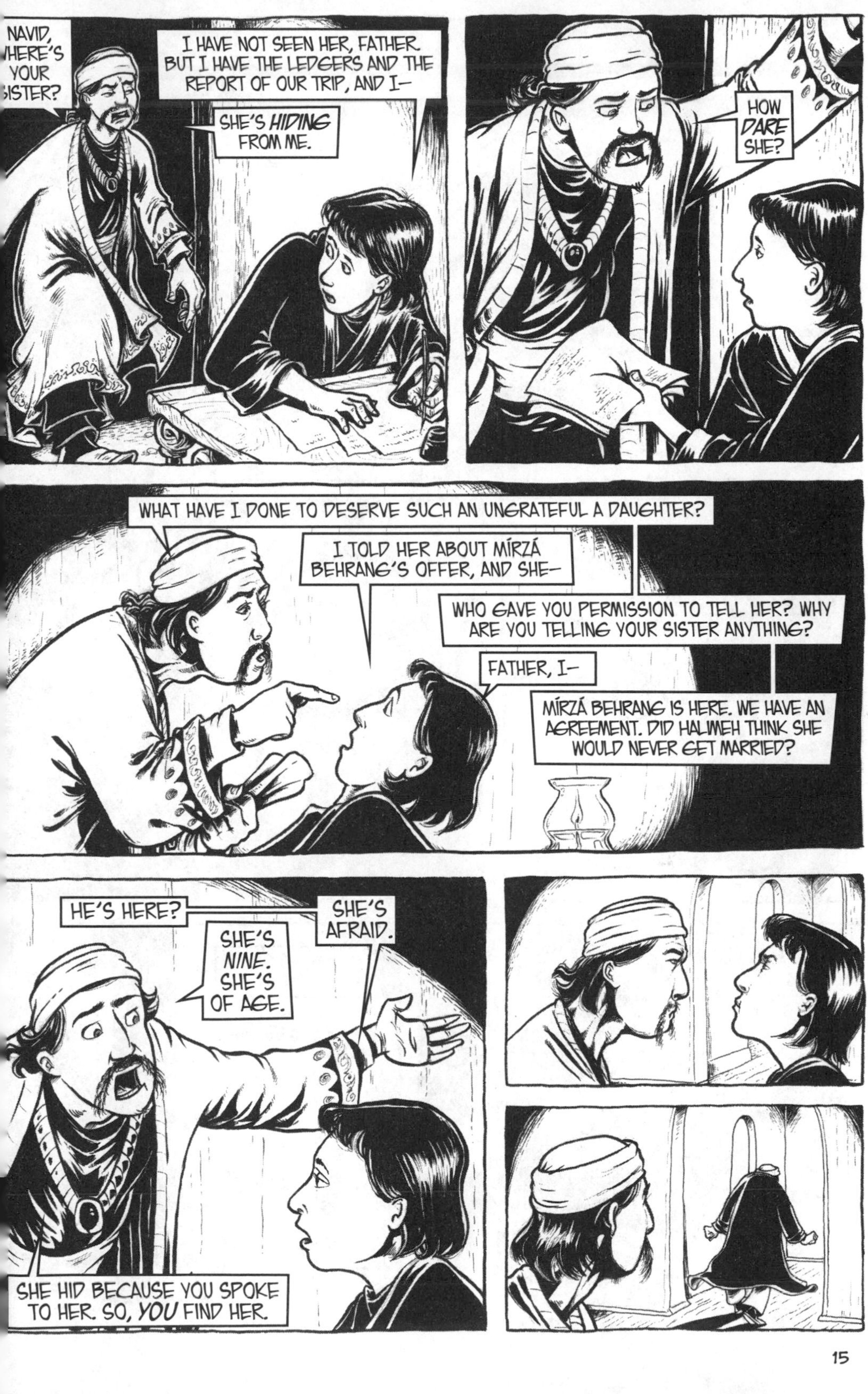
NAVID, WHERE'S YOUR SISTER?
I HAVE NOT SEEN HER, FATHER. BUT I HAVE THE LEDGERS AND THE REPORT OF OUR TRIP, AND I—
SHE'S HIDING FROM ME.
HOW DARE SHE?
WHAT HAVE I DONE TO DESERVE SUCH AN UNGRATEFUL A DAUGHTER?
I TOLD HER ABOUT MÍRZÁ BEHRANG'S OFFER, AND SHE—
WHO GAVE YOU PERMISSION TO TELL HER? WHY ARE YOU TELLING YOUR SISTER ANYTHING?
FATHER, I—
MÍRZÁ BEHRANG IS HERE. WE HAVE AN AGREEMENT. DID HALIMEH THINK SHE WOULD NEVER GET MARRIED?
HE'S HERE?
SHE'S AFRAID.
SHE'S NINE. SHE'S OF AGE.
SHE HID BECAUSE YOU SPOKE TO HER. SO, YOU FIND HER.

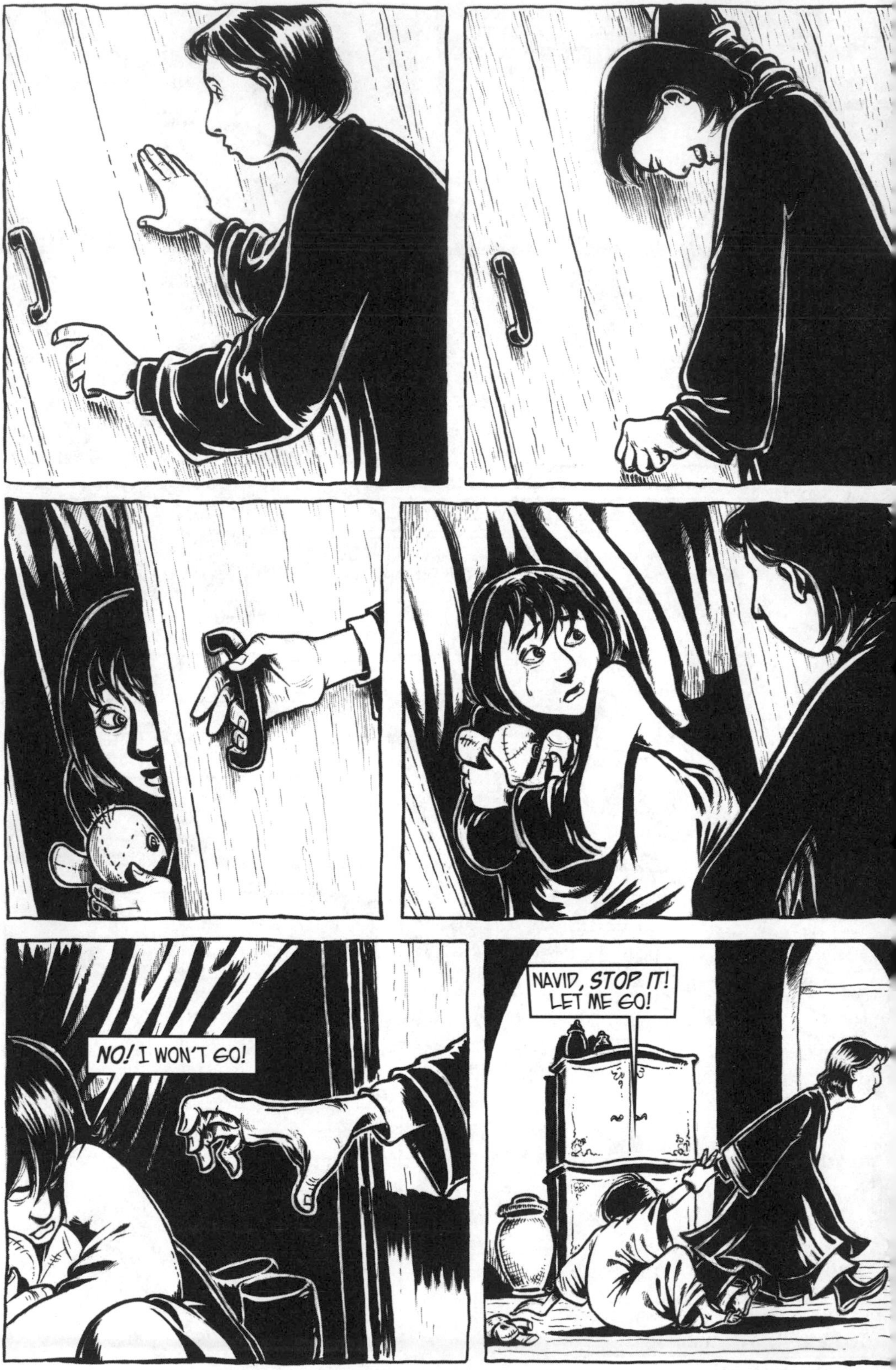
NO! I WON'T GO!
NAVID, STOP IT! LET ME GO!

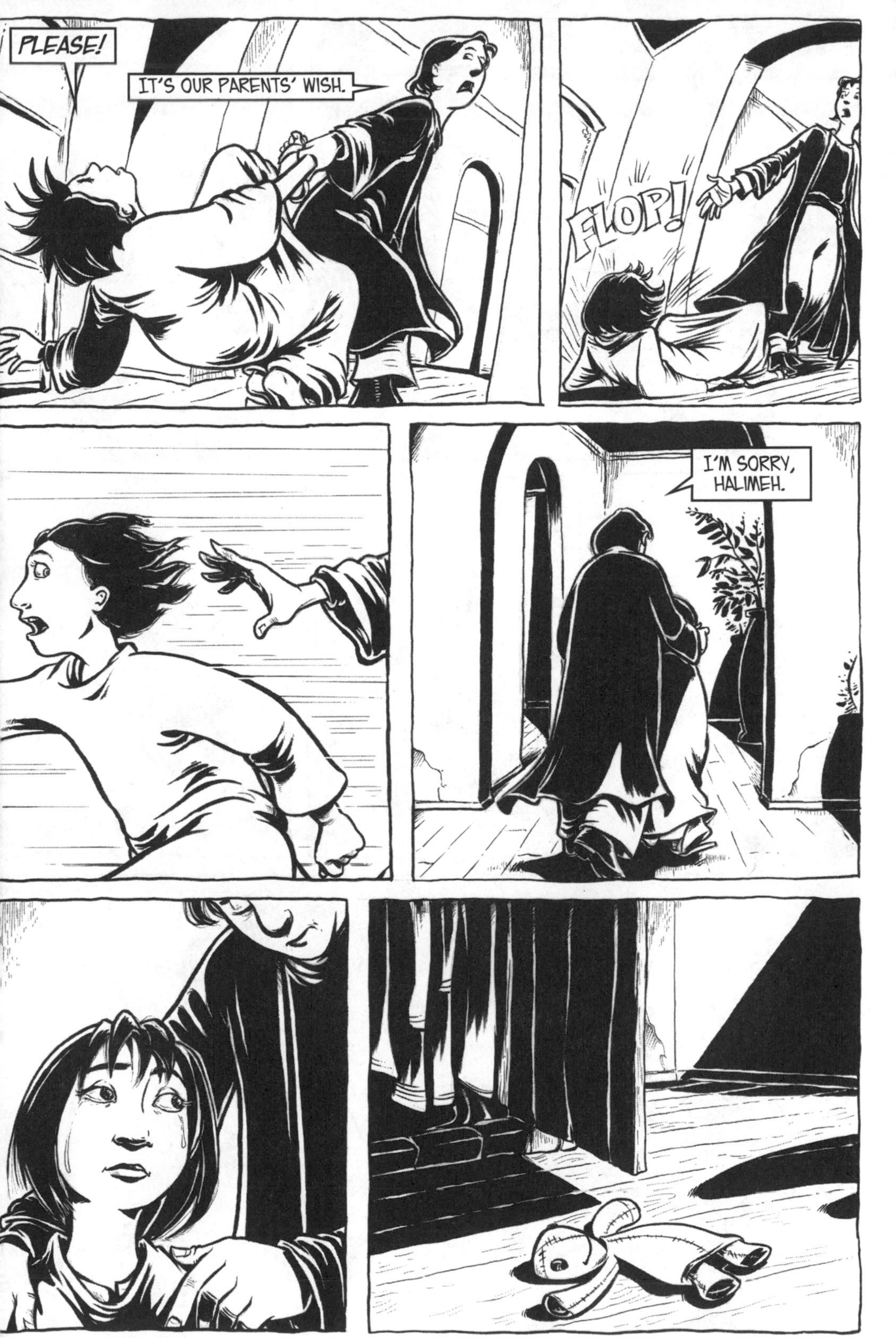
PLEASE!
IT'S OUR PARENTS' WISH.
FLOP!
I'M SORRY, HALIMEH.

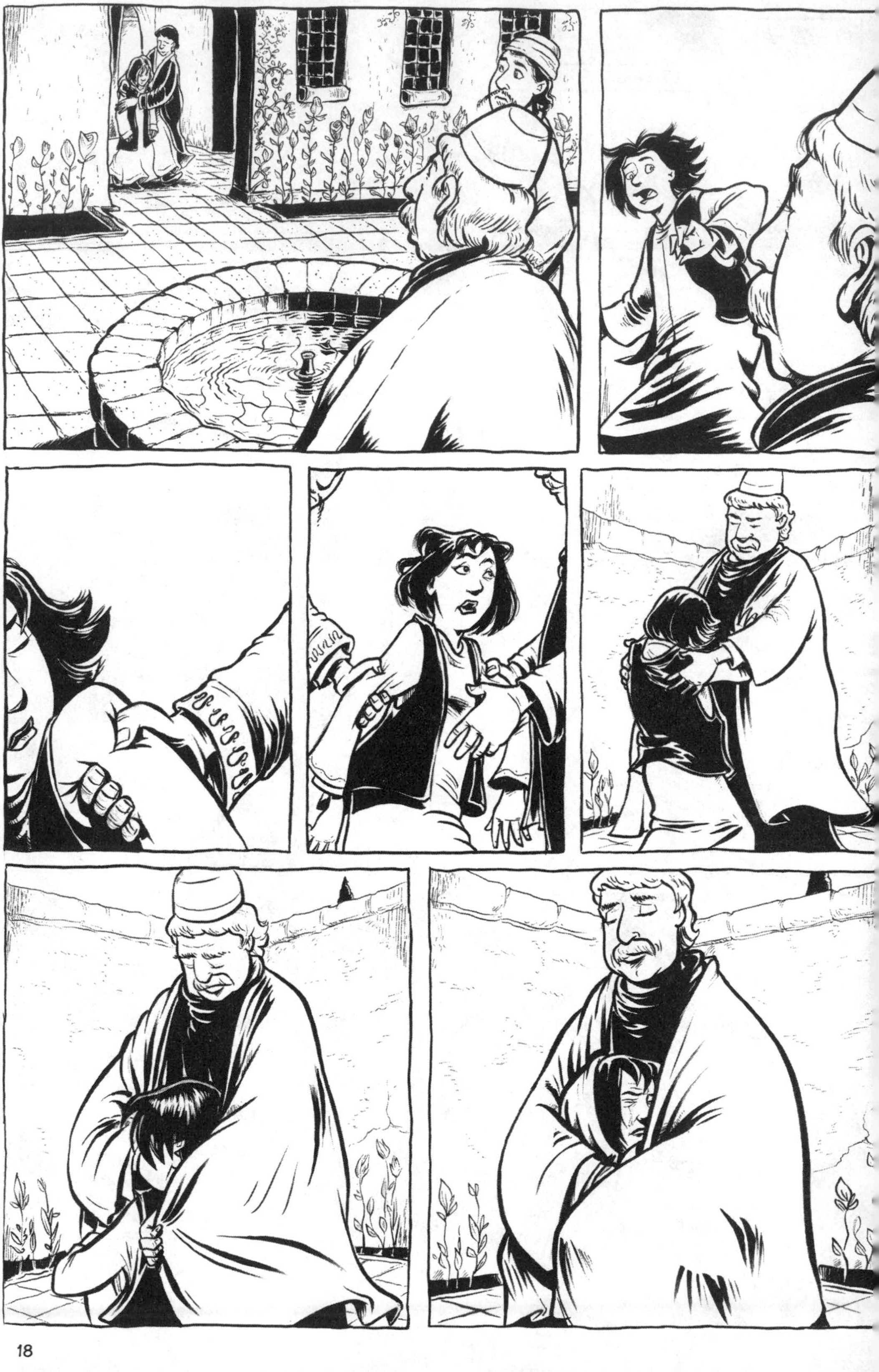

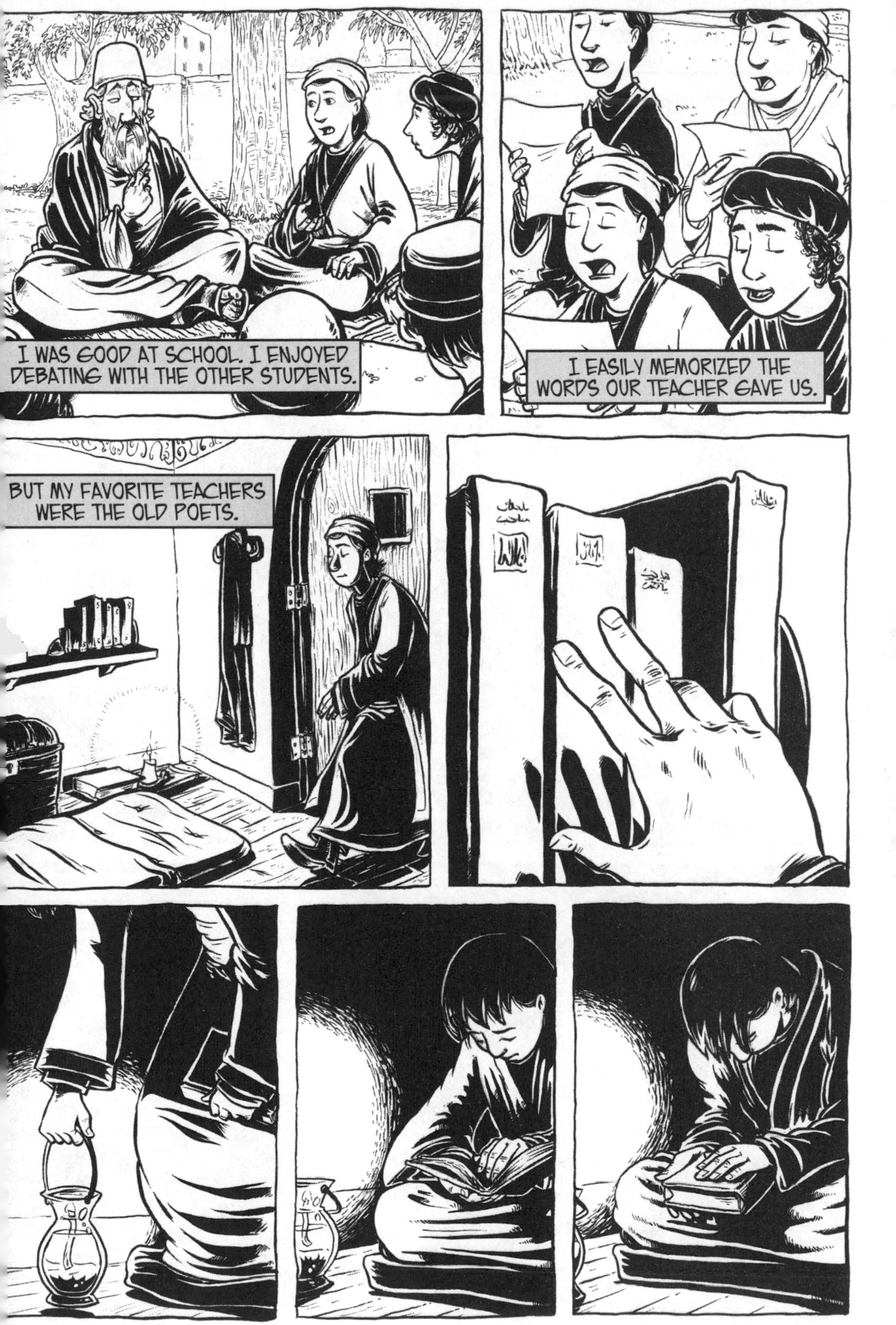
I WAS GOOD AT SCHOOL. I ENJOYED DEBATING WITH THE OTHER STUDENTS.
I EASILY MEMORIZED THE WORDS OUR TEACHER GAVE US.
BUT MY FAVORITE TEACHERS WERE THE OLD POETS.

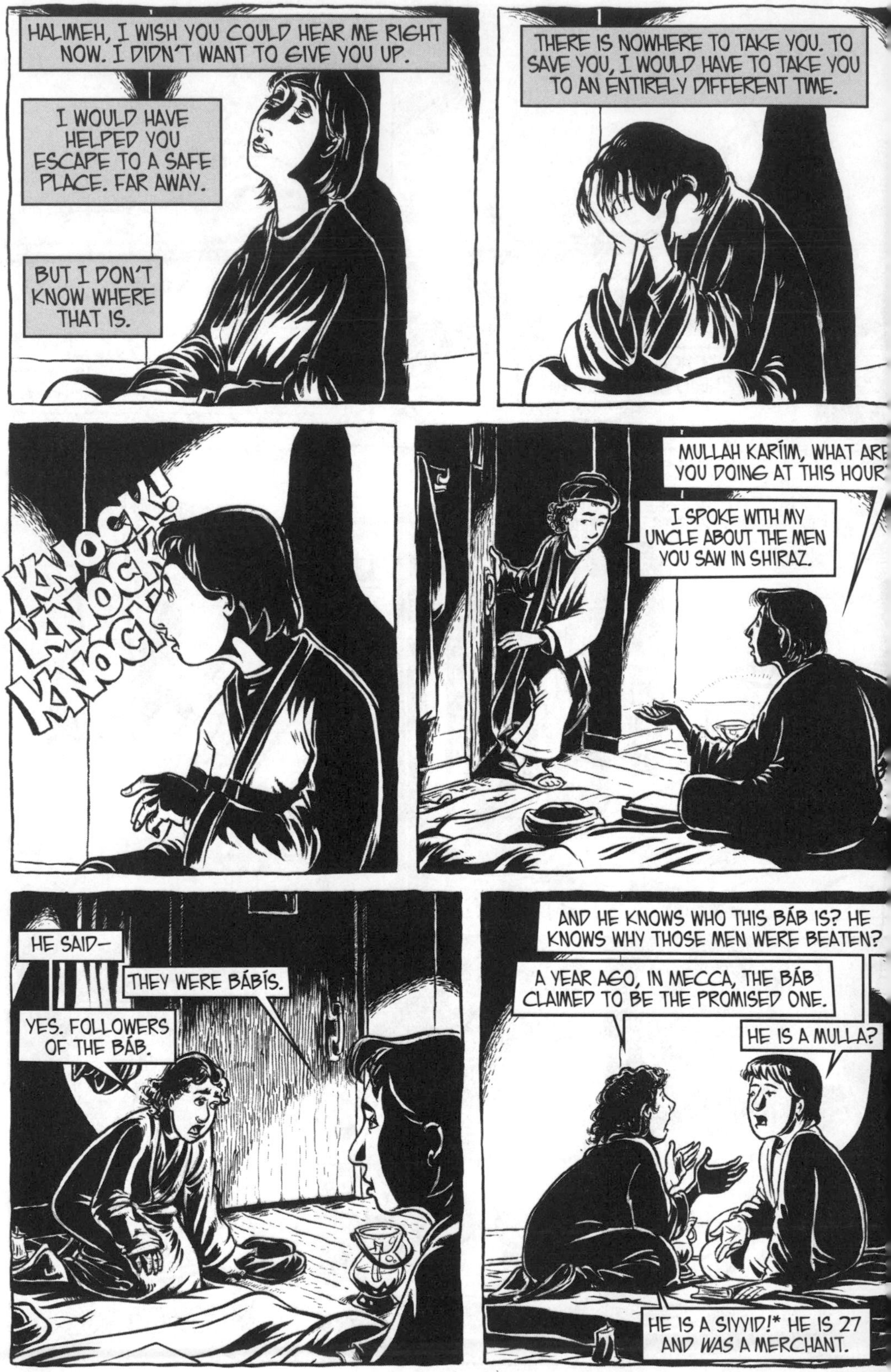
HALIMEH, I WISH YOU COULD HEAR ME RIGHT NOW. I DIDN'T WANT TO GIVE YOU UP.
I WOULD HAVE HELPED YOU ESCAPE TO A SAFE PLACE. FAR AWAY.
BUT I DON'T KNOW WHERE THAT IS.
THERE IS NOWHERE TO TAKE YOU. TO SAVE YOU, I WOULD HAVE TO TAKE YOU TO AN ENTIRELY DIFFERENT TIME.
KNOCK! KNOCK! KNOCK!
MULLAH KARÍM, WHAT ARE YOU DOING AT THIS HOUR
I SPOKE WITH MY UNCLE ABOUT THE MEN YOU SAW IN SHIRAZ.
HE SAID—
THEY WERE BÁBÍS.
YES. FOLLOWERS OF THE BÁB.
AND HE KNOWS WHO THIS BÁB IS? HE KNOWS WHY THOSE MEN WERE BEATEN?
A YEAR AGO, IN MECCA, THE BÁB CLAIMED TO BE THE PROMISED ONE.
HE IS A MULLA?
HE IS A SIYYID!* HE IS 27 AND *WAS* A MERCHANT.

*A DESCENDANT OF MUHAMM

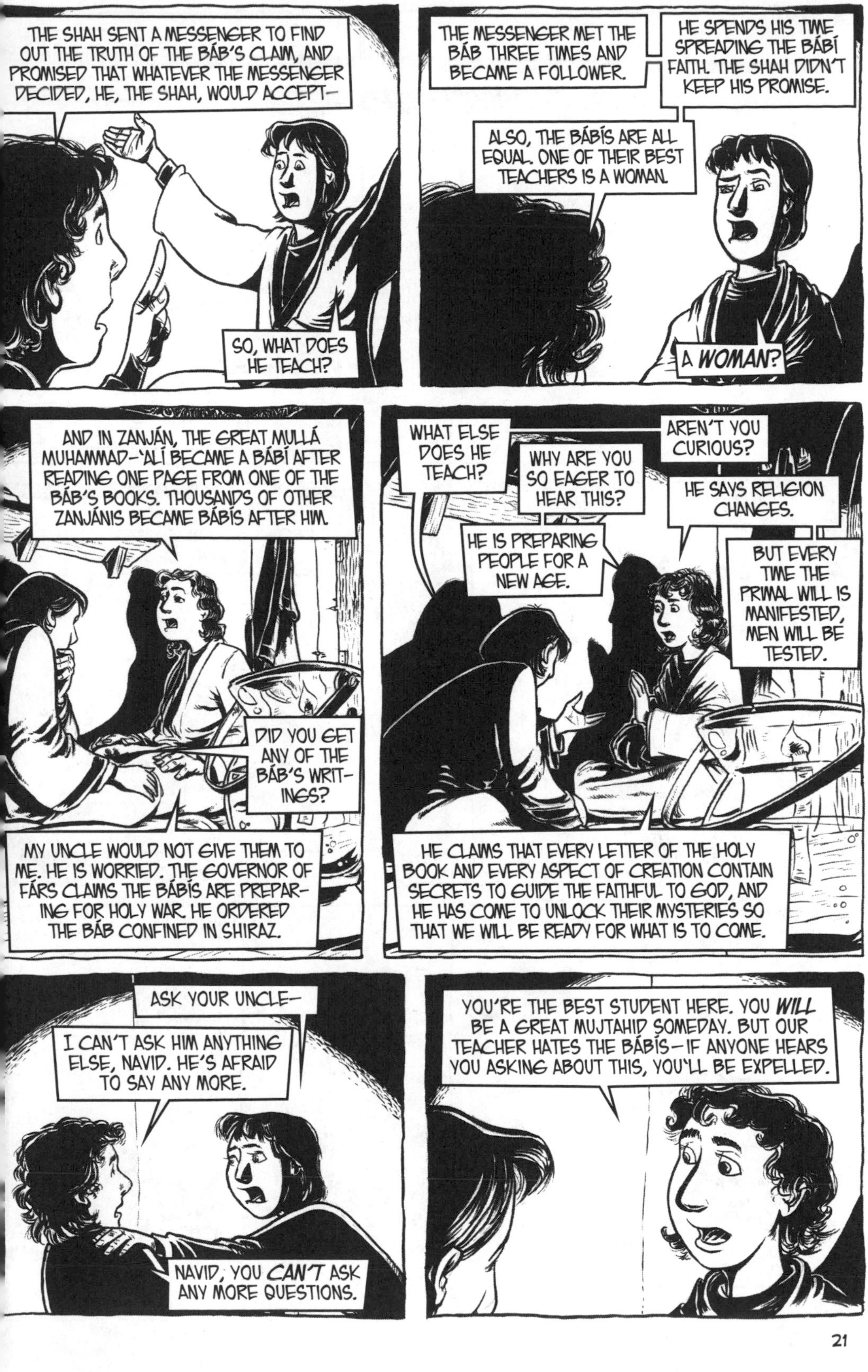
THE SHAH SENT A MESSENGER TO FIND OUT THE TRUTH OF THE BÁB'S CLAIM, AND PROMISED THAT WHATEVER THE MESSENGER DECIDED, HE, THE SHAH, WOULD ACCEPT–
SO, WHAT DOES HE TEACH?
THE MESSENGER MET THE BÁB THREE TIMES AND BECAME A FOLLOWER.
HE SPENDS HIS TIME SPREADING THE BÁBÍ FAITH. THE SHAH DIDN'T KEEP HIS PROMISE.
ALSO, THE BÁBÍS ARE ALL EQUAL. ONE OF THEIR BEST TEACHERS IS A WOMAN.
A *WOMAN*?
AND IN ZANJÁN, THE GREAT MULLÁ MUHAMMAD–'ALÍ BECAME A BÁBÍ AFTER READING ONE PAGE FROM ONE OF THE BÁB'S BOOKS. THOUSANDS OF OTHER ZANJÁNIS BECAME BÁBÍS AFTER HIM.
DID YOU GET ANY OF THE BÁB'S WRITINGS?
MY UNCLE WOULD NOT GIVE THEM TO ME. HE IS WORRIED. THE GOVERNOR OF FÁRS CLAIMS THE BÁBÍS ARE PREPARING FOR HOLY WAR. HE ORDERED THE BÁB CONFINED IN SHIRAZ.
WHAT ELSE DOES HE TEACH?
AREN'T YOU CURIOUS?
WHY ARE YOU SO EAGER TO HEAR THIS?
HE SAYS RELIGION CHANGES.
HE IS PREPARING PEOPLE FOR A NEW AGE.
BUT EVERY TIME THE PRIMAL WILL IS MANIFESTED, MEN WILL BE TESTED.
HE CLAIMS THAT EVERY LETTER OF THE HOLY BOOK AND EVERY ASPECT OF CREATION CONTAIN SECRETS TO GUIDE THE FAITHFUL TO GOD, AND HE HAS COME TO UNLOCK THEIR MYSTERIES SO THAT WE WILL BE READY FOR WHAT IS TO COME.
ASK YOUR UNCLE–
I CAN'T ASK HIM ANYTHING ELSE, NAVID. HE'S AFRAID TO SAY ANY MORE.
NAVID, YOU *CAN'T* ASK ANY MORE QUESTIONS.
YOU'RE THE BEST STUDENT HERE. YOU *WILL* BE A GREAT MUJTAHID SOMEDAY. BUT OUR TEACHER HATES THE BÁBÍS– IF ANYONE HEARS YOU ASKING ABOUT THIS, YOU'LL BE EXPELLED.

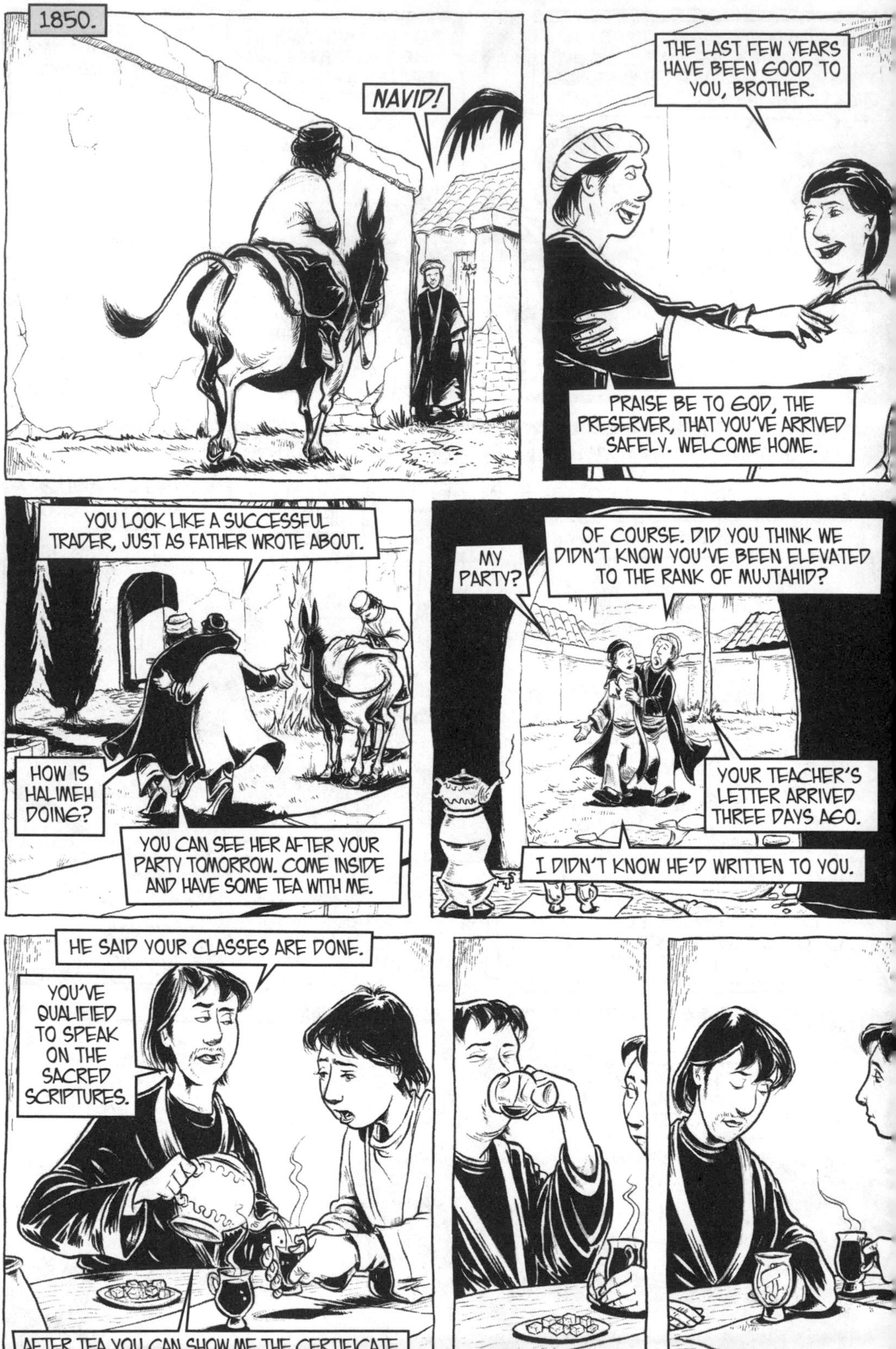
1850.
NAVID!
THE LAST FEW YEARS HAVE BEEN GOOD TO YOU, BROTHER.
PRAISE BE TO GOD, THE PRESERVER, THAT YOU'VE ARRIVED SAFELY. WELCOME HOME.
YOU LOOK LIKE A SUCCESSFUL TRADER, JUST AS FATHER WROTE ABOUT.
HOW IS HALIMEH DOING?
YOU CAN SEE HER AFTER YOUR PARTY TOMORROW. COME INSIDE AND HAVE SOME TEA WITH ME.
MY PARTY?
OF COURSE. DID YOU THINK WE DIDN'T KNOW YOU'VE BEEN ELEVATED TO THE RANK OF MUJTAHID?
YOUR TEACHER'S LETTER ARRIVED THREE DAYS AGO.
I DIDN'T KNOW HE'D WRITTEN TO YOU.
HE SAID YOUR CLASSES ARE DONE.
YOU'VE QUALIFIED TO SPEAK ON THE SACRED SCRIPTURES.
AFTER TEA YOU CAN SHOW ME THE CERTIFICATE.

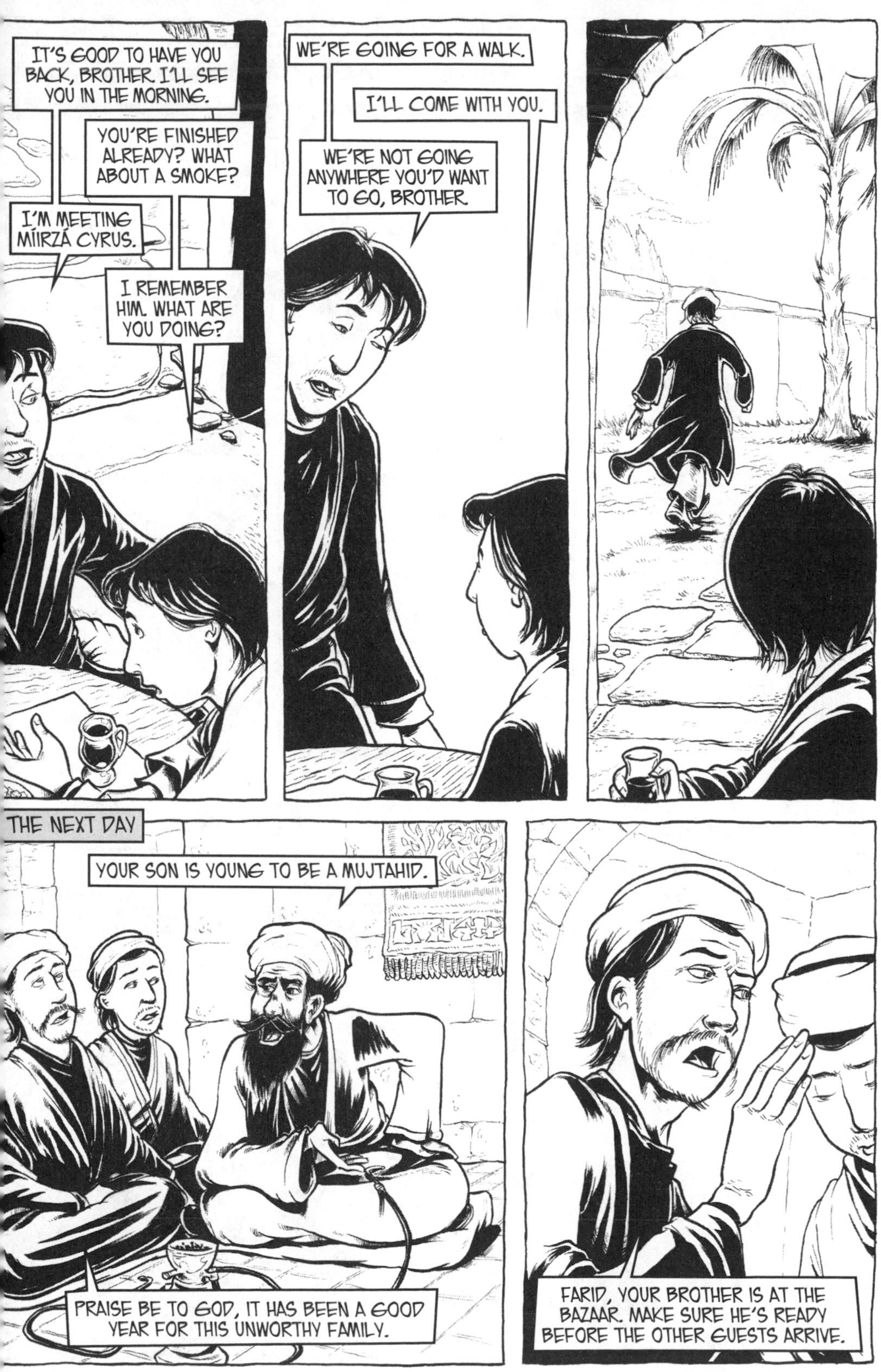
IT'S GOOD TO HAVE YOU BACK, BROTHER. I'LL SEE YOU IN THE MORNING.
YOU'RE FINISHED ALREADY? WHAT ABOUT A SMOKE?
I'M MEETING MÍIRZÁ CYRUS.
I REMEMBER HIM. WHAT ARE YOU DOING?
WE'RE GOING FOR A WALK.
I'LL COME WITH YOU.
WE'RE NOT GOING ANYWHERE YOU'D WANT TO GO, BROTHER.
THE NEXT DAY
YOUR SON IS YOUNG TO BE A MUJTAHID.
PRAISE BE TO GOD, IT HAS BEEN A GOOD YEAR FOR THIS UNWORTHY FAMILY.
FARID, YOUR BROTHER IS AT THE BAZAAR. MAKE SURE HE'S READY BEFORE THE OTHER GUESTS ARRIVE.

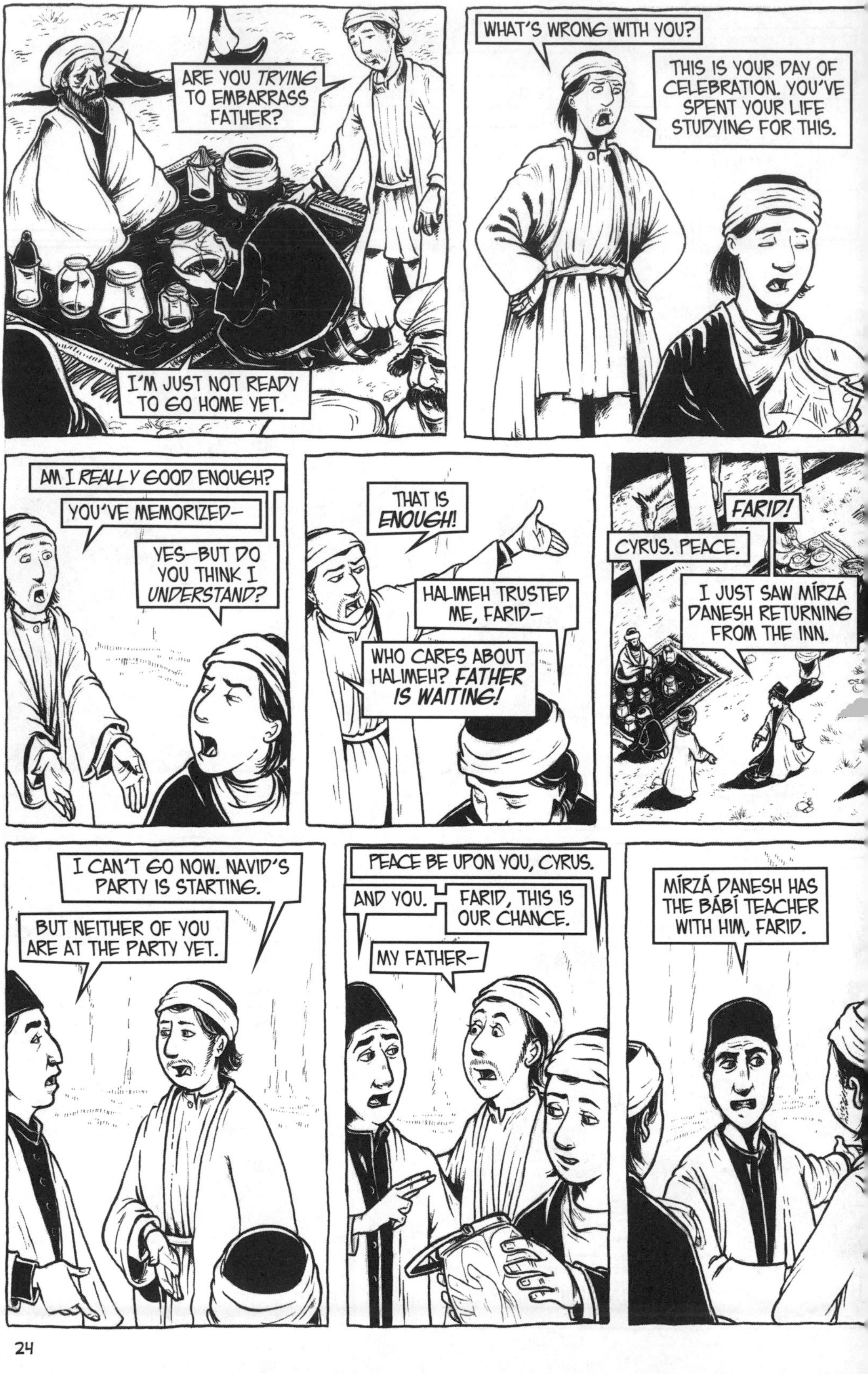
ARE YOU *TRYING* TO EMBARRASS FATHER?
I'M JUST NOT READY TO GO HOME YET.
WHAT'S WRONG WITH YOU?
THIS IS YOUR DAY OF CELEBRATION. YOU'VE SPENT YOUR LIFE STUDYING FOR THIS.
AM I *REALLY* GOOD ENOUGH?
YOU'VE MEMORIZED—
YES—BUT DO YOU THINK I *UNDERSTAND?*
THAT IS *ENOUGH!*
HALIMEH TRUSTED ME, FARID—
WHO CARES ABOUT HALIMEH? *FATHER IS WAITING!*
FARID!
CYRUS. PEACE.
I JUST SAW MÍRZÁ DANESH RETURNING FROM THE INN.
I CAN'T GO NOW. NAVID'S PARTY IS STARTING.
BUT NEITHER OF YOU ARE AT THE PARTY YET.
PEACE BE UPON YOU, CYRUS.
AND YOU.
FARID, THIS IS OUR CHANCE.
MY FATHER—
MÍRZÁ DANESH HAS THE BÁBÍ TEACHER WITH HIM, FARID.

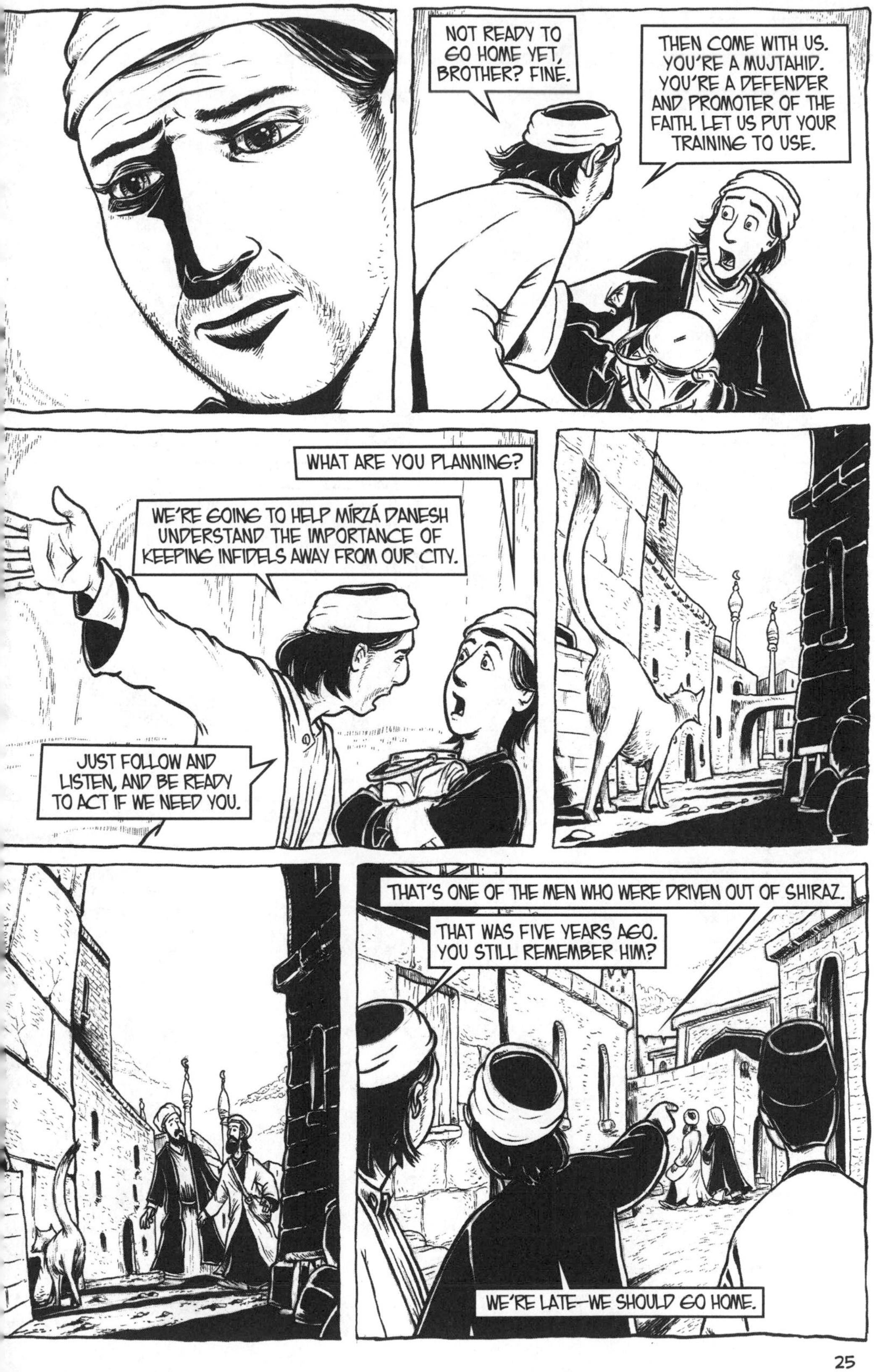
NOT READY TO GO HOME YET, BROTHER? FINE.
THEN COME WITH US. YOU'RE A MUJTAHID. YOU'RE A DEFENDER AND PROMOTER OF THE FAITH. LET US PUT YOUR TRAINING TO USE.
WHAT ARE YOU PLANNING?
WE'RE GOING TO HELP MÍRZÁ DANESH UNDERSTAND THE IMPORTANCE OF KEEPING INFIDELS AWAY FROM OUR CITY.
JUST FOLLOW AND LISTEN, AND BE READY TO ACT IF WE NEED YOU.
THAT'S ONE OF THE MEN WHO WERE DRIVEN OUT OF SHIRAZ.
THAT WAS FIVE YEARS AGO. YOU STILL REMEMBER HIM?
WE'RE LATE—WE SHOULD GO HOME.

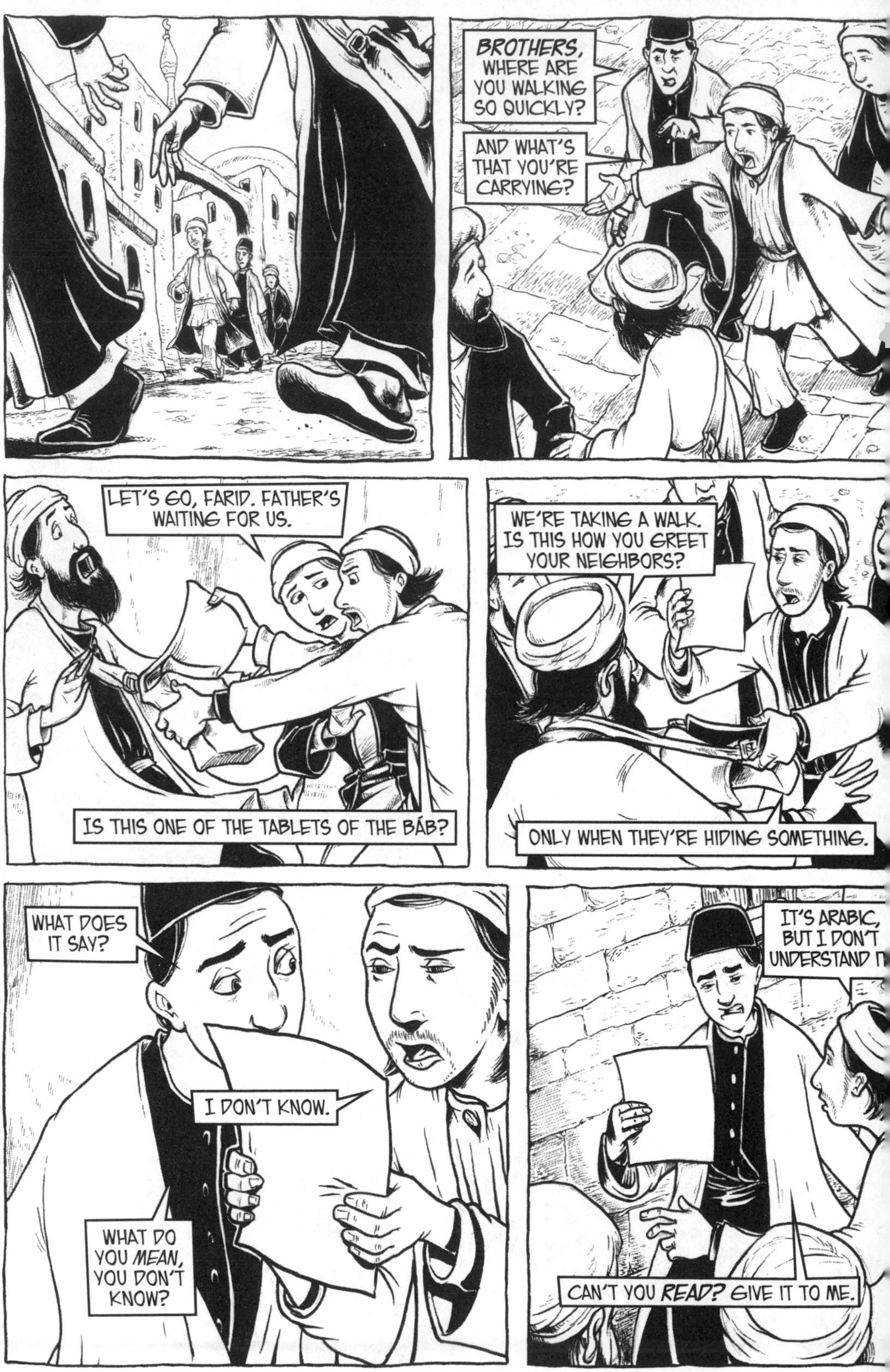
BROTHERS, WHERE ARE YOU WALKING SO QUICKLY?
AND WHAT'S THAT YOU'RE CARRYING?
LET'S GO, FARID. FATHER'S WAITING FOR US.
IS THIS ONE OF THE TABLETS OF THE BÁB?
WE'RE TAKING A WALK. IS THIS HOW YOU GREET YOUR NEIGHBORS?
ONLY WHEN THEY'RE HIDING SOMETHING.
WHAT DOES IT SAY?
I DON'T KNOW.
WHAT DO YOU MEAN, YOU DON'T KNOW?
IT'S ARABIC, BUT I DON'T UNDERSTAND IT
CAN'T YOU READ? GIVE IT TO ME.

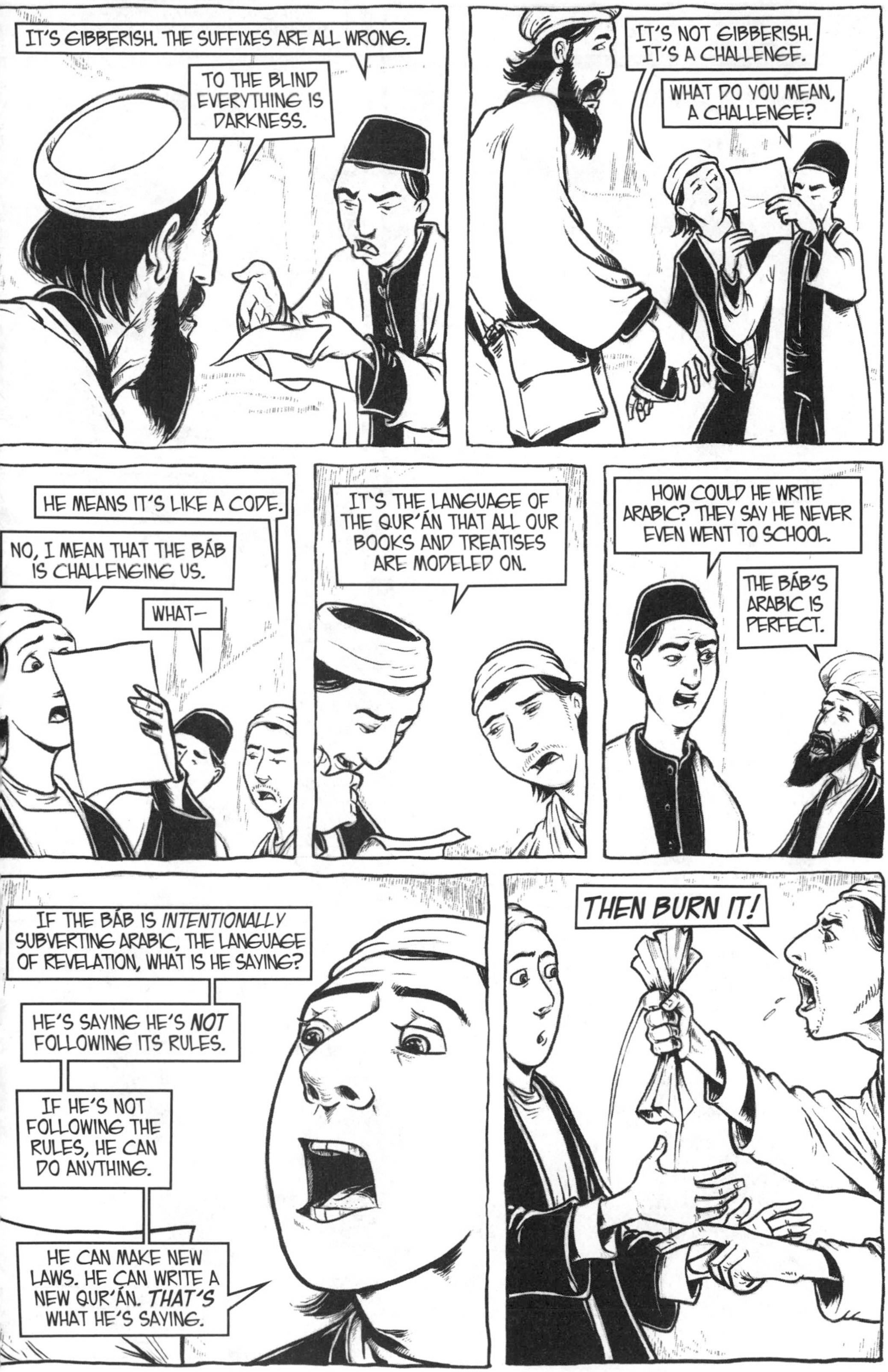
IT'S GIBBERISH. THE SUFFIXES ARE ALL WRONG.
TO THE BLIND EVERYTHING IS DARKNESS.
IT'S NOT GIBBERISH. IT'S A CHALLENGE.
WHAT DO YOU MEAN, A CHALLENGE?
HE MEANS IT'S LIKE A CODE.
NO, I MEAN THAT THE BÁB IS CHALLENGING US.
WHAT—
IT'S THE LANGUAGE OF THE QUR'ÁN THAT ALL OUR BOOKS AND TREATISES ARE MODELED ON.
HOW COULD HE WRITE ARABIC? THEY SAY HE NEVER EVEN WENT TO SCHOOL.
THE BÁB'S ARABIC IS PERFECT.
IF THE BÁB IS *INTENTIONALLY* SUBVERTING ARABIC, THE LANGUAGE OF REVELATION, WHAT IS HE SAYING?
HE'S SAYING HE'S ***NOT*** FOLLOWING ITS RULES.
IF HE'S NOT FOLLOWING THE RULES, HE CAN DO ANYTHING.
HE CAN MAKE NEW LAWS. HE CAN WRITE A NEW QUR'ÁN. *THAT'S* WHAT HE'S SAYING.
THEN BURN IT!

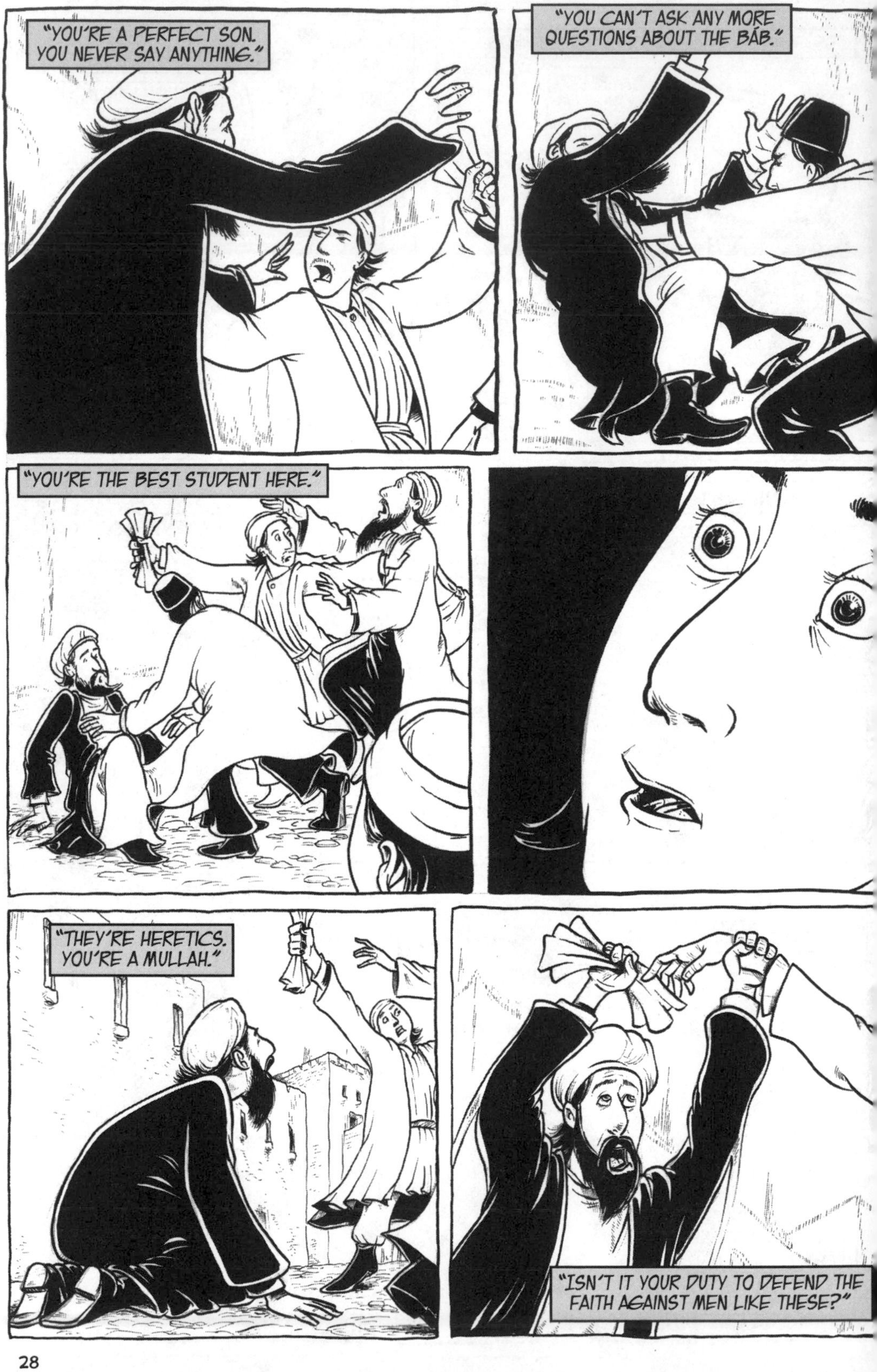
"YOU'RE A PERFECT SON. YOU NEVER SAY ANYTHING."
"YOU CAN'T ASK ANY MORE QUESTIONS ABOUT THE BÁB."
"YOU'RE THE BEST STUDENT HERE."
"THEY'RE HERETICS. YOU'RE A MULLAH."
"ISN'T IT YOUR DUTY TO DEFEND THE FAITH AGAINST MEN LIKE THESE?"

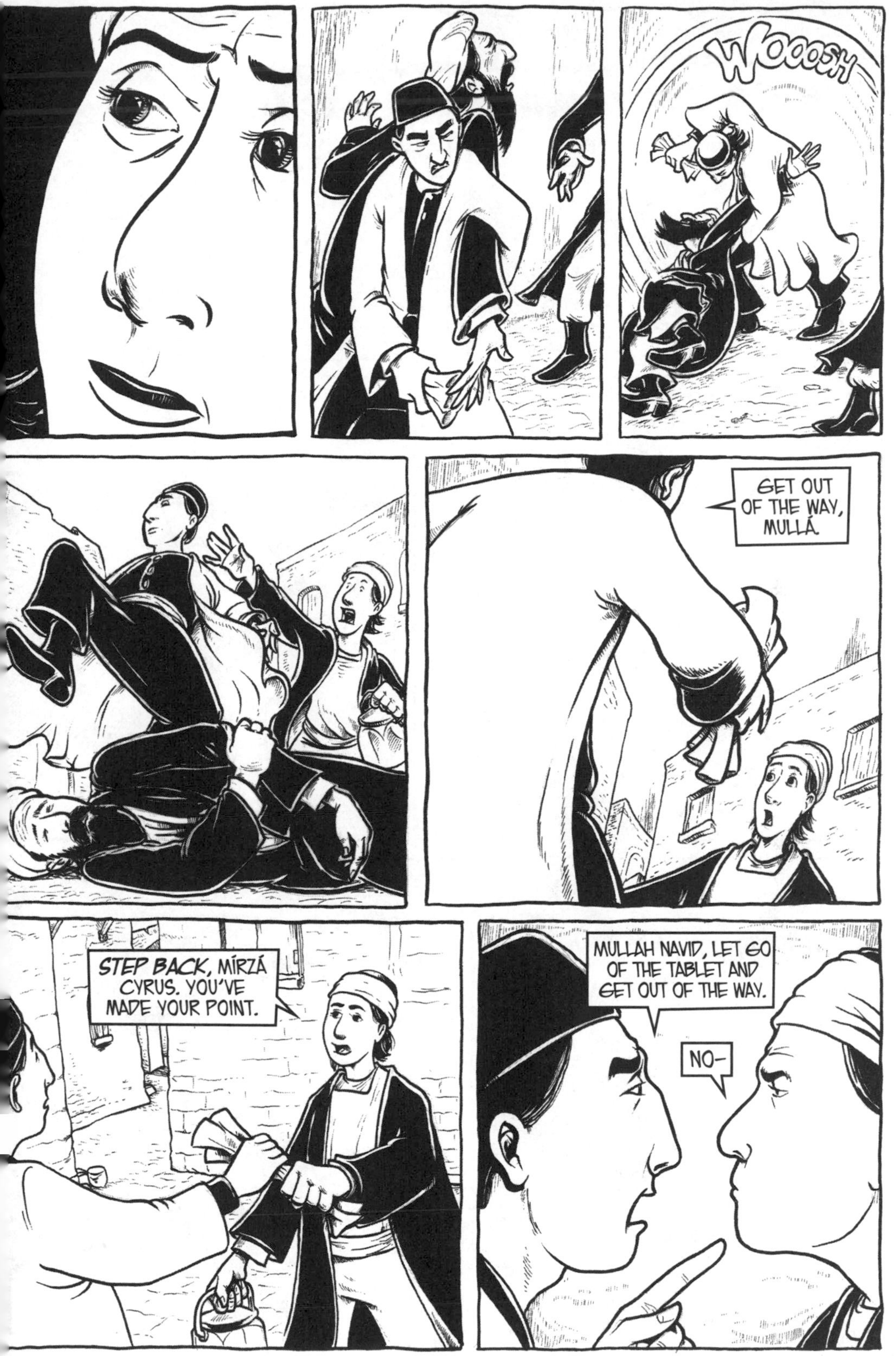
WOOOSH
GET OUT OF THE WAY, MULLÁ.
STEP BACK, MÍRZÁ CYRUS. YOU'VE MADE YOUR POINT.
MULLAH NAVID, LET GO OF THE TABLET AND GET OUT OF THE WAY.
NO–

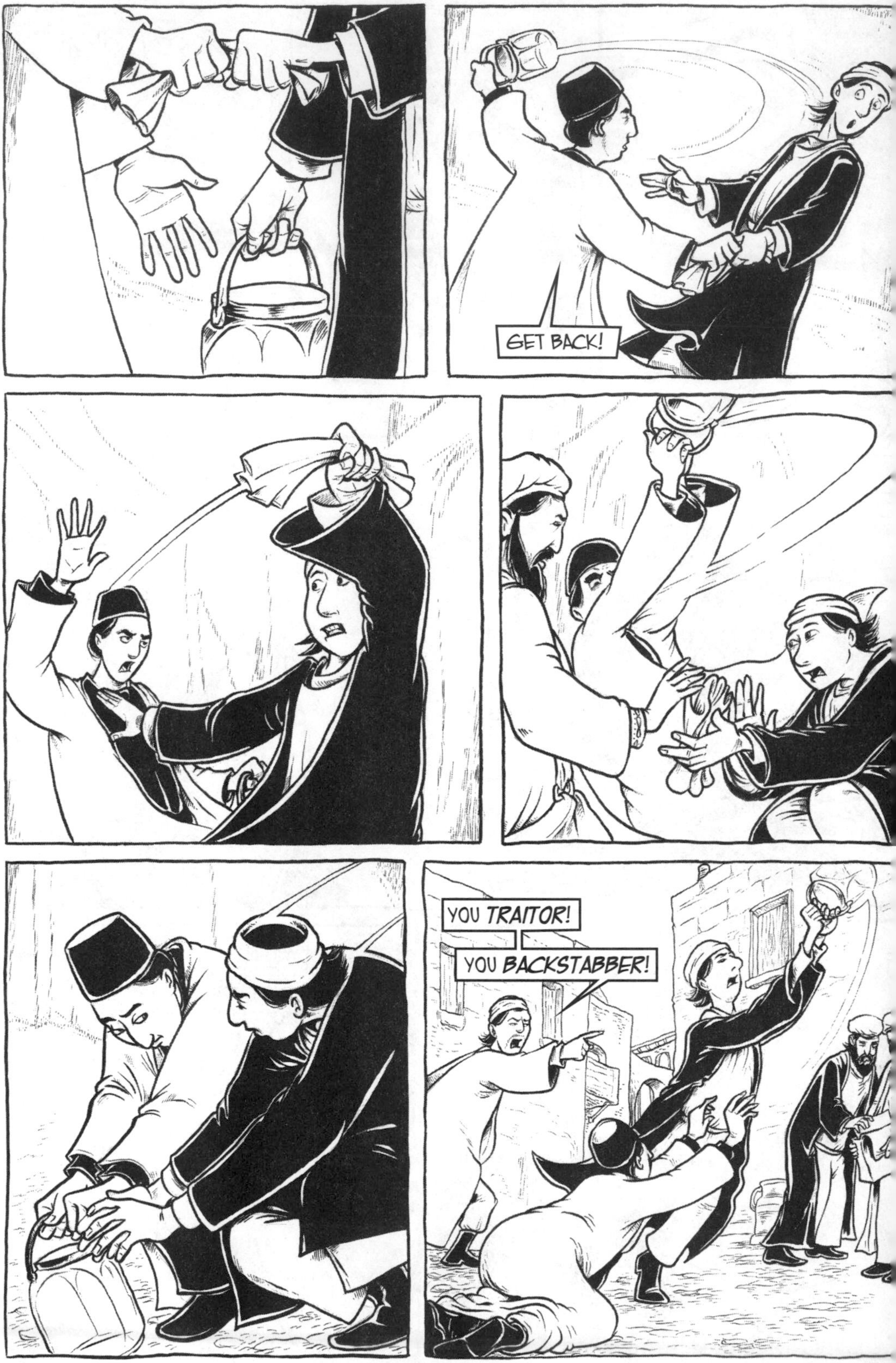
GET BACK!
YOU TRAITOR!
YOU BACKSTABBER!

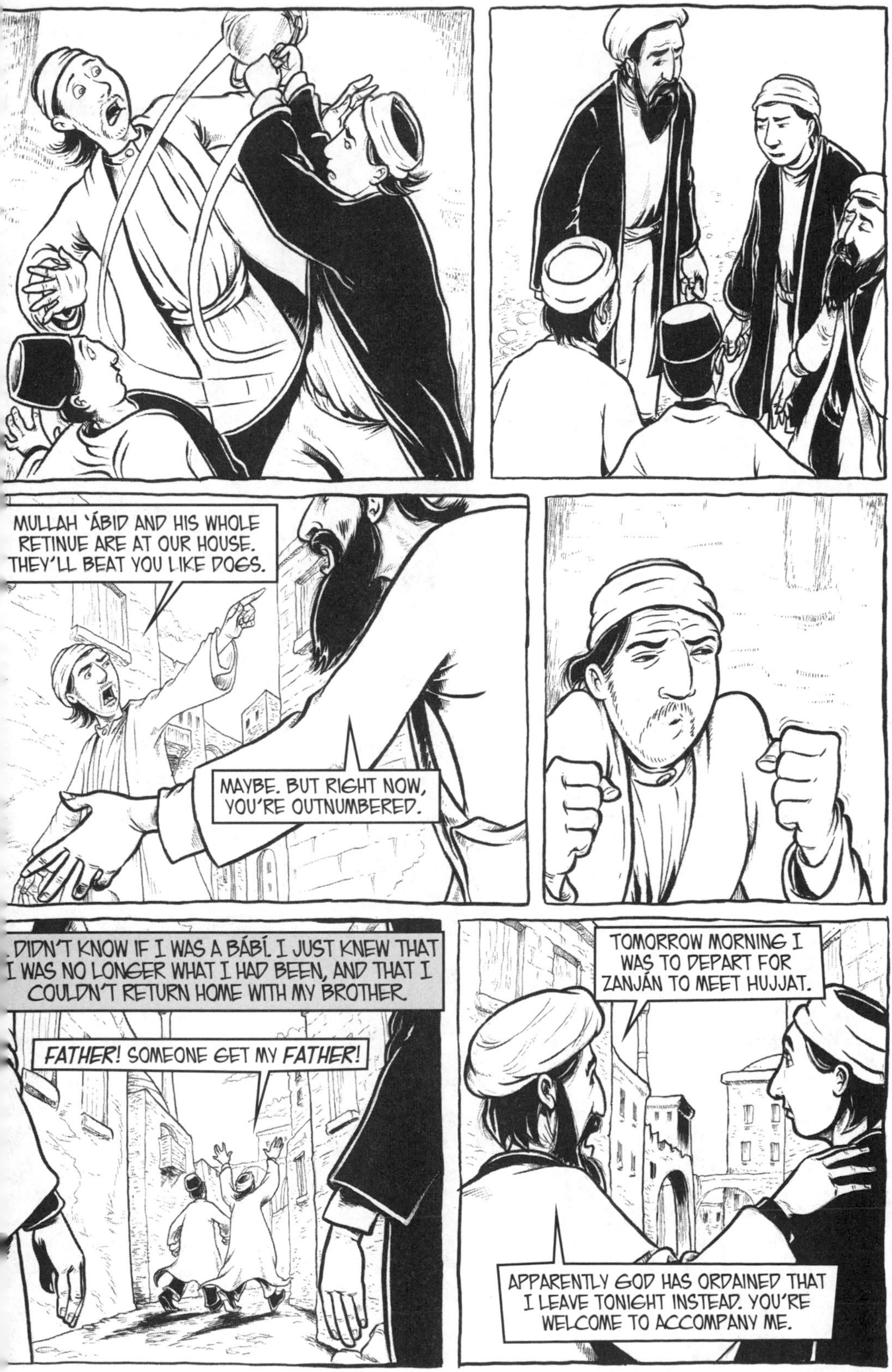
MULLAH 'ÁBID AND HIS WHOLE RETINUE ARE AT OUR HOUSE. THEY'LL BEAT YOU LIKE DOGS.
MAYBE. BUT RIGHT NOW, YOU'RE OUTNUMBERED.
DIDN'T KNOW IF I WAS A BÁBÍ. I JUST KNEW THAT I WAS NO LONGER WHAT I HAD BEEN, AND THAT I COULDN'T RETURN HOME WITH MY BROTHER.
FATHER! SOMEONE GET MY FATHER!
TOMORROW MORNING I WAS TO DEPART FOR ZANJÁN TO MEET HUJJAT.
APPARENTLY GOD HAS ORDAINED THAT I LEAVE TONIGHT INSTEAD. YOU'RE WELCOME TO ACCOMPANY ME.

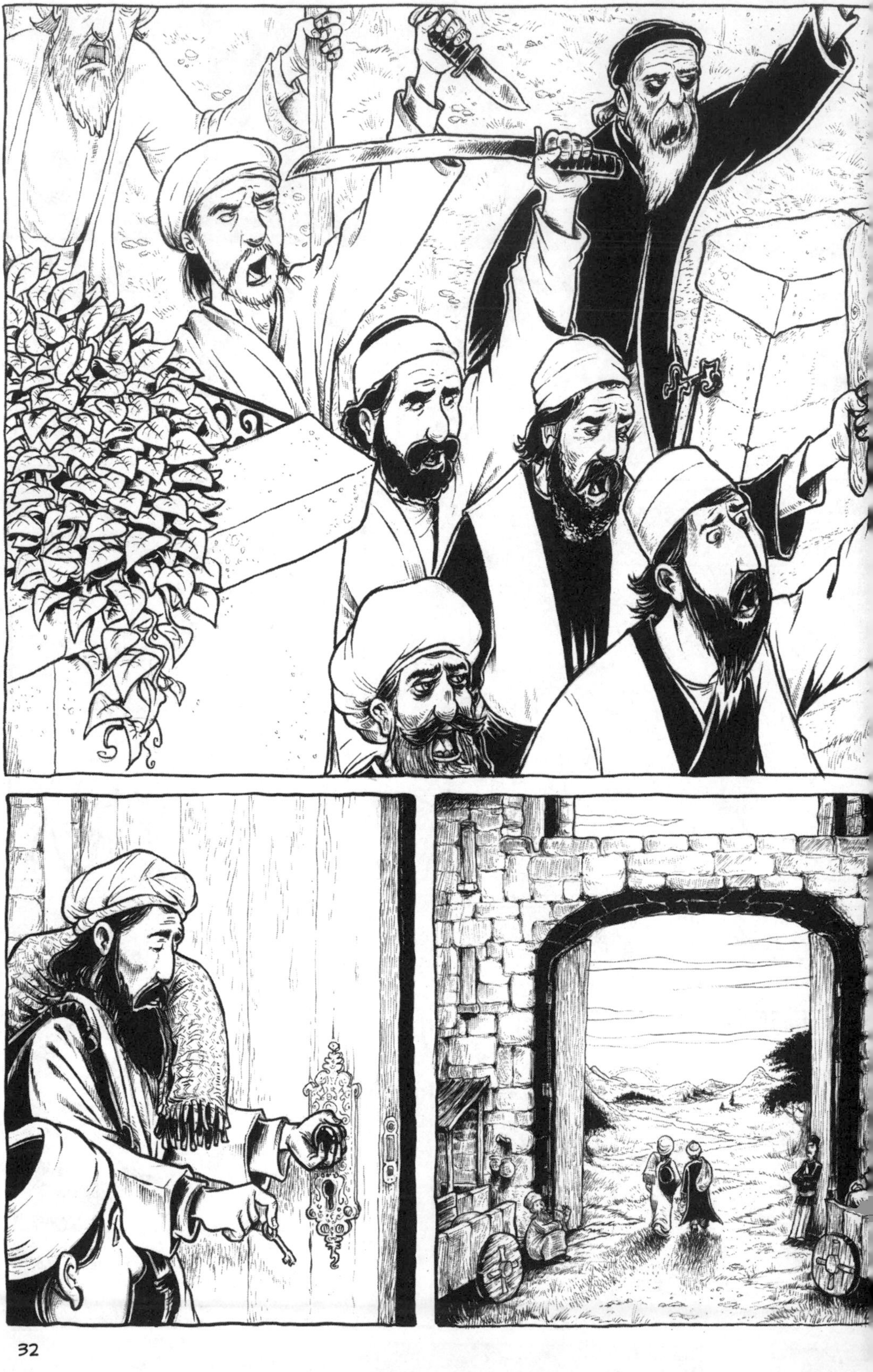

2: PRIEST

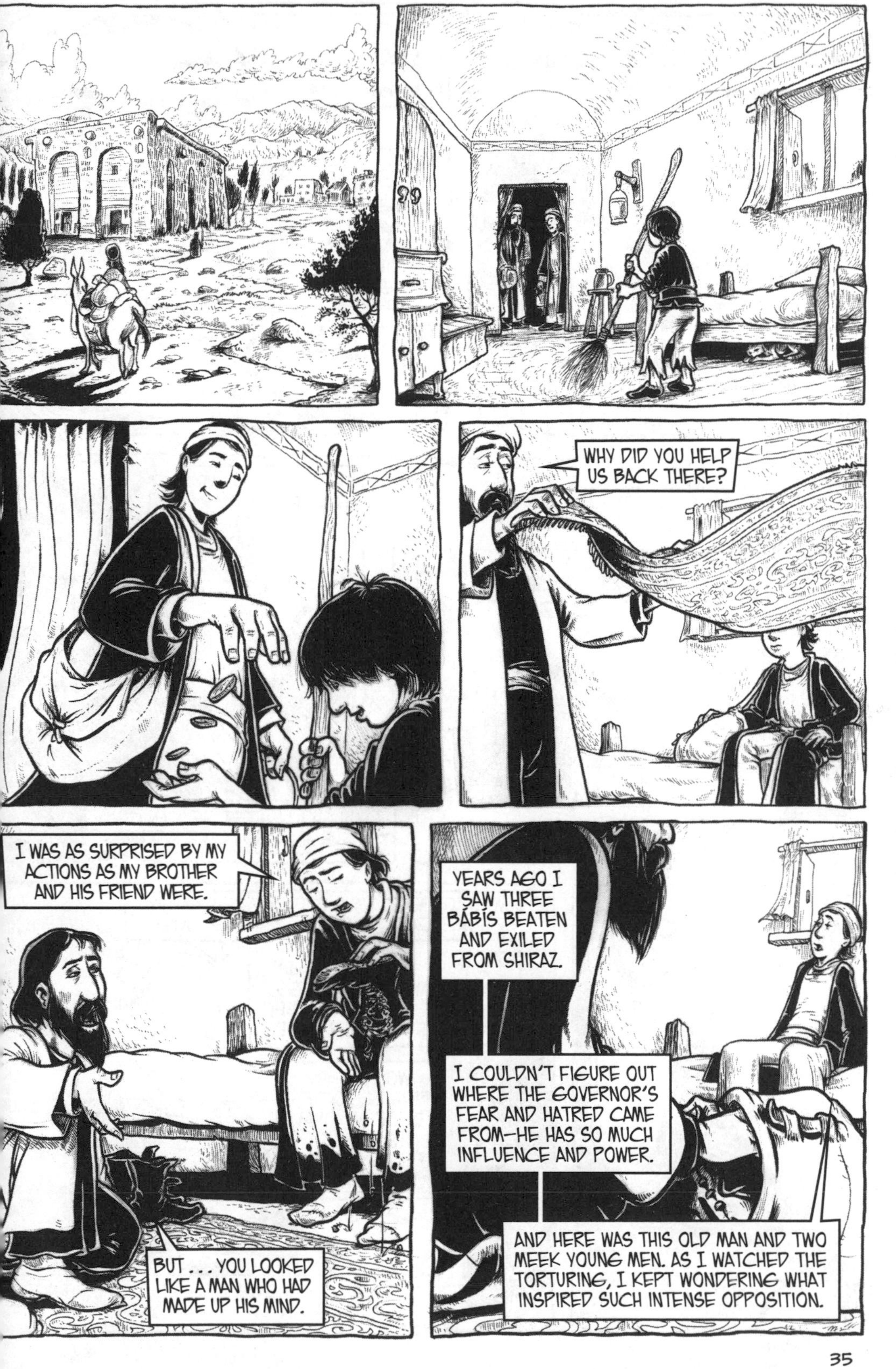
WHY DID YOU HELP US BACK THERE?
I WAS AS SURPRISED BY MY ACTIONS AS MY BROTHER AND HIS FRIEND WERE.
BUT . . . YOU LOOKED LIKE A MAN WHO HAD MADE UP HIS MIND.
YEARS AGO I SAW THREE BÁBÍS BEATEN AND EXILED FROM SHIRAZ.
I COULDN'T FIGURE OUT WHERE THE GOVERNOR'S FEAR AND HATRED CAME FROM—HE HAS SO MUCH INFLUENCE AND POWER.
AND HERE WAS THIS OLD MAN AND TWO MEEK YOUNG MEN. AS I WATCHED THE TORTURING, I KEPT WONDERING WHAT INSPIRED SUCH INTENSE OPPOSITION.

AFTERWARDS, I LOOKED INTO THE EYES OF THE OLD MAN, AND I KNEW.

THEY WERE THE EYES OF SOMEONE WHO'S SEEN INTO OTHER WORLDS. HE'S SEEN PARADISE IN THIS LIFE. HIS CERTAINTY— THAT WAS WHAT THEY WERE AFRAID OF.

I'D NEVER SEEN THAT LOOK AGAIN, FROM MY TEACHER OR MY CLASSMATES OR ANY- WHERE ELSE.

ALL THESE YEARS I'VE BEEN WAIT- ING TO SEE IT AGAIN. AND THEN LAST NIGHT I SAW IT AGAIN—

IN YOU.

THE FIRST THING WE'LL HAVE TO DO IN THE MORNING IS BUY SOME TEA. WHAT TYPE OF MEN TRAVEL WITHOUT TEA?

THERE WERE MITIGATING CIRCUMSTANCES.

TEA IS TEA. ARE WE MEN OF PERSIA OR AREN'T WE? THERE ARE NO MITIGATING CIRCUMSTANCES.

YOU SHOULD REST. WE CAN CON- TINUE TALKING IN THE MORNING.

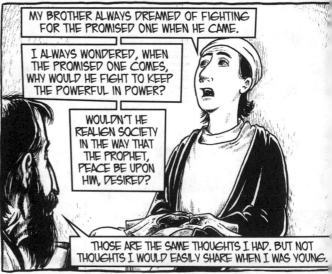

MY BROTHER ALWAYS DREAMED OF FIGHTING FOR THE PROMISED ONE WHEN HE CAME.

I ALWAYS WONDERED, WHEN THE PROMISED ONE COMES, WHY WOULD HE FIGHT TO KEEP THE POWERFUL IN POWER?

WOULDN'T HE REALIGN SOCIETY IN THE WAY THAT THE PROPHET, PEACE BE UPON HIM, DESIRED?

THOSE ARE THE SAME THOUGHTS I HAD. BUT NOT THOUGHTS I WOULD EASILY SHARE WHEN I WAS YOUNG.

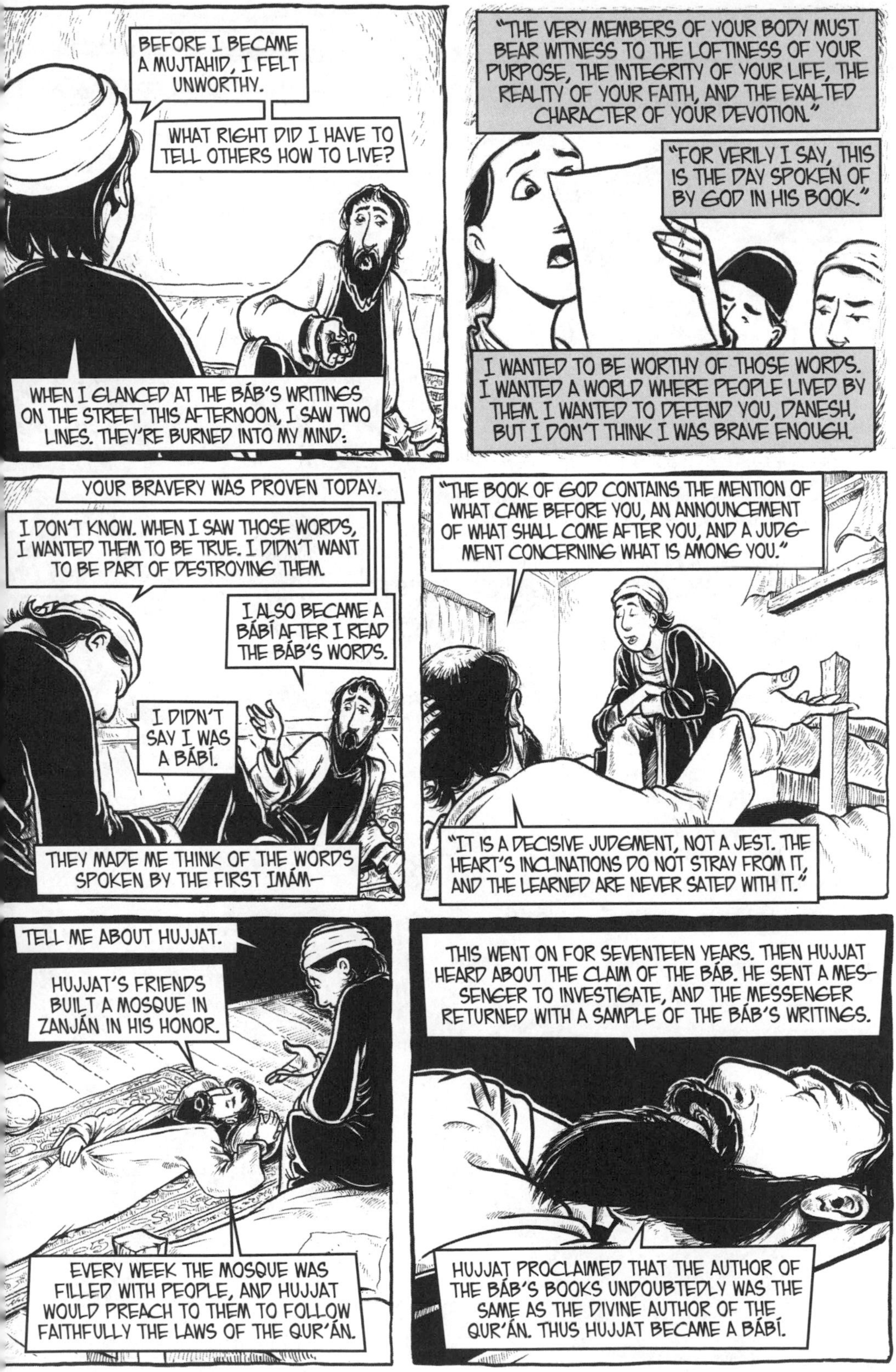
BEFORE I BECAME A MUJTAHID, I FELT UNWORTHY.
WHAT RIGHT DID I HAVE TO TELL OTHERS HOW TO LIVE?
WHEN I GLANCED AT THE BÁB'S WRITINGS ON THE STREET THIS AFTERNOON, I SAW TWO LINES. THEY'RE BURNED INTO MY MIND:
"THE VERY MEMBERS OF YOUR BODY MUST BEAR WITNESS TO THE LOFTINESS OF YOUR PURPOSE, THE INTEGRITY OF YOUR LIFE, THE REALITY OF YOUR FAITH, AND THE EXALTED CHARACTER OF YOUR DEVOTION."
"FOR VERILY I SAY, THIS IS THE DAY SPOKEN OF BY GOD IN HIS BOOK."
I WANTED TO BE WORTHY OF THOSE WORDS. I WANTED A WORLD WHERE PEOPLE LIVED BY THEM. I WANTED TO DEFEND YOU, DANESH, BUT I DON'T THINK I WAS BRAVE ENOUGH.
YOUR BRAVERY WAS PROVEN TODAY.
I DON'T KNOW. WHEN I SAW THOSE WORDS, I WANTED THEM TO BE TRUE. I DIDN'T WANT TO BE PART OF DESTROYING THEM.
I ALSO BECAME A BÁBÍ AFTER I READ THE BÁB'S WORDS.
I DIDN'T SAY I WAS A BÁBÍ.
THEY MADE ME THINK OF THE WORDS SPOKEN BY THE FIRST IMÁM—
"THE BOOK OF GOD CONTAINS THE MENTION OF WHAT CAME BEFORE YOU, AN ANNOUNCEMENT OF WHAT SHALL COME AFTER YOU, AND A JUDGEMENT CONCERNING WHAT IS AMONG YOU."
"IT IS A DECISIVE JUDGEMENT, NOT A JEST. THE HEART'S INCLINATIONS DO NOT STRAY FROM IT, AND THE LEARNED ARE NEVER SATED WITH IT."
TELL ME ABOUT HUJJAT.
HUJJAT'S FRIENDS BUILT A MOSQUE IN ZANJÁN IN HIS HONOR.
EVERY WEEK THE MOSQUE WAS FILLED WITH PEOPLE, AND HUJJAT WOULD PREACH TO THEM TO FOLLOW FAITHFULLY THE LAWS OF THE QUR'ÁN.
THIS WENT ON FOR SEVENTEEN YEARS. THEN HUJJAT HEARD ABOUT THE CLAIM OF THE BÁB. HE SENT A MESSENGER TO INVESTIGATE, AND THE MESSENGER RETURNED WITH A SAMPLE OF THE BÁB'S WRITINGS.
HUJJAT PROCLAIMED THAT THE AUTHOR OF THE BÁB'S BOOKS UNDOUBTEDLY WAS THE SAME AS THE DIVINE AUTHOR OF THE QUR'ÁN. THUS HUJJAT BECAME A BÁBÍ.

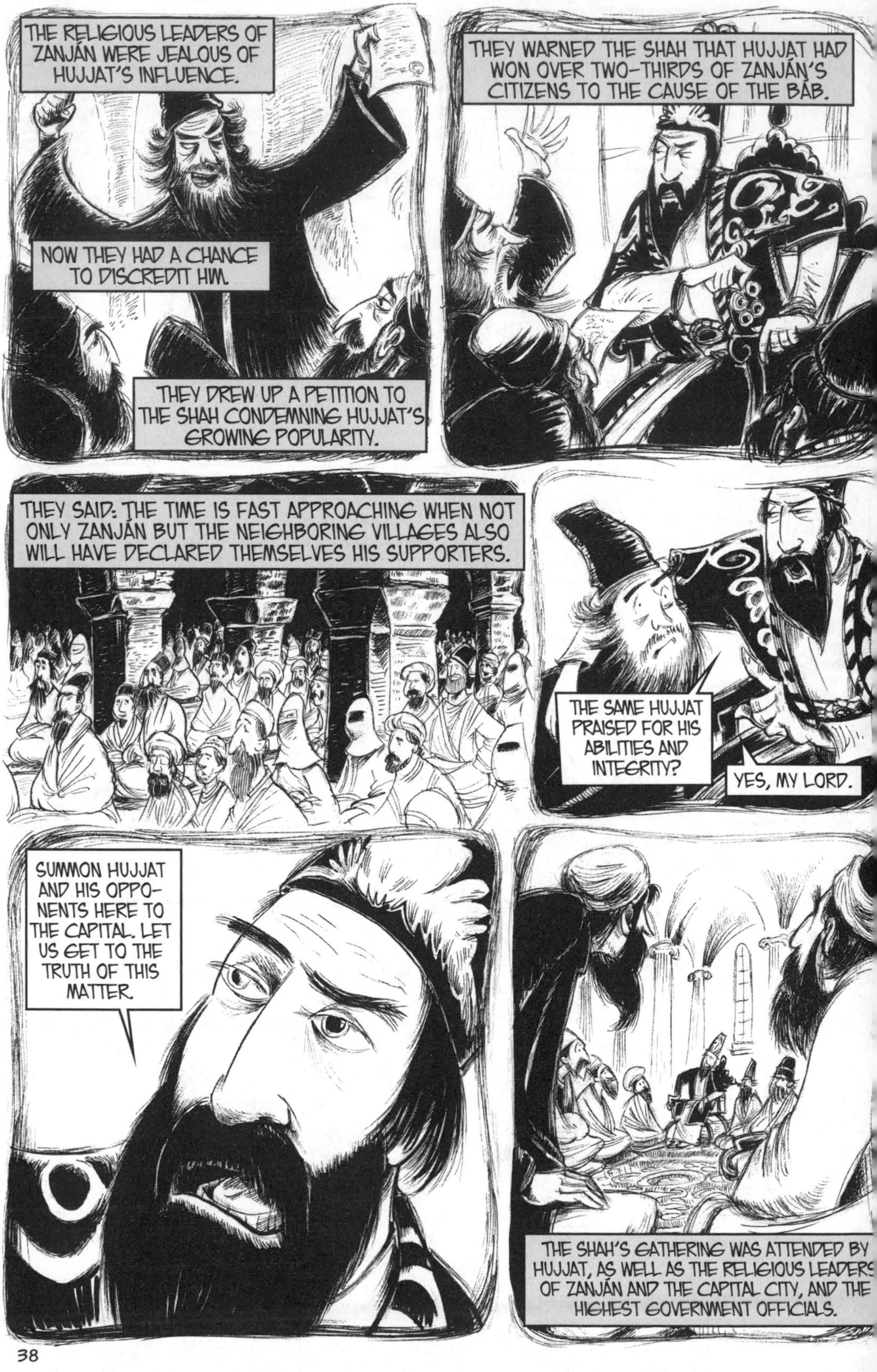
THE RELIGIOUS LEADERS OF ZANJÁN WERE JEALOUS OF HUJJAT'S INFLUENCE.
NOW THEY HAD A CHANCE TO DISCREDIT HIM.
THEY DREW UP A PETITION TO THE SHAH CONDEMNING HUJJAT'S GROWING POPULARITY.
THEY WARNED THE SHAH THAT HUJJAT HAD WON OVER TWO-THIRDS OF ZANJÁN'S CITIZENS TO THE CAUSE OF THE BÁB.
THEY SAID: THE TIME IS FAST APPROACHING WHEN NOT ONLY ZANJÁN BUT THE NEIGHBORING VILLAGES ALSO WILL HAVE DECLARED THEMSELVES HIS SUPPORTERS.
THE SAME HUJJAT PRAISED FOR HIS ABILITIES AND INTEGRITY?
YES, MY LORD.
SUMMON HUJJAT AND HIS OPPONENTS HERE TO THE CAPITAL. LET US GET TO THE TRUTH OF THIS MATTER.
THE SHAH'S GATHERING WAS ATTENDED BY HUJJAT, AS WELL AS THE RELIGIOUS LEADERS OF ZANJÁN AND THE CAPITAL CITY, AND THE HIGHEST GOVERNMENT OFFICIALS.

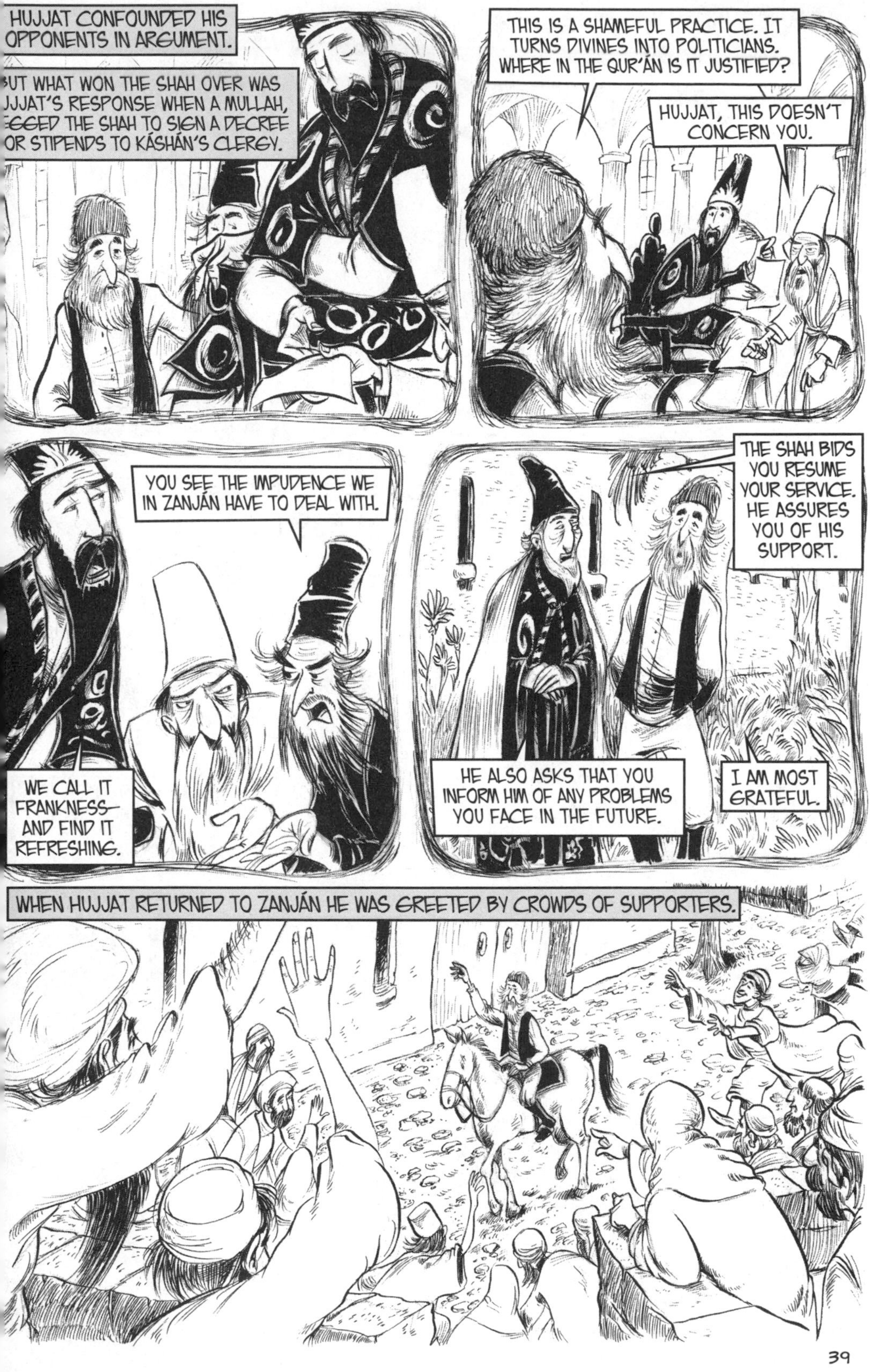

HUJJAT CONFOUNDED HIS OPPONENTS IN ARGUMENT.
UT WHAT WON THE SHAH OVER WAS UJJAT'S RESPONSE WHEN A MULLAH, EGGED THE SHAH TO SIGN A DECREE OR STIPENDS TO KÁSHÁN'S CLERGY.
THIS IS A SHAMEFUL PRACTICE. IT TURNS DIVINES INTO POLITICIANS. WHERE IN THE QUR'ÁN IS IT JUSTIFIED?
HUJJAT, THIS DOESN'T CONCERN YOU.
YOU SEE THE IMPUDENCE WE IN ZANJÁN HAVE TO DEAL WITH.
WE CALL IT FRANKNESS— AND FIND IT REFRESHING.
THE SHAH BIDS YOU RESUME YOUR SERVICE. HE ASSURES YOU OF HIS SUPPORT.
HE ALSO ASKS THAT YOU INFORM HIM OF ANY PROBLEMS YOU FACE IN THE FUTURE.
I AM MOST GRATEFUL.
WHEN HUJJAT RETURNED TO ZANJÁN HE WAS GREETED BY CROWDS OF SUPPORTERS.

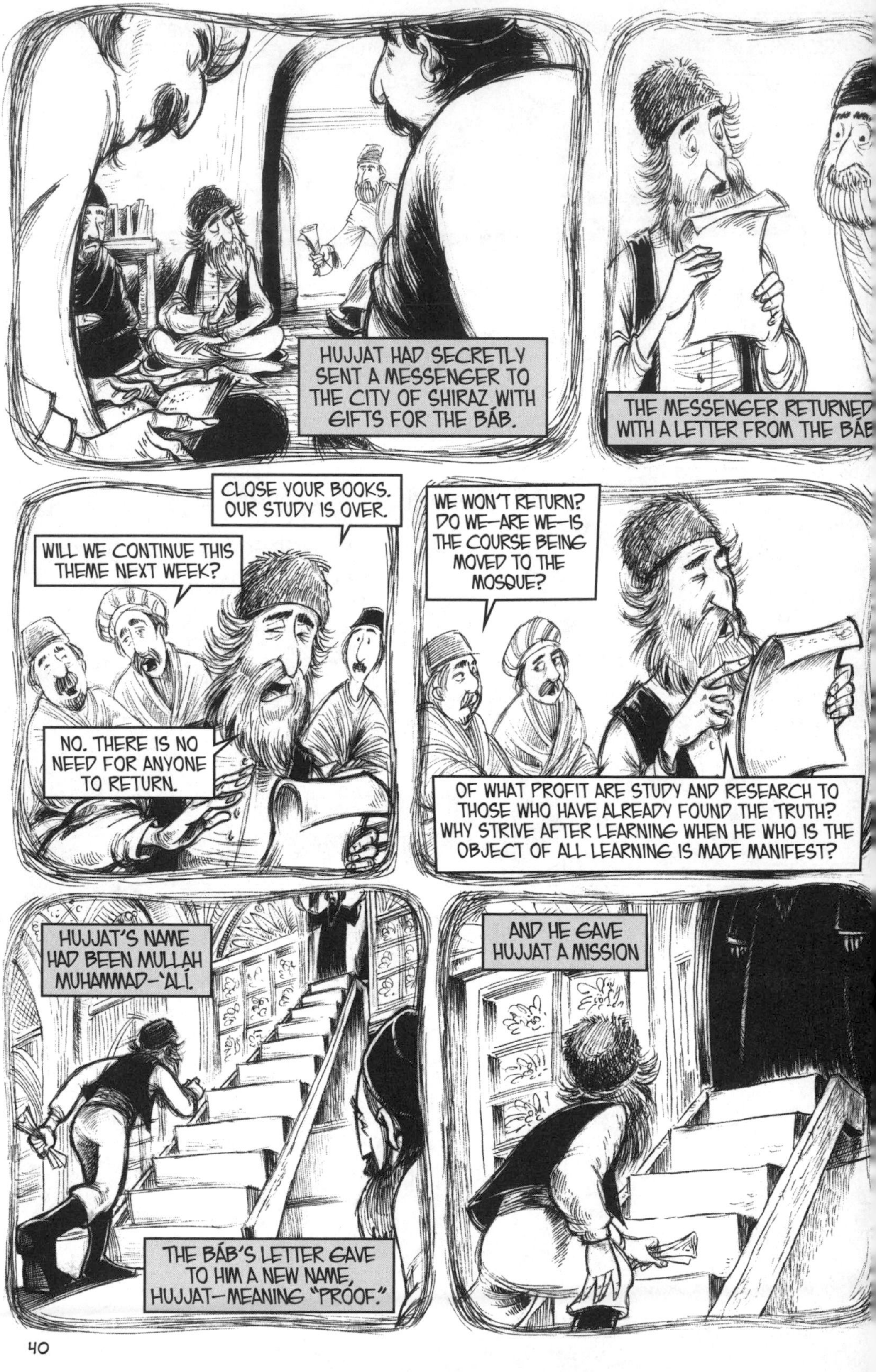
HUJJAT HAD SECRETLY SENT A MESSENGER TO THE CITY OF SHIRAZ WITH GIFTS FOR THE BÁB.
THE MESSENGER RETURNED WITH A LETTER FROM THE BÁB
CLOSE YOUR BOOKS. OUR STUDY IS OVER.
WILL WE CONTINUE THIS THEME NEXT WEEK?
NO. THERE IS NO NEED FOR ANYONE TO RETURN.
WE WON'T RETURN? DO WE—ARE WE—IS THE COURSE BEING MOVED TO THE MOSQUE?
OF WHAT PROFIT ARE STUDY AND RESEARCH TO THOSE WHO HAVE ALREADY FOUND THE TRUTH? WHY STRIVE AFTER LEARNING WHEN HE WHO IS THE OBJECT OF ALL LEARNING IS MADE MANIFEST?
HUJJAT'S NAME HAD BEEN MULLAH MUHAMMAD-'ALÍ.
THE BÁB'S LETTER GAVE TO HIM A NEW NAME, HUJJAT—MEANING "PROOF."
AND HE GAVE HUJJAT A MISSION

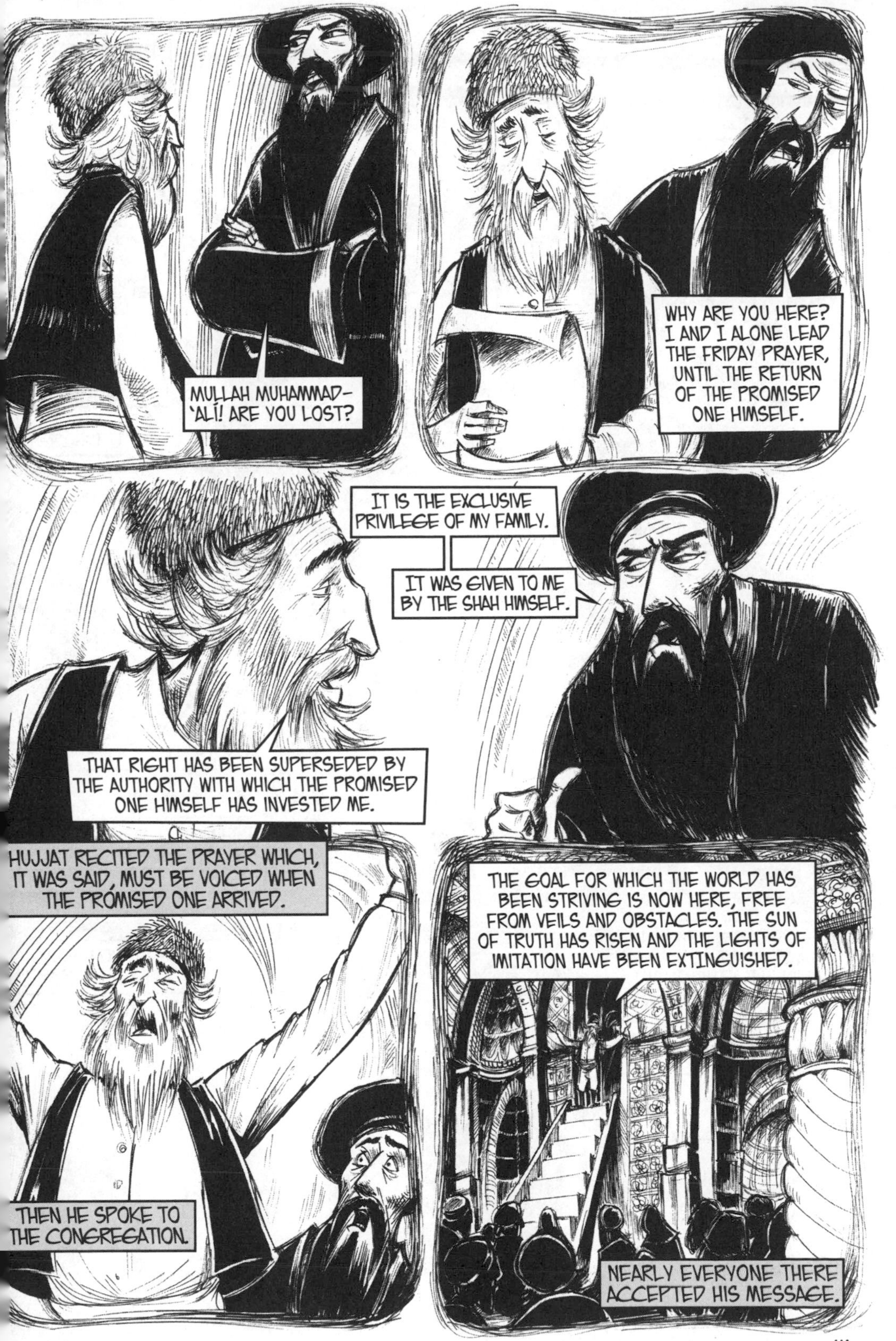

MULLAH MUHAMMAD-'ALÍ! ARE YOU LOST?
WHY ARE YOU HERE? I AND I ALONE LEAD THE FRIDAY PRAYER, UNTIL THE RETURN OF THE PROMISED ONE HIMSELF.
IT IS THE EXCLUSIVE PRIVILEGE OF MY FAMILY.
IT WAS GIVEN TO ME BY THE SHAH HIMSELF.
THAT RIGHT HAS BEEN SUPERSEDED BY THE AUTHORITY WITH WHICH THE PROMISED ONE HIMSELF HAS INVESTED ME.
HUJJAT RECITED THE PRAYER WHICH, IT WAS SAID, MUST BE VOICED WHEN THE PROMISED ONE ARRIVED.
THEN HE SPOKE TO THE CONGREGATION.
THE GOAL FOR WHICH THE WORLD HAS BEEN STRIVING IS NOW HERE, FREE FROM VEILS AND OBSTACLES. THE SUN OF TRUTH HAS RISEN AND THE LIGHTS OF IMITATION HAVE BEEN EXTINGUISHED.
NEARLY EVERYONE THERE ACCEPTED HIS MESSAGE.

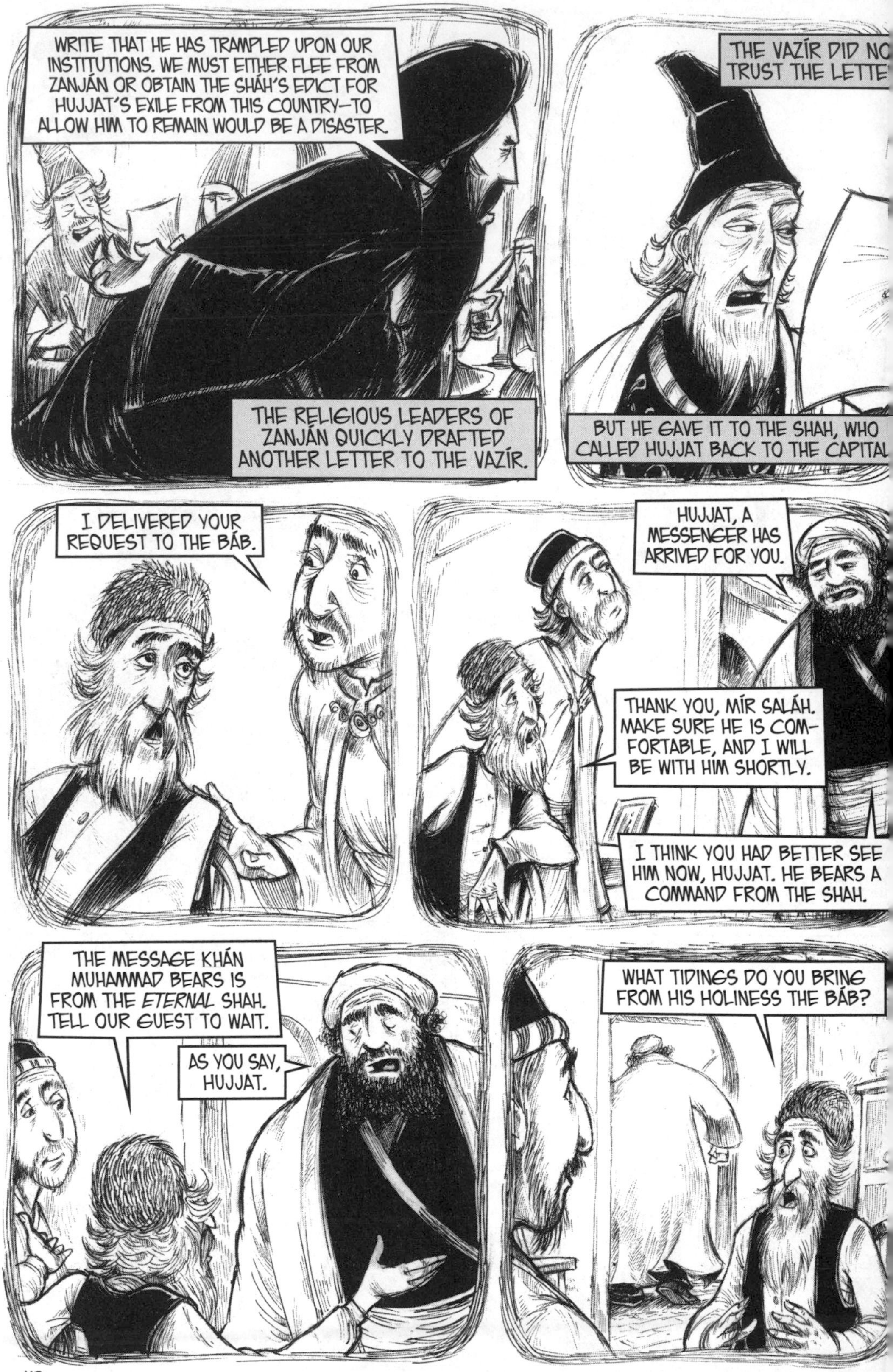
WRITE THAT HE HAS TRAMPLED UPON OUR INSTITUTIONS. WE MUST EITHER FLEE FROM ZANJÁN OR OBTAIN THE SHÁH'S EDICT FOR HUJJAT'S EXILE FROM THIS COUNTRY—TO ALLOW HIM TO REMAIN WOULD BE A DISASTER.
THE RELIGIOUS LEADERS OF ZANJÁN QUICKLY DRAFTED ANOTHER LETTER TO THE VAZÍR.
THE VAZÍR DID NO
TRUST THE LETTE
BUT HE GAVE IT TO THE SHAH, WHO CALLED HUJJAT BACK TO THE CAPITAL
I DELIVERED YOUR REQUEST TO THE BÁB.
HUJJAT, A MESSENGER HAS ARRIVED FOR YOU.
THANK YOU, MÍR SALÁH. MAKE SURE HE IS COM-FORTABLE, AND I WILL BE WITH HIM SHORTLY.
I THINK YOU HAD BETTER SEE HIM NOW, HUJJAT. HE BEARS A COMMAND FROM THE SHAH.
THE MESSAGE KHÁN MUHAMMAD BEARS IS FROM THE *ETERNAL* SHAH. TELL OUR GUEST TO WAIT.
AS YOU SAY, HUJJAT.
WHAT TIDINGS DO YOU BRING FROM HIS HOLINESS THE BÁB?

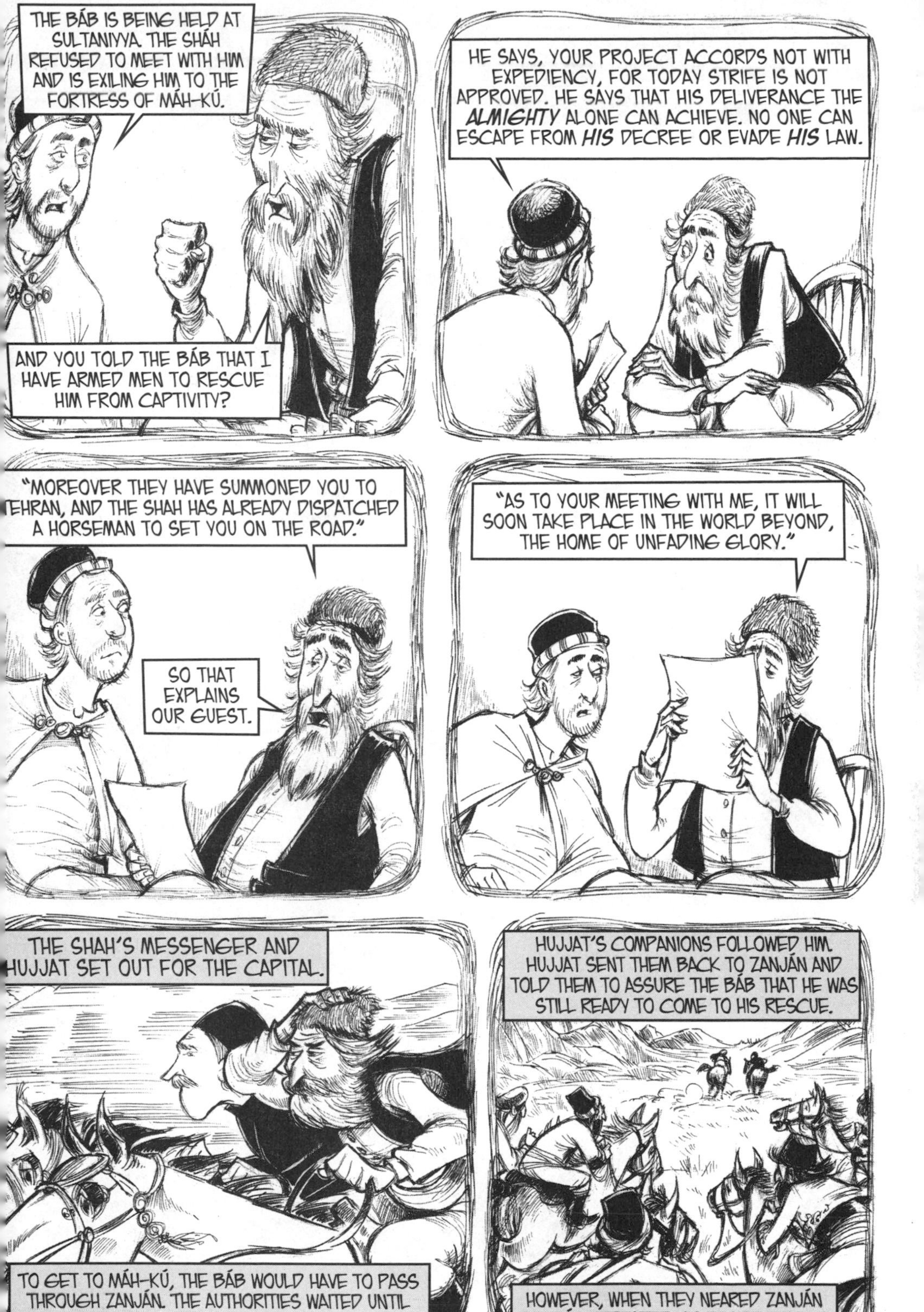

THE BÁB IS BEING HELD AT SULTANIYYA. THE SHÁH REFUSED TO MEET WITH HIM AND IS EXILING HIM TO THE FORTRESS OF MÁH-KÚ.
AND YOU TOLD THE BÁB THAT I HAVE ARMED MEN TO RESCUE HIM FROM CAPTIVITY?
HE SAYS, YOUR PROJECT ACCORDS NOT WITH EXPEDIENCY, FOR TODAY STRIFE IS NOT APPROVED. HE SAYS THAT HIS DELIVERANCE THE ALMIGHTY ALONE CAN ACHIEVE. NO ONE CAN ESCAPE FROM HIS DECREE OR EVADE HIS LAW.
"MOREOVER THEY HAVE SUMMONED YOU TO EHRAN, AND THE SHAH HAS ALREADY DISPATCHED A HORSEMAN TO SET YOU ON THE ROAD."
SO THAT EXPLAINS OUR GUEST.
"AS TO YOUR MEETING WITH ME, IT WILL SOON TAKE PLACE IN THE WORLD BEYOND, THE HOME OF UNFADING GLORY."
THE SHAH'S MESSENGER AND HUJJAT SET OUT FOR THE CAPITAL.
TO GET TO MÁH-KÚ, THE BÁB WOULD HAVE TO PASS THROUGH ZANJÁN. THE AUTHORITIES WAITED UNTIL HUJJAT SET OUT WITH THE MESSENGER BEFORE SENDING ON THE BÁB, AFRAID OF WHAT MIGHT TAKE PLACE SHOULD HUJJAT AND THE BÁB MEET.
HUJJAT'S COMPANIONS FOLLOWED HIM. HUJJAT SENT THEM BACK TO ZANJÁN AND TOLD THEM TO ASSURE THE BÁB THAT HE WAS STILL READY TO COME TO HIS RESCUE.
HOWEVER, WHEN THEY NEARED ZANJÁN THE BÁB REPEATED HIS DESIRE THAT NO ONE SHOULD ATTEMPT TO FREE HIM.

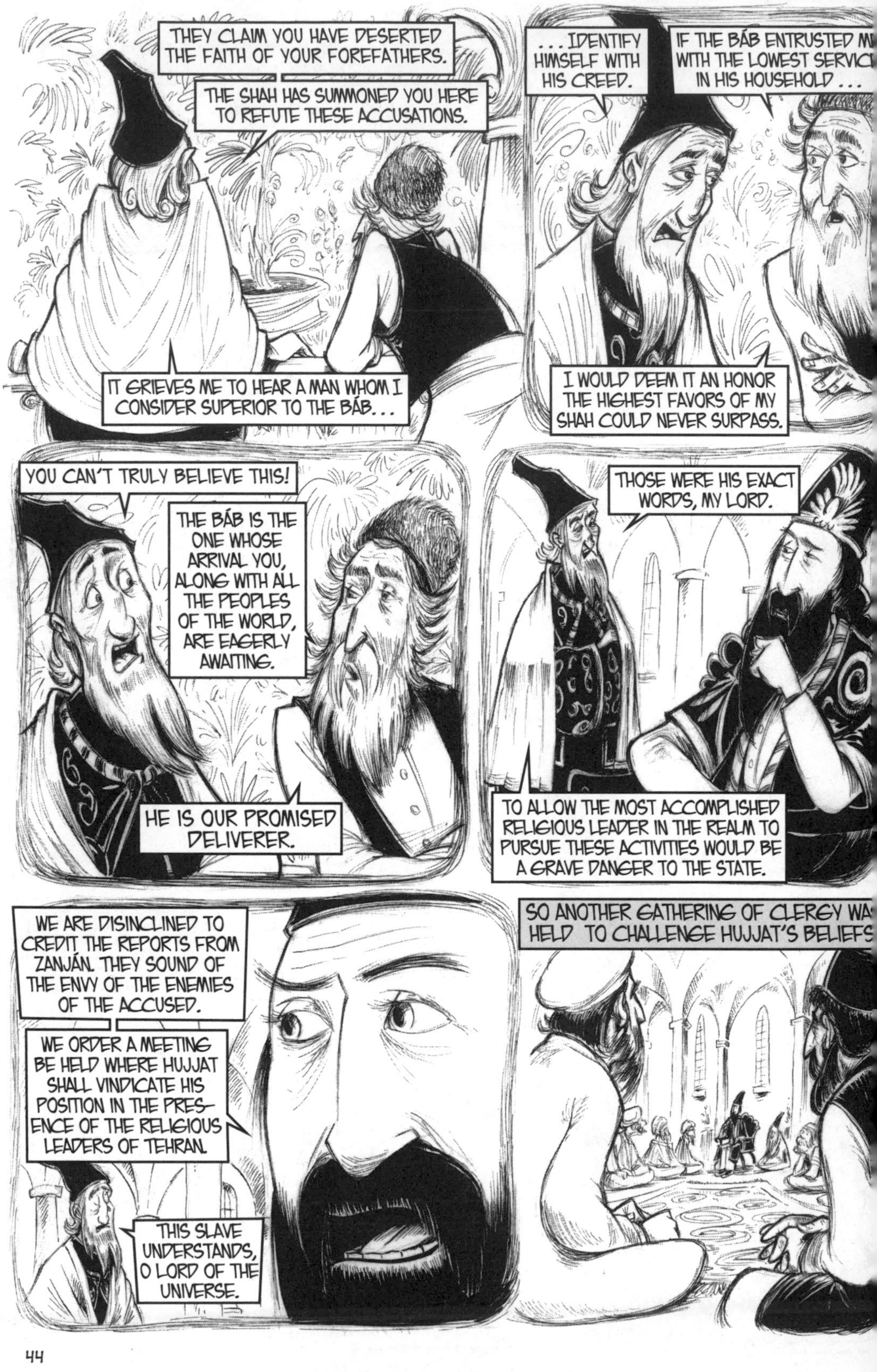

THEY CLAIM YOU HAVE DESERTED THE FAITH OF YOUR FOREFATHERS.
THE SHAH HAS SUMMONED YOU HERE TO REFUTE THESE ACCUSATIONS.
IT GRIEVES ME TO HEAR A MAN WHOM I CONSIDER SUPERIOR TO THE BÁB . . .
. . . IDENTIFY HIMSELF WITH HIS CREED.
IF THE BÁB ENTRUSTED M
WITH THE LOWEST SERVIC
IN HIS HOUSEHOLD . . .
I WOULD DEEM IT AN HONOR THE HIGHEST FAVORS OF MY SHAH COULD NEVER SURPASS.
YOU CAN'T TRULY BELIEVE THIS!
THE BÁB IS THE ONE WHOSE ARRIVAL YOU, ALONG WITH ALL THE PEOPLES OF THE WORLD, ARE EAGERLY AWAITING.
HE IS OUR PROMISED DELIVERER.
THOSE WERE HIS EXACT WORDS, MY LORD.
TO ALLOW THE MOST ACCOMPLISHED RELIGIOUS LEADER IN THE REALM TO PURSUE THESE ACTIVITIES WOULD BE A GRAVE DANGER TO THE STATE.
WE ARE DISINCLINED TO CREDIT THE REPORTS FROM ZANJÁN. THEY SOUND OF THE ENVY OF THE ENEMIES OF THE ACCUSED.
WE ORDER A MEETING BE HELD WHERE HUJJAT SHALL VINDICATE HIS POSITION IN THE PRES-ENCE OF THE RELIGIOUS LEADERS OF TEHRAN.
THIS SLAVE UNDERSTANDS, O LORD OF THE UNIVERSE.
SO ANOTHER GATHERING OF CLERGY WA
HELD TO CHALLENGE HUJJAT'S BELIEFS

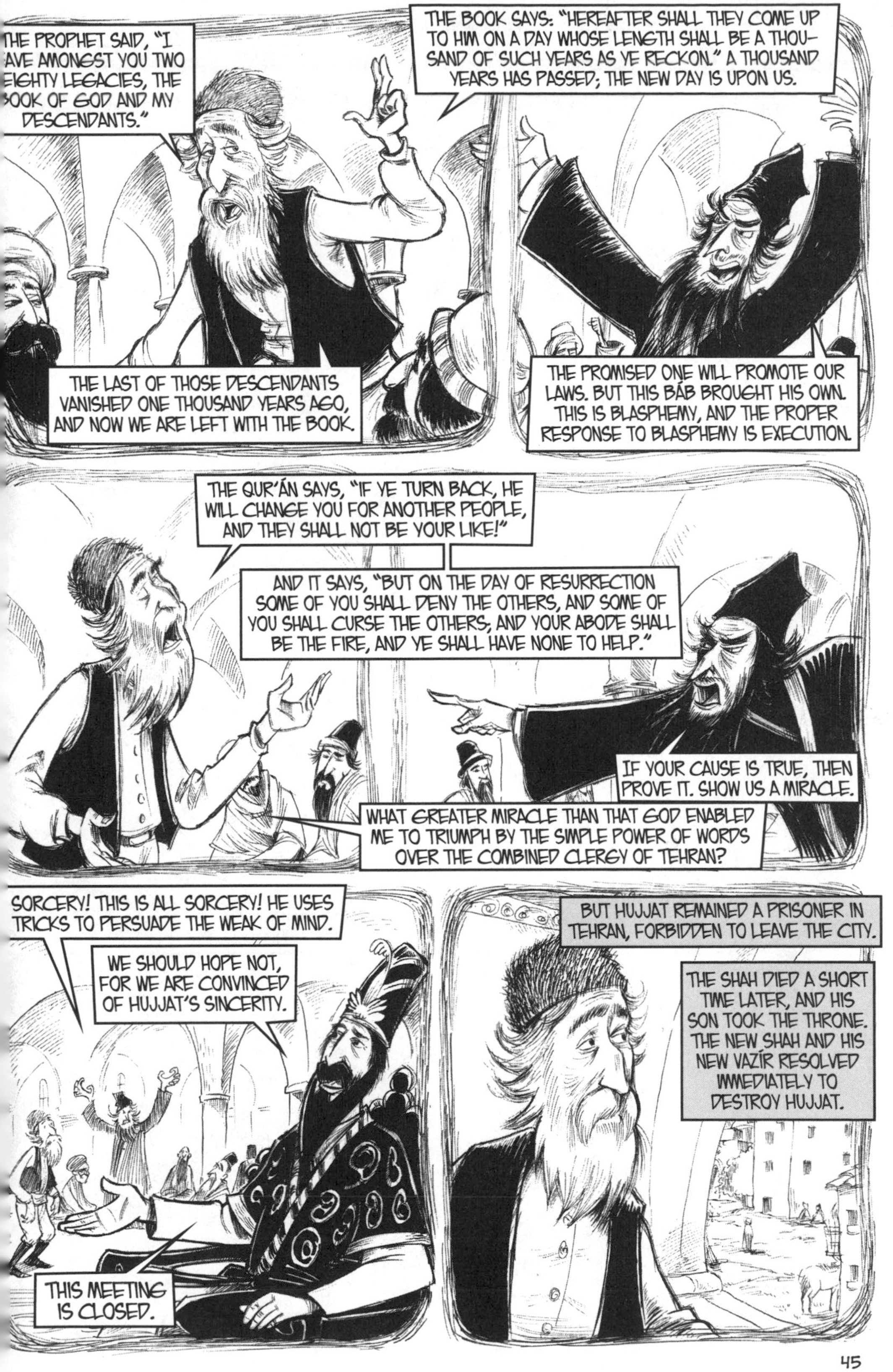
THE PROPHET SAID, "I [L]EAVE AMONGST YOU TWO [W]EIGHTY LEGACIES, THE [B]OOK OF GOD AND MY DESCENDANTS."
THE LAST OF THOSE DESCENDANTS VANISHED ONE THOUSAND YEARS AGO, AND NOW WE ARE LEFT WITH THE BOOK.
THE BOOK SAYS: "HEREAFTER SHALL THEY COME UP TO HIM ON A DAY WHOSE LENGTH SHALL BE A THOUSAND OF SUCH YEARS AS YE RECKON." A THOUSAND YEARS HAS PASSED; THE NEW DAY IS UPON US.
THE PROMISED ONE WILL PROMOTE OUR LAWS. BUT THIS BÁB BROUGHT HIS OWN. THIS IS BLASPHEMY, AND THE PROPER RESPONSE TO BLASPHEMY IS EXECUTION.
THE QUR'ÁN SAYS, "IF YE TURN BACK, HE WILL CHANGE YOU FOR ANOTHER PEOPLE, AND THEY SHALL NOT BE YOUR LIKE!"
AND IT SAYS, "BUT ON THE DAY OF RESURRECTION SOME OF YOU SHALL DENY THE OTHERS, AND SOME OF YOU SHALL CURSE THE OTHERS; AND YOUR ABODE SHALL BE THE FIRE, AND YE SHALL HAVE NONE TO HELP."
IF YOUR CAUSE IS TRUE, THEN PROVE IT. SHOW US A MIRACLE.
WHAT GREATER MIRACLE THAN THAT GOD ENABLED ME TO TRIUMPH BY THE SIMPLE POWER OF WORDS OVER THE COMBINED CLERGY OF TEHRAN?
SORCERY! THIS IS ALL SORCERY! HE USES TRICKS TO PERSUADE THE WEAK OF MIND.
WE SHOULD HOPE NOT, FOR WE ARE CONVINCED OF HUJJAT'S SINCERITY.
THIS MEETING IS CLOSED.
BUT HUJJAT REMAINED A PRISONER IN TEHRAN, FORBIDDEN TO LEAVE THE CITY.
THE SHAH DIED A SHORT TIME LATER, AND HIS SON TOOK THE THRONE. THE NEW SHAH AND HIS NEW VAZÍR RESOLVED IMMEDIATELY TO DESTROY HUJJAT.

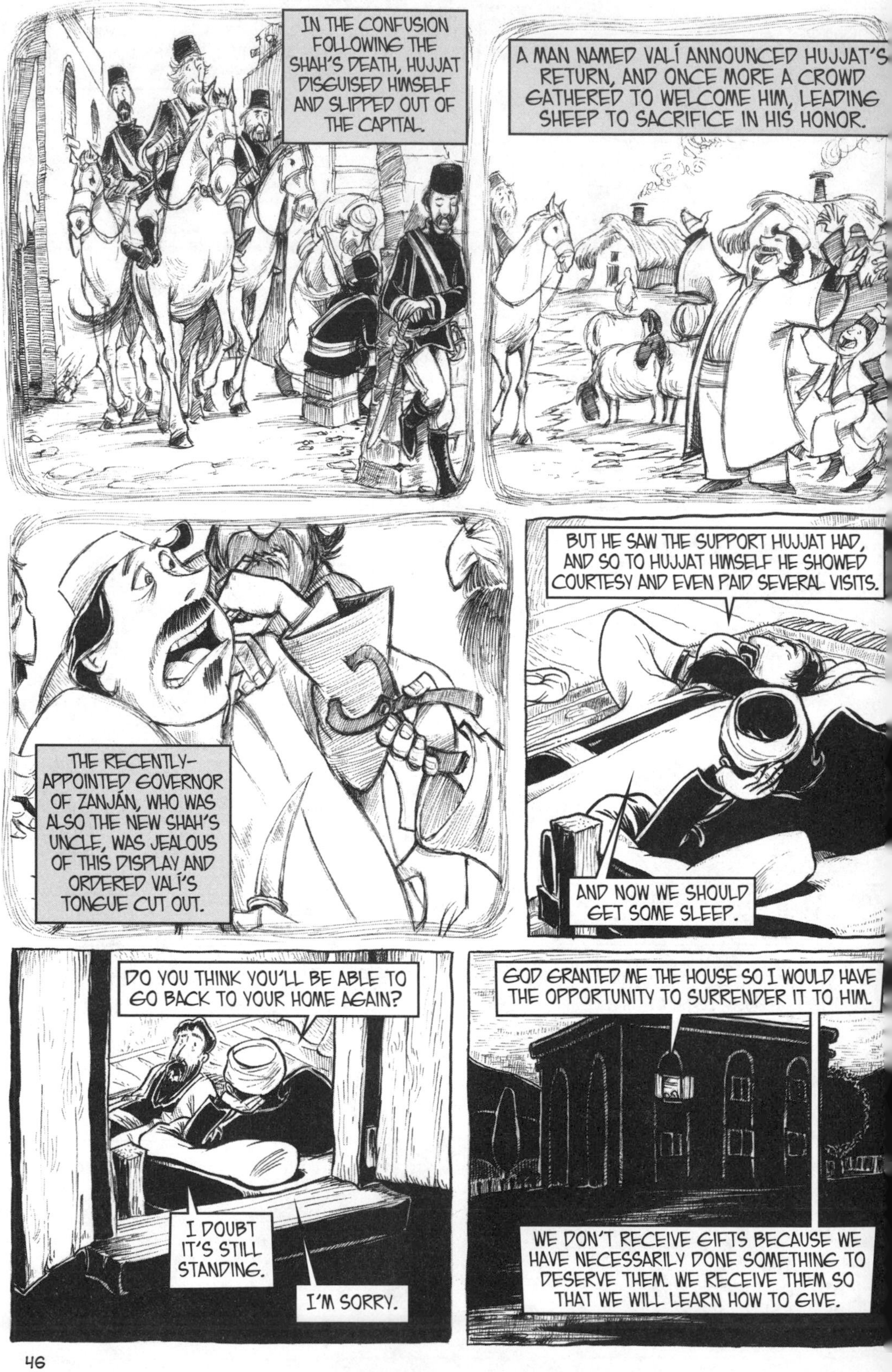

IN THE CONFUSION FOLLOWING THE SHAH'S DEATH, HUJJAT DISGUISED HIMSELF AND SLIPPED OUT OF THE CAPITAL.
A MAN NAMED VALÍ ANNOUNCED HUJJAT'S RETURN, AND ONCE MORE A CROWD GATHERED TO WELCOME HIM, LEADING SHEEP TO SACRIFICE IN HIS HONOR.
THE RECENTLY-APPOINTED GOVERNOR OF ZANJÁN, WHO WAS ALSO THE NEW SHAH'S UNCLE, WAS JEALOUS OF THIS DISPLAY AND ORDERED VALÍ'S TONGUE CUT OUT.
BUT HE SAW THE SUPPORT HUJJAT HAD, AND SO TO HUJJAT HIMSELF HE SHOWED COURTESY AND EVEN PAID SEVERAL VISITS.
AND NOW WE SHOULD GET SOME SLEEP.
DO YOU THINK YOU'LL BE ABLE TO GO BACK TO YOUR HOME AGAIN?
I DOUBT IT'S STILL STANDING.
I'M SORRY.
GOD GRANTED ME THE HOUSE SO I WOULD HAVE THE OPPORTUNITY TO SURRENDER IT TO HIM.
WE DON'T RECEIVE GIFTS BECAUSE WE HAVE NECESSARILY DONE SOMETHING TO DESERVE THEM. WE RECEIVE THEM SO THAT WE WILL LEARN HOW TO GIVE.

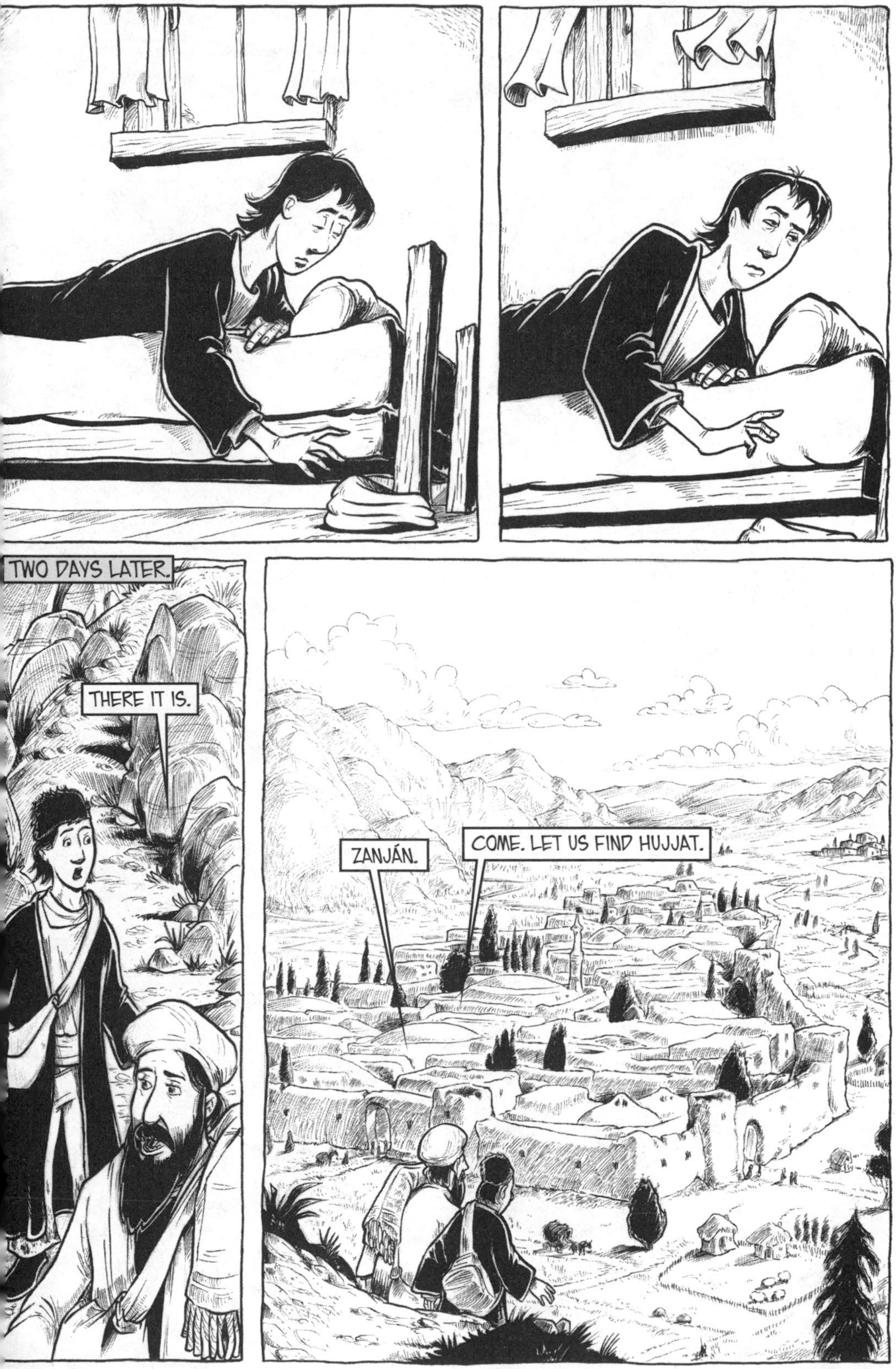
TWO DAYS LATER.
THERE IT IS.
ZANJÁN.
COME. LET US FIND HUJJAT.

3: APOSTLE

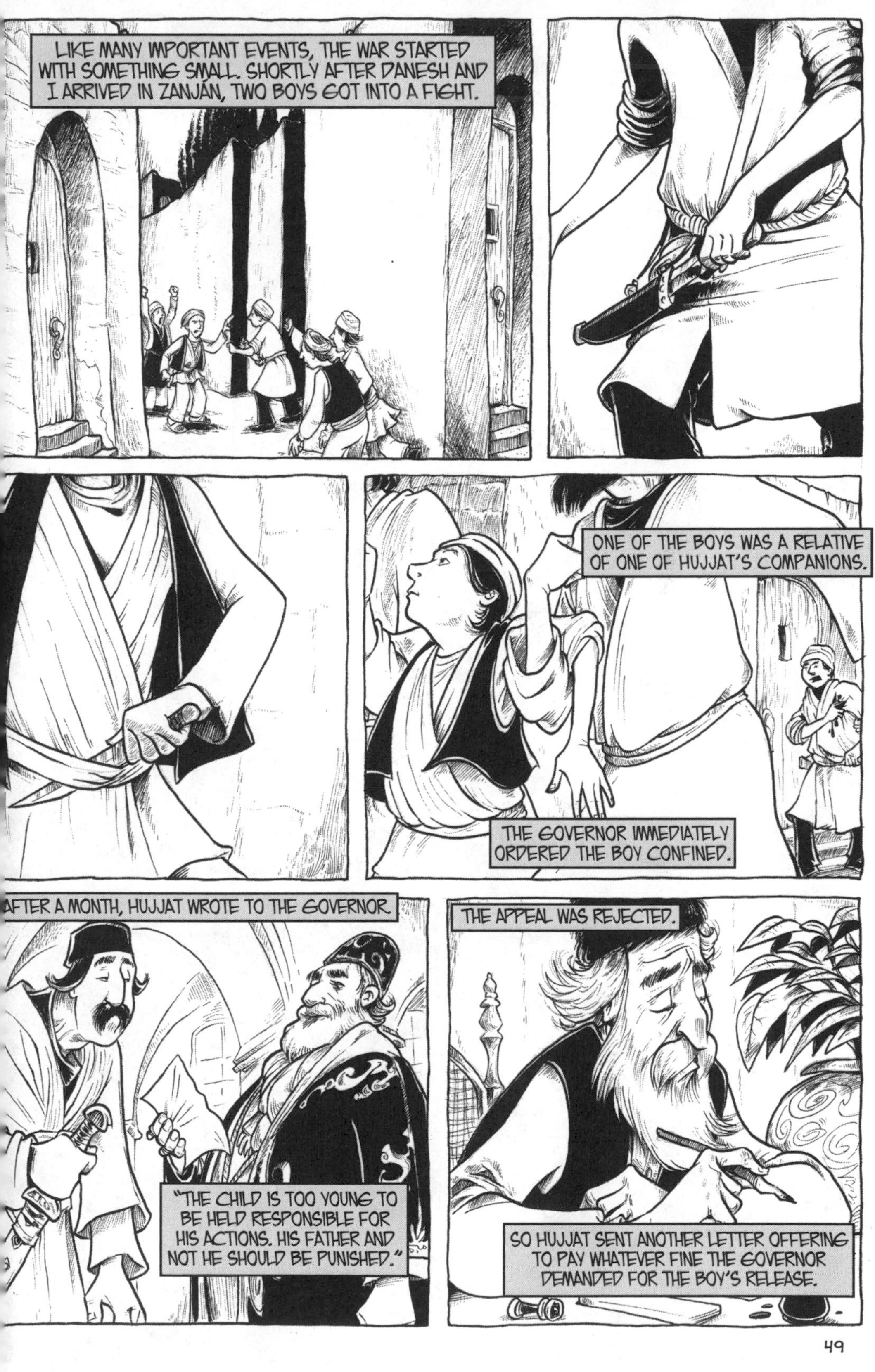
LIKE MANY IMPORTANT EVENTS, THE WAR STARTED WITH SOMETHING SMALL. SHORTLY AFTER DANESH AND I ARRIVED IN ZANJÁN, TWO BOYS GOT INTO A FIGHT.
ONE OF THE BOYS WAS A RELATIVE OF ONE OF HUJJAT'S COMPANIONS.
THE GOVERNOR IMMEDIATELY ORDERED THE BOY CONFINED.
AFTER A MONTH, HUJJAT WROTE TO THE GOVERNOR.
"THE CHILD IS TOO YOUNG TO BE HELD RESPONSIBLE FOR HIS ACTIONS. HIS FATHER AND NOT HE SHOULD BE PUNISHED."
THE APPEAL WAS REJECTED.
SO HUJJAT SENT ANOTHER LETTER OFFERING TO PAY WHATEVER FINE THE GOVERNOR DEMANDED FOR THE BOY'S RELEASE.

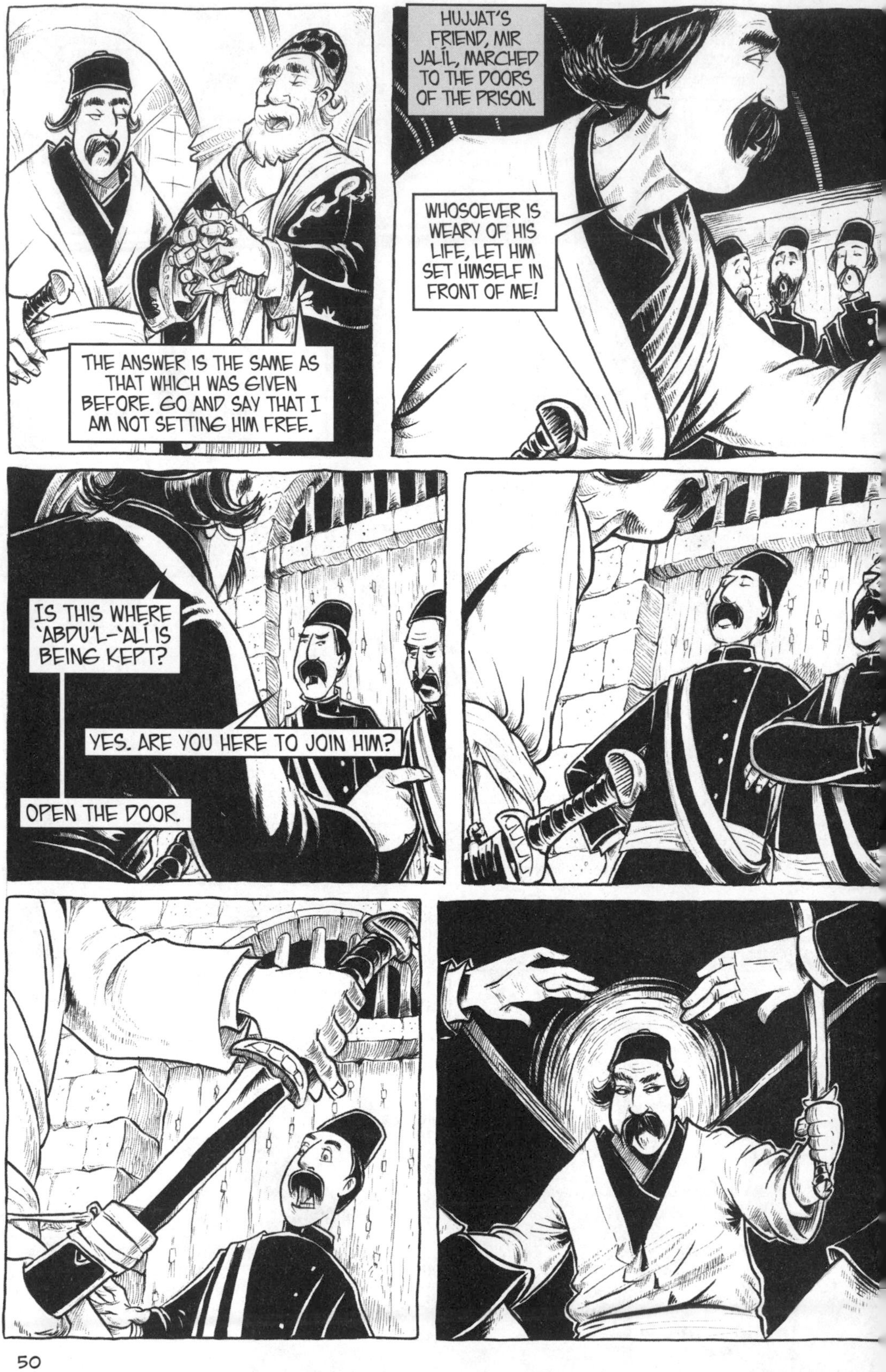
THE ANSWER IS THE SAME AS THAT WHICH WAS GIVEN BEFORE. GO AND SAY THAT I AM NOT SETTING HIM FREE.
HUJJAT'S FRIEND, MIR JALÍL, MARCHED TO THE DOORS OF THE PRISON.
WHOSOEVER IS WEARY OF HIS LIFE, LET HIM SET HIMSELF IN FRONT OF ME!
IS THIS WHERE 'ABDU'L-'ALÍ IS BEING KEPT?
YES. ARE YOU HERE TO JOIN HIM?
OPEN THE DOOR.

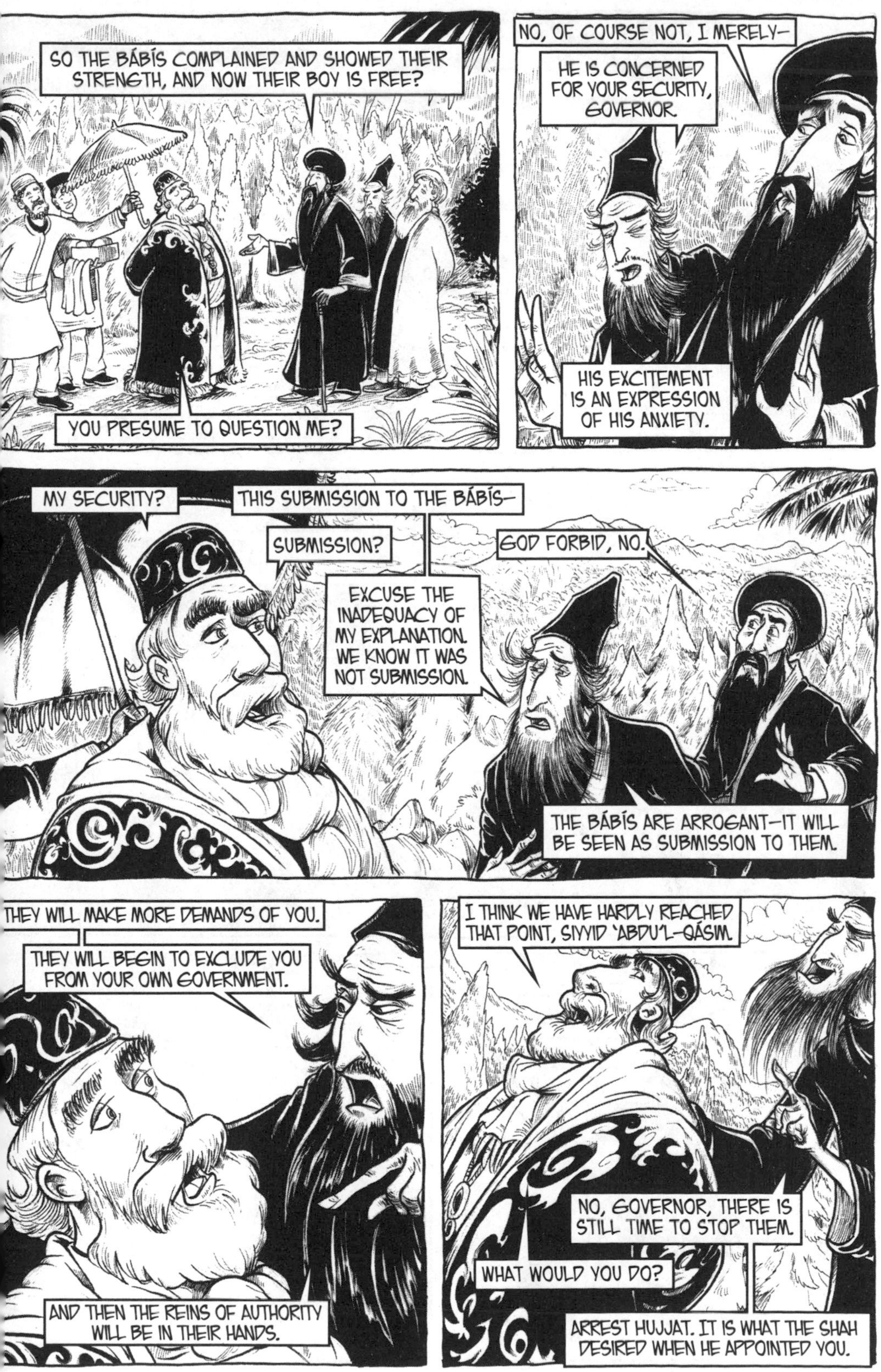
SO THE BÁBÍS COMPLAINED AND SHOWED THEIR STRENGTH, AND NOW THEIR BOY IS FREE?
YOU PRESUME TO QUESTION ME?
NO, OF COURSE NOT, I MERELY—
HE IS CONCERNED FOR YOUR SECURITY, GOVERNOR.
HIS EXCITEMENT IS AN EXPRESSION OF HIS ANXIETY.
MY SECURITY?
THIS SUBMISSION TO THE BÁBÍS—
SUBMISSION?
EXCUSE THE INADEQUACY OF MY EXPLANATION. WE KNOW IT WAS NOT SUBMISSION.
GOD FORBID, NO.
THE BÁBÍS ARE ARROGANT—IT WILL BE SEEN AS SUBMISSION TO THEM.
THEY WILL MAKE MORE DEMANDS OF YOU.
THEY WILL BEGIN TO EXCLUDE YOU FROM YOUR OWN GOVERNMENT.
AND THEN THE REINS OF AUTHORITY WILL BE IN THEIR HANDS.
I THINK WE HAVE HARDLY REACHED THAT POINT, SIYYID 'ABDU'L-QÁSIM.
NO, GOVERNOR, THERE IS STILL TIME TO STOP THEM.
WHAT WOULD YOU DO?
ARREST HUJJAT. IT IS WHAT THE SHAH DESIRED WHEN HE APPOINTED YOU.

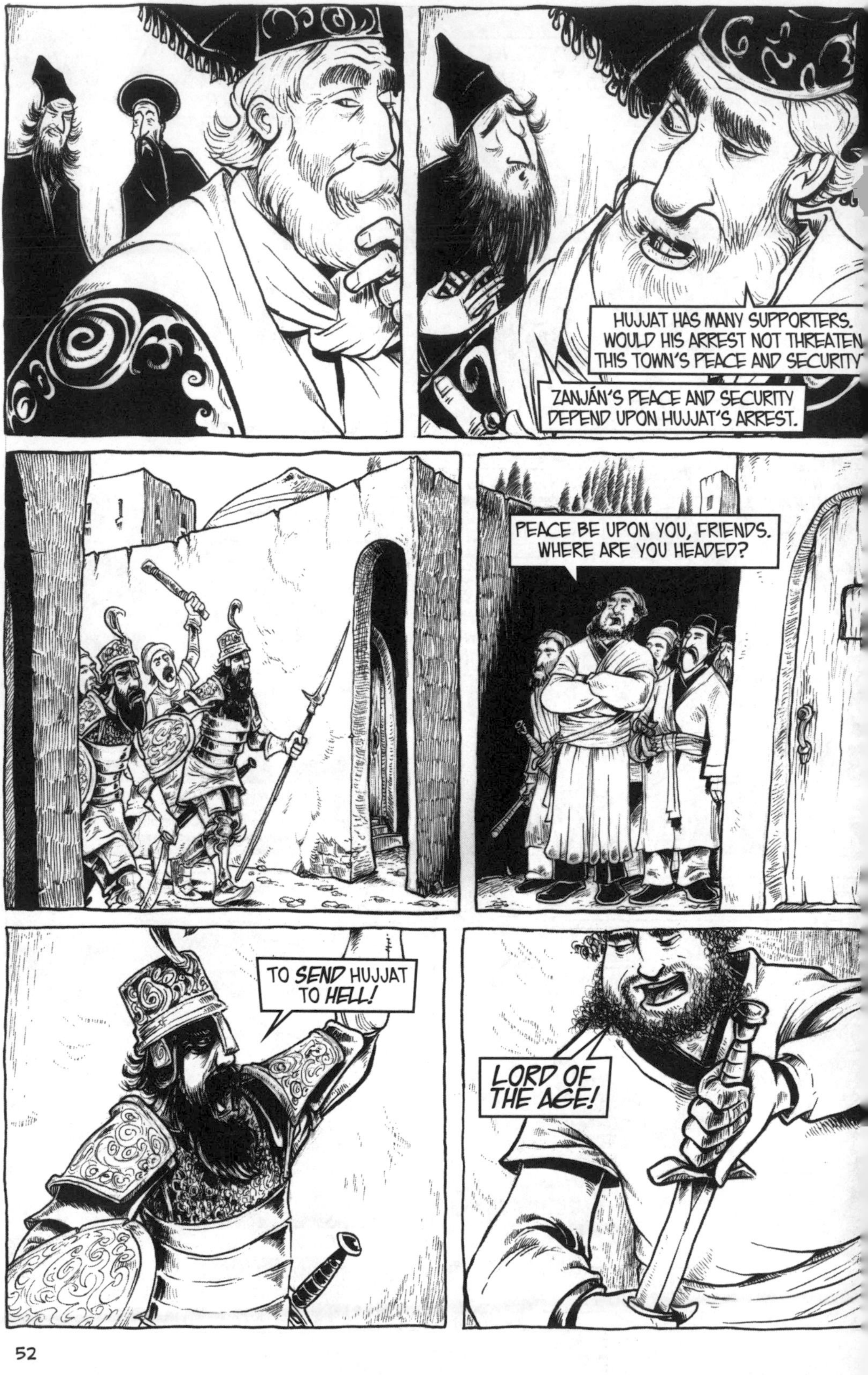
HUJJAT HAS MANY SUPPORTERS. WOULD HIS ARREST NOT THREATEN THIS TOWN'S PEACE AND SECURITY?
ZANJÁN'S PEACE AND SECURITY DEPEND UPON HUJJAT'S ARREST.
PEACE BE UPON YOU, FRIENDS. WHERE ARE YOU HEADED?
TO *SEND* HUJJAT TO *HELL!*
LORD OF THE AGE!

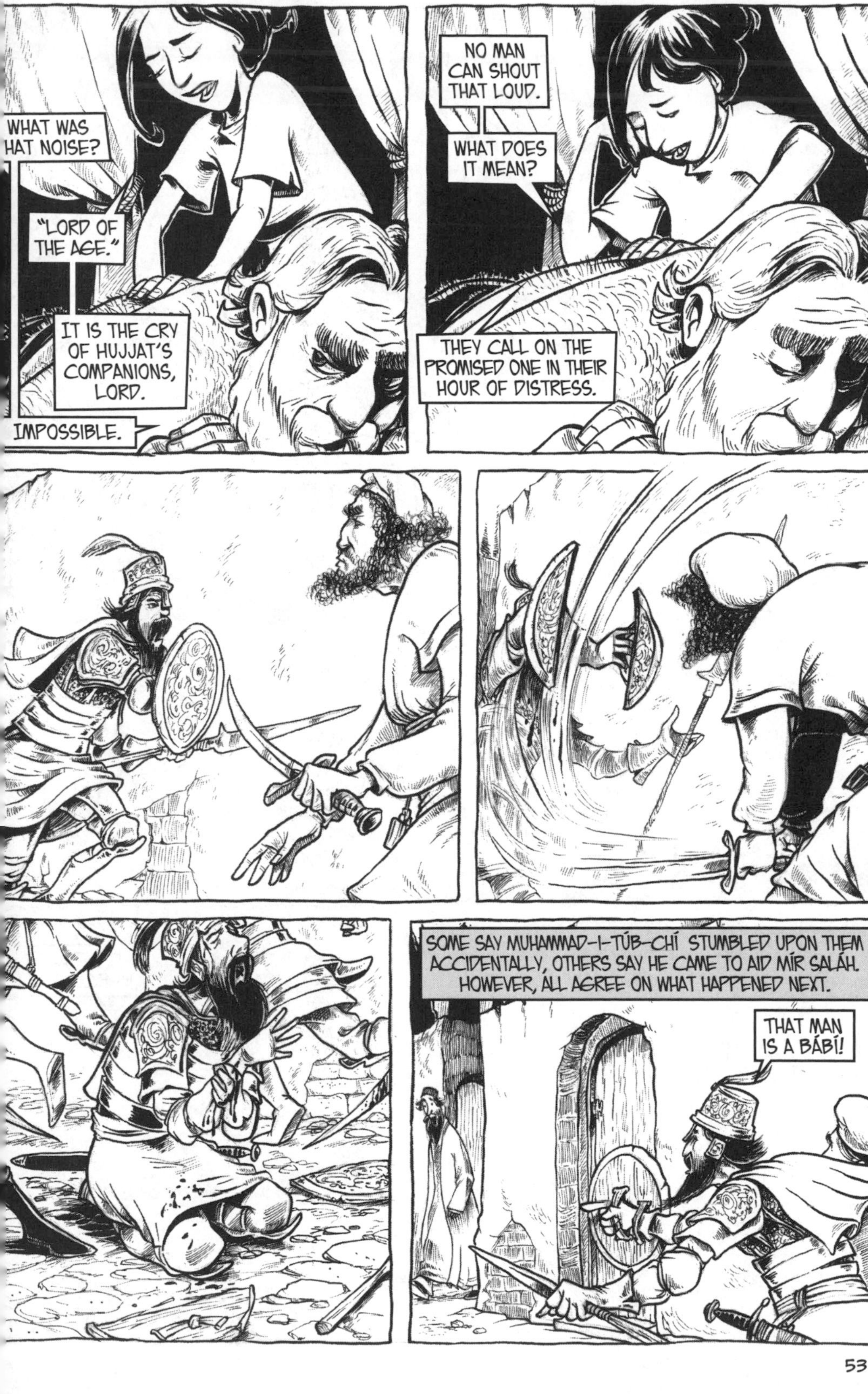

WHAT WAS
HAT NOISE?
"LORD OF THE AGE."
IT IS THE CRY OF HUJJAT'S COMPANIONS, LORD.
IMPOSSIBLE.
NO MAN CAN SHOUT THAT LOUD.
WHAT DOES IT MEAN?
THEY CALL ON THE PROMISED ONE IN THEIR HOUR OF DISTRESS.
SOME SAY MUHAMMAD-I-TÚB-CHÍ STUMBLED UPON THEM ACCIDENTALLY, OTHERS SAY HE CAME TO AID MÍR SALÁH. HOWEVER, ALL AGREE ON WHAT HAPPENED NEXT.
THAT MAN IS A BÁBÍ!

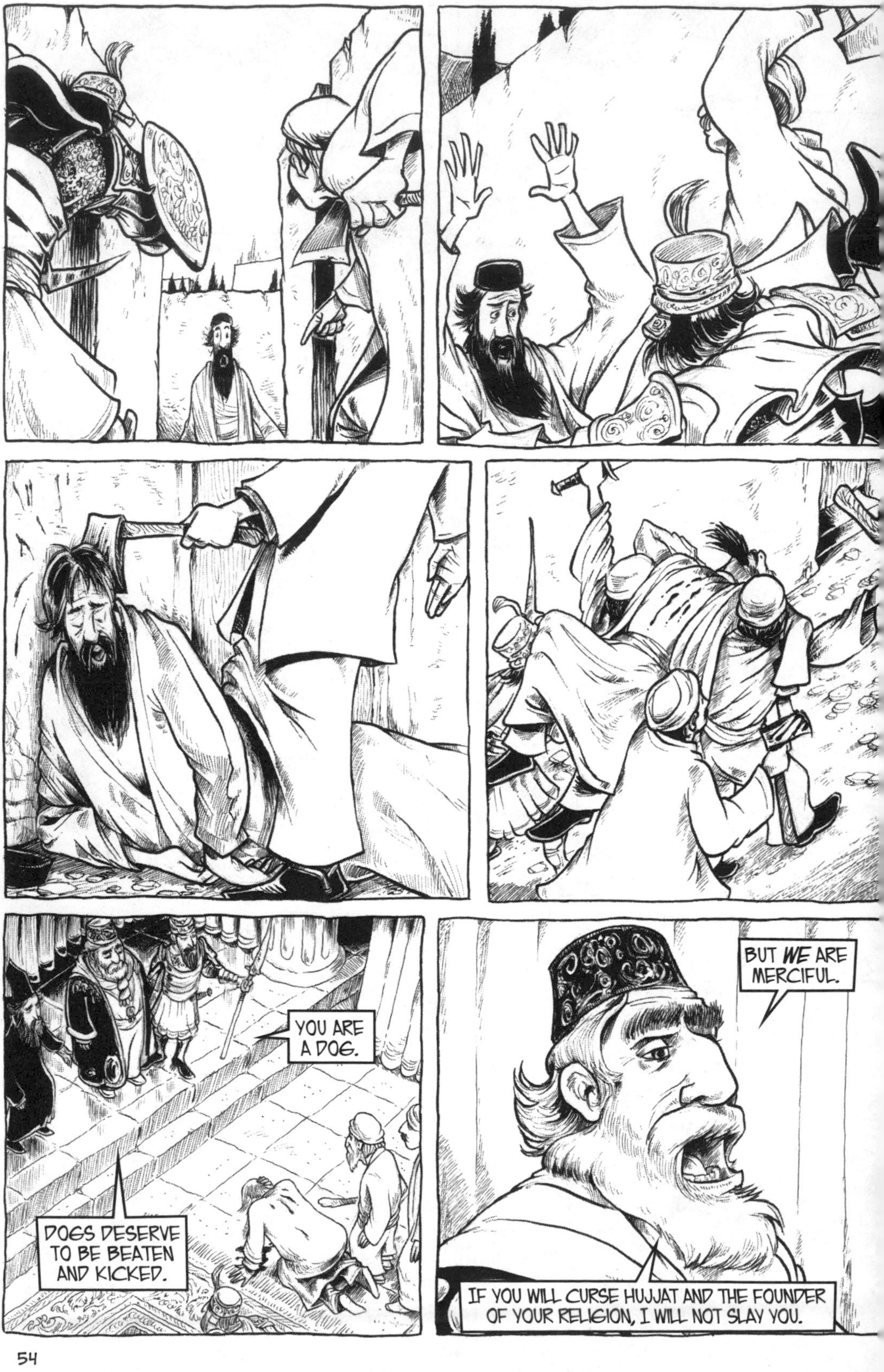
YOU ARE A DOG.
DOGS DESERVE TO BE BEATEN AND KICKED.
BUT WE ARE MERCIFUL.
IF YOU WILL CURSE HUJJAT AND THE FOUNDER OF YOUR RELIGION, I WILL NOT SLAY YOU.

CURSES BE UPON THINE OWN FOUL NATURE!

O FRIENDS, *THIS* IS HOLY WAR!

STAND ASIDE, 'ABDU'L-QÁSIM.

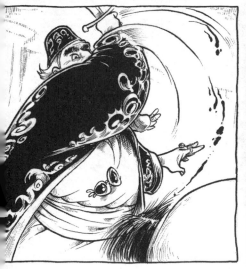

MY FRIENDS, TONIGHT WE WILL ALL SWEAR AN OATH TO GOD.

WE WILL NOT REST UNTIL THIS HERESY IS ENTIRELY DESTROYED.

THEY'VE KILLED MUHAMMAD-I-TÚB-CHÍ.

I KNOW.

WE *MUST* AVENGE HIS DEATH. IT IS TIME TO DECLARE HOLY WAR.

AND HAVE HUNDREDS MORE DIE?

NO!

NOT UNDER ANY CIRCUMSTANCE.

I HEARD ABOUT THIS FROM MÍR SALÁH WHEN HE CAME FOR A VISIT.

WE WERE THE GUESTS OF A BÁBÍ, MÍRZÁ IMAN

HE WAS A BAKER WHO BELIEVED EVERY PROBLEM COULD BE SOLVED BY HUMOR AND BOLD ACTION.

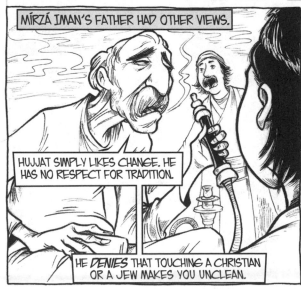

MÍRZÁ IMAN'S FATHER HAD OTHER VIEWS.

HUJJAT SIMPLY LIKES CHANGE. HE HAS NO RESPECT FOR TRADITION.

HE *DENIES* THAT TOUCHING A CHRISTIAN OR A JEW MAKES YOU UNCLEAN.

HE THREATENS THEIR CORRUPTION. YOU REMEMBER THE CARAVANSERAI WHERE THE CLERGY MADE MONEY BY GRANTING TEMPO RARY MARRIAGES? HUJJAT PUT AN END TO I

BAH!

THAT IS WHY THE DIVINES ARE ANGRY.

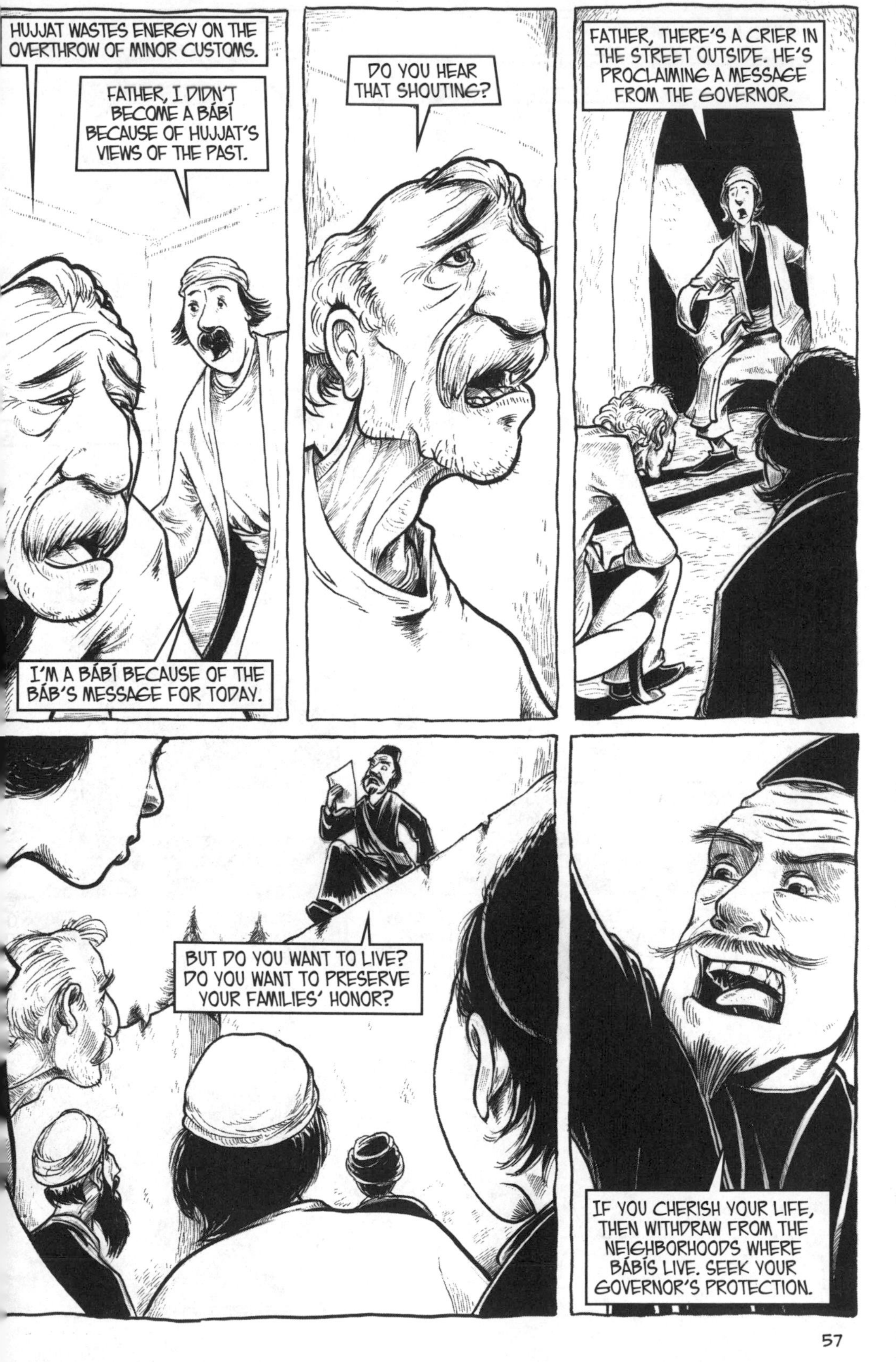
HUJJAT WASTES ENERGY ON THE OVERTHROW OF MINOR CUSTOMS.
FATHER, I DIDN'T BECOME A BÁBÍ BECAUSE OF HUJJAT'S VIEWS OF THE PAST.
I'M A BÁBÍ BECAUSE OF THE BÁB'S MESSAGE FOR TODAY.
DO YOU HEAR THAT SHOUTING?
FATHER, THERE'S A CRIER IN THE STREET OUTSIDE. HE'S PROCLAIMING A MESSAGE FROM THE GOVERNOR.
BUT DO YOU WANT TO LIVE? DO YOU WANT TO PRESERVE YOUR FAMILIES' HONOR?
IF YOU CHERISH YOUR LIFE, THEN WITHDRAW FROM THE NEIGHBORHOODS WHERE BÁBÍS LIVE. SEEK YOUR GOVERNOR'S PROTECTION.

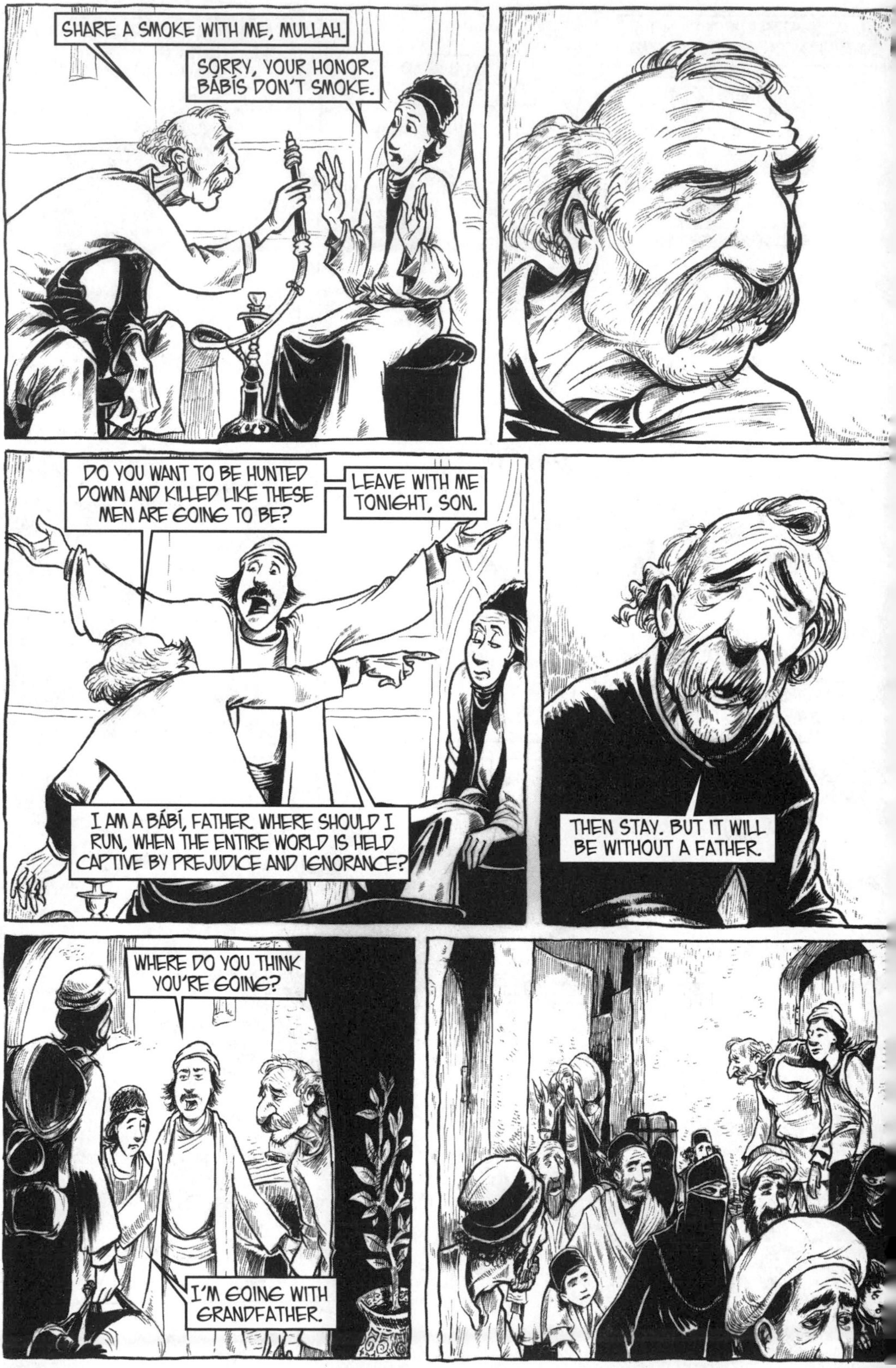
SHARE A SMOKE WITH ME, MULLAH.
SORRY, YOUR HONOR. BÁBÍS DON'T SMOKE.
DO YOU WANT TO BE HUNTED DOWN AND KILLED LIKE THESE MEN ARE GOING TO BE?
LEAVE WITH ME TONIGHT, SON.
I AM A BÁBÍ, FATHER. WHERE SHOULD I RUN, WHEN THE ENTIRE WORLD IS HELD CAPTIVE BY PREJUDICE AND IGNORANCE?
THEN STAY. BUT IT WILL BE WITHOUT A FATHER.
WHERE DO YOU THINK YOU'RE GOING?
I'M GOING WITH GRANDFATHER.

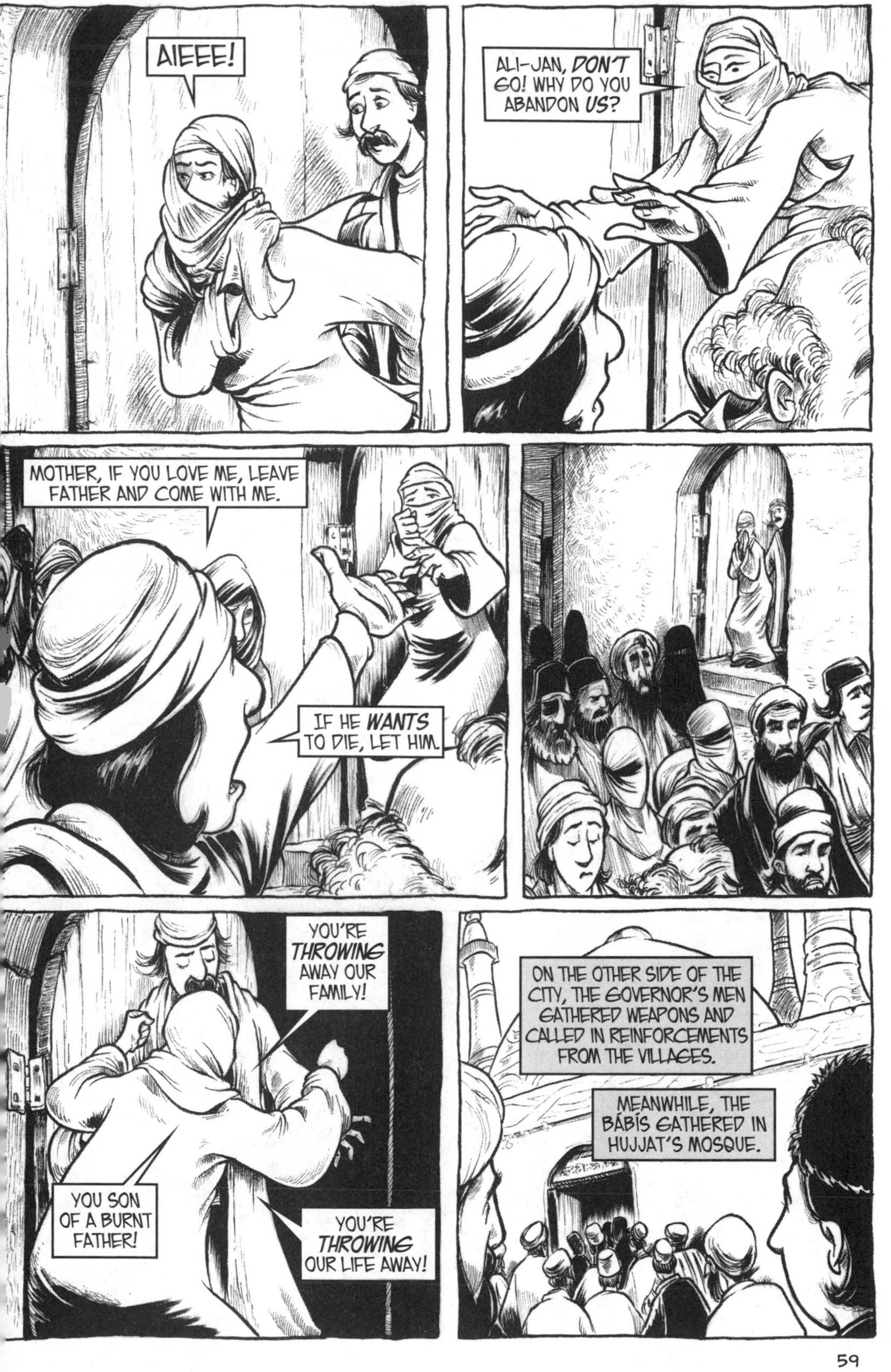
AIEEE!
ALI-JAN, DON'T GO! WHY DO YOU ABANDON US?
MOTHER, IF YOU LOVE ME, LEAVE FATHER AND COME WITH ME.
IF HE WANTS TO DIE, LET HIM.
YOU'RE THROWING AWAY OUR FAMILY!
YOU SON OF A BURNT FATHER!
YOU'RE THROWING OUR LIFE AWAY!
ON THE OTHER SIDE OF THE CITY, THE GOVERNOR'S MEN GATHERED WEAPONS AND CALLED IN REINFORCEMENTS FROM THE VILLAGES.
MEANWHILE, THE BÁBÍS GATHERED IN HUJJAT'S MOSQUE.

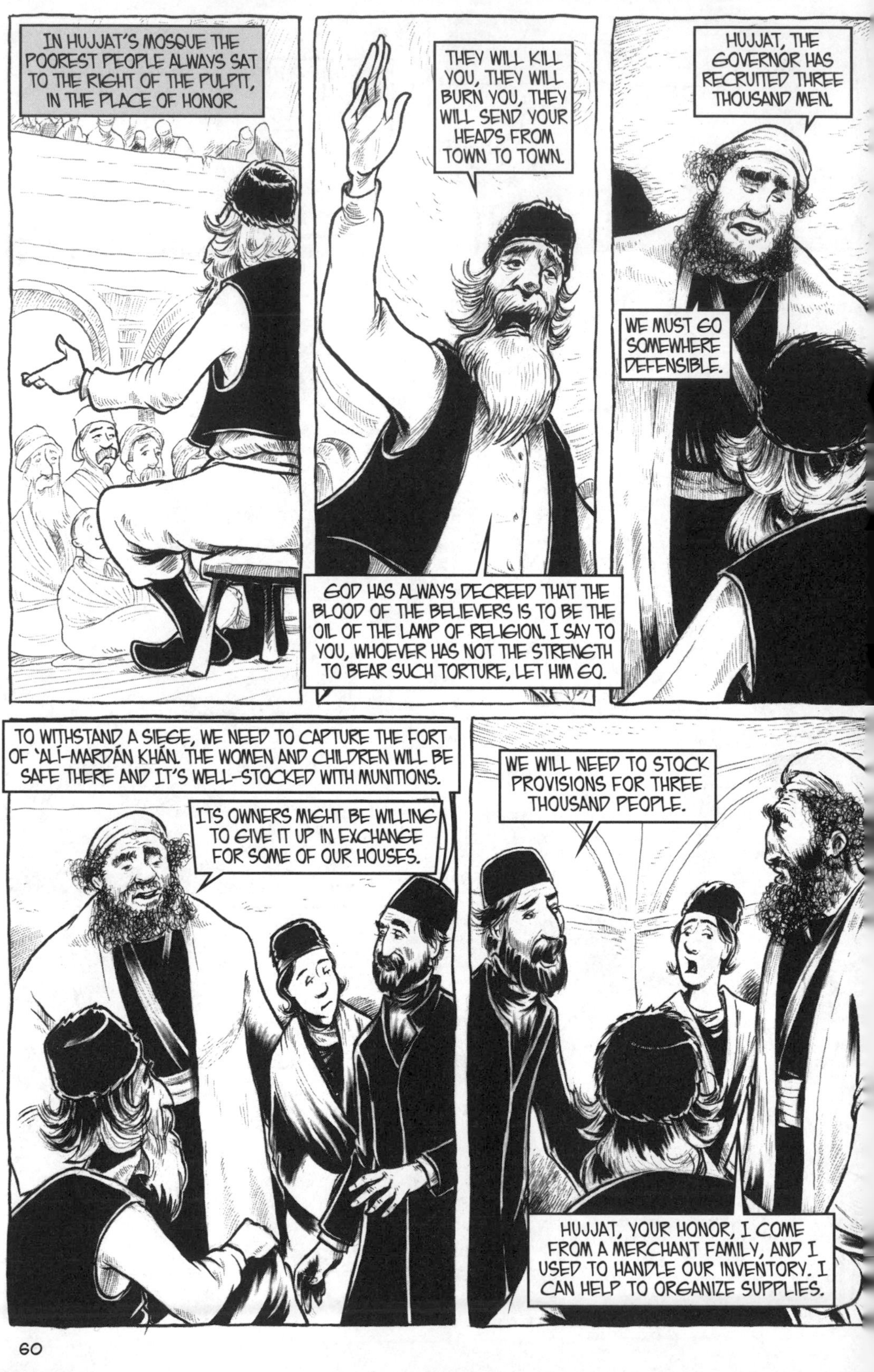

IN HUJJAT'S MOSQUE THE POOREST PEOPLE ALWAYS SAT TO THE RIGHT OF THE PULPIT, IN THE PLACE OF HONOR.
THEY WILL KILL YOU, THEY WILL BURN YOU, THEY WILL SEND YOUR HEADS FROM TOWN TO TOWN.
GOD HAS ALWAYS DECREED THAT THE BLOOD OF THE BELIEVERS IS TO BE THE OIL OF THE LAMP OF RELIGION. I SAY TO YOU, WHOEVER HAS NOT THE STRENGTH TO BEAR SUCH TORTURE, LET HIM GO.
HUJJAT, THE GOVERNOR HAS RECRUITED THREE THOUSAND MEN.
WE MUST GO SOMEWHERE DEFENSIBLE.
TO WITHSTAND A SIEGE, WE NEED TO CAPTURE THE FORT OF 'ALÍ-MARDÁN KHÁN. THE WOMEN AND CHILDREN WILL BE SAFE THERE AND IT'S WELL-STOCKED WITH MUNITIONS.
ITS OWNERS MIGHT BE WILLING TO GIVE IT UP IN EXCHANGE FOR SOME OF OUR HOUSES.
WE WILL NEED TO STOCK PROVISIONS FOR THREE THOUSAND PEOPLE.
HUJJAT, YOUR HONOR, I COME FROM A MERCHANT FAMILY, AND I USED TO HANDLE OUR INVENTORY. I CAN HELP TO ORGANIZE SUPPLIES.

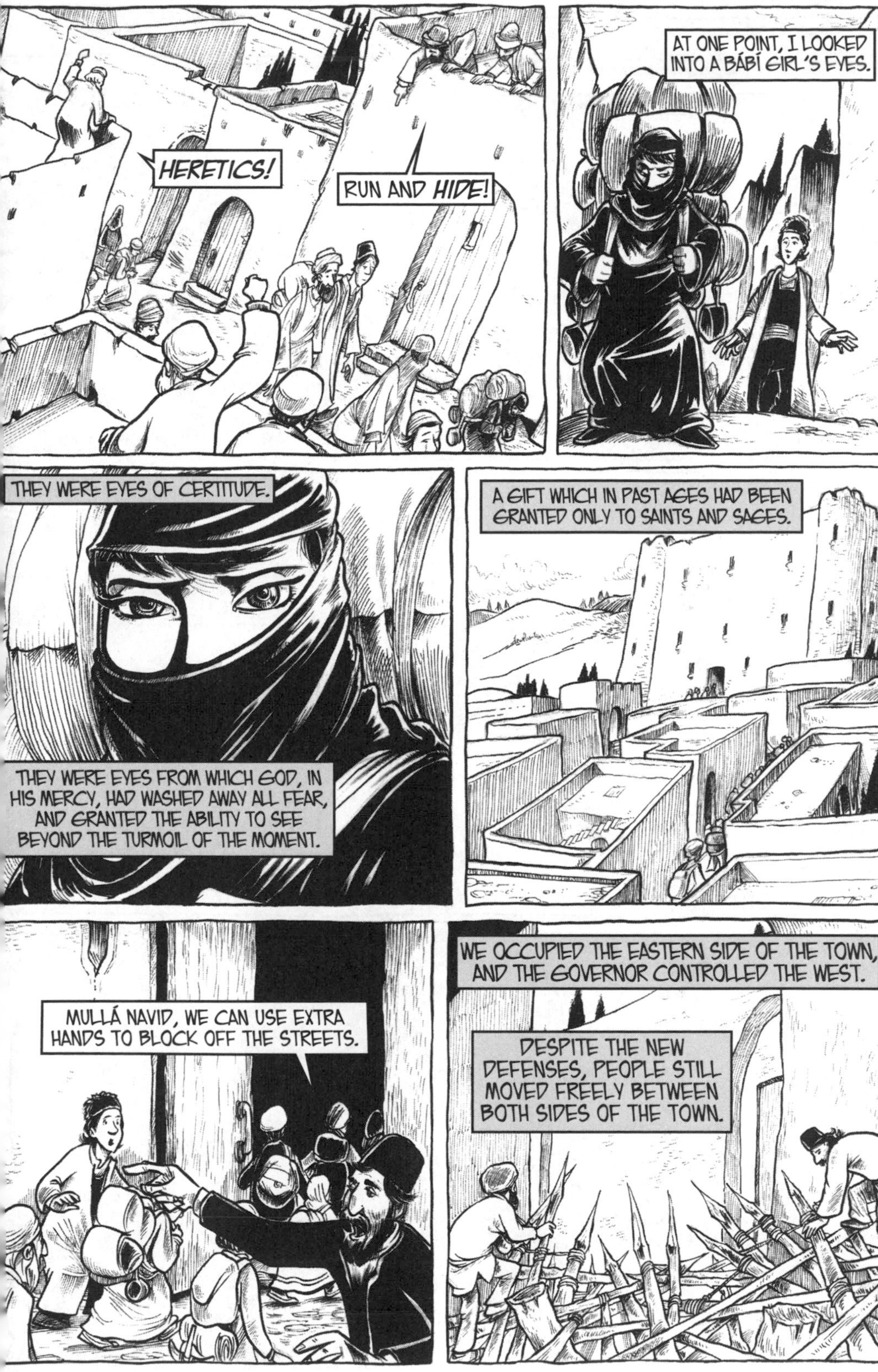
HERETICS!
RUN AND HIDE!
AT ONE POINT, I LOOKED INTO A BÁBÍ GIRL'S EYES.
THEY WERE EYES OF CERTITUDE.
THEY WERE EYES FROM WHICH GOD, IN HIS MERCY, HAD WASHED AWAY ALL FEAR, AND GRANTED THE ABILITY TO SEE BEYOND THE TURMOIL OF THE MOMENT.
A GIFT WHICH IN PAST AGES HAD BEEN GRANTED ONLY TO SAINTS AND SAGES.
MULLÁ NAVID, WE CAN USE EXTRA HANDS TO BLOCK OFF THE STREETS.
WE OCCUPIED THE EASTERN SIDE OF THE TOWN, AND THE GOVERNOR CONTROLLED THE WEST.
DESPITE THE NEW DEFENSES, PEOPLE STILL MOVED FREELY BETWEEN BOTH SIDES OF THE TOWN.

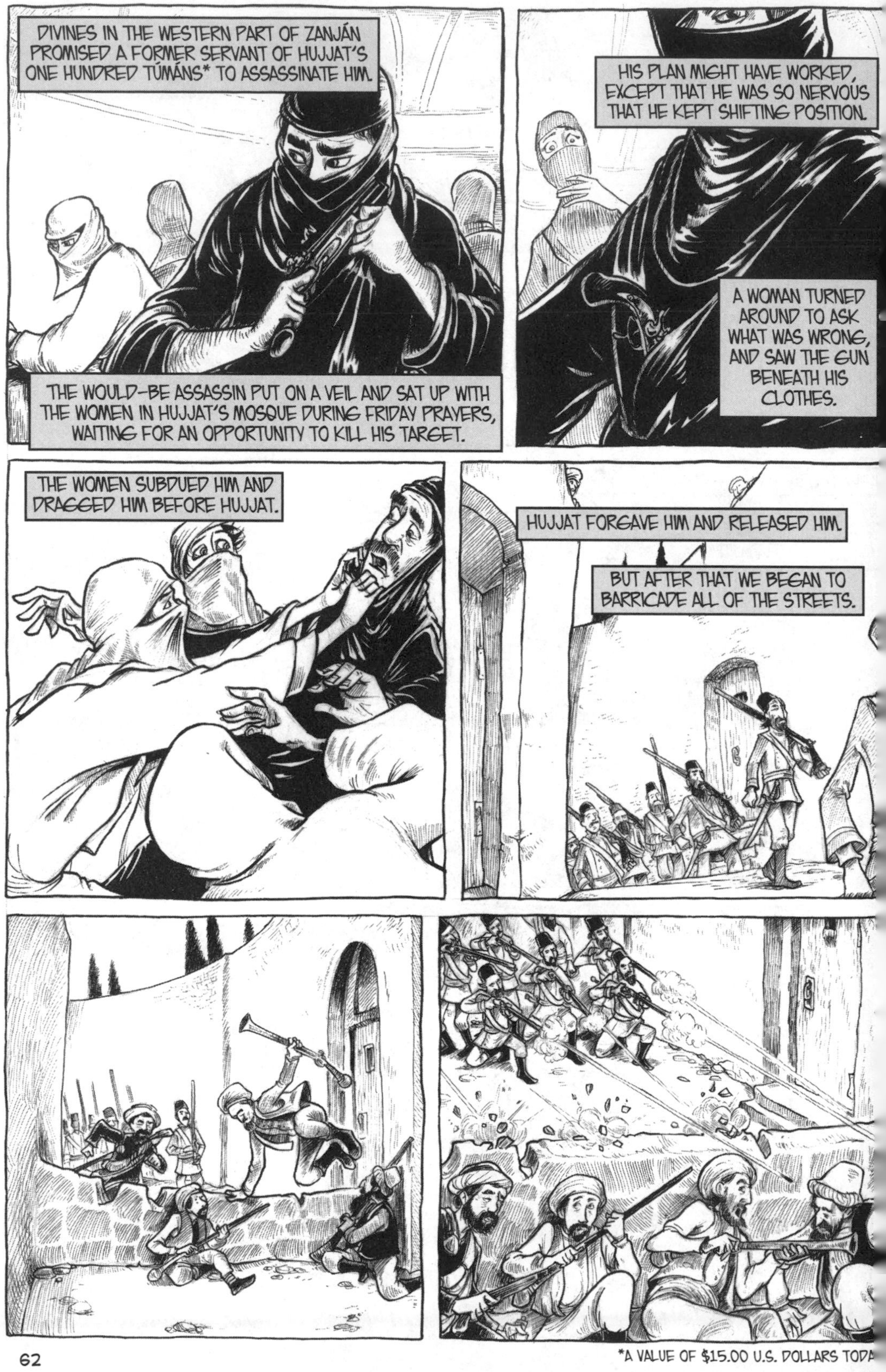
DIVINES IN THE WESTERN PART OF ZANJÁN PROMISED A FORMER SERVANT OF HUJJAT'S ONE HUNDRED TÚMÁNS* TO ASSASSINATE HIM.
THE WOULD-BE ASSASSIN PUT ON A VEIL AND SAT UP WITH THE WOMEN IN HUJJAT'S MOSQUE DURING FRIDAY PRAYERS, WAITING FOR AN OPPORTUNITY TO KILL HIS TARGET.
HIS PLAN MIGHT HAVE WORKED, EXCEPT THAT HE WAS SO NERVOUS THAT HE KEPT SHIFTING POSITION.
A WOMAN TURNED AROUND TO ASK WHAT WAS WRONG, AND SAW THE GUN BENEATH HIS CLOTHES.
THE WOMEN SUBDUED HIM AND DRAGGED HIM BEFORE HUJJAT.
HUJJAT FORGAVE HIM AND RELEASED HIM.
BUT AFTER THAT WE BEGAN TO BARRICADE ALL OF THE STREETS.

*A VALUE OF $15.00 U.S. DOLLARS TODA

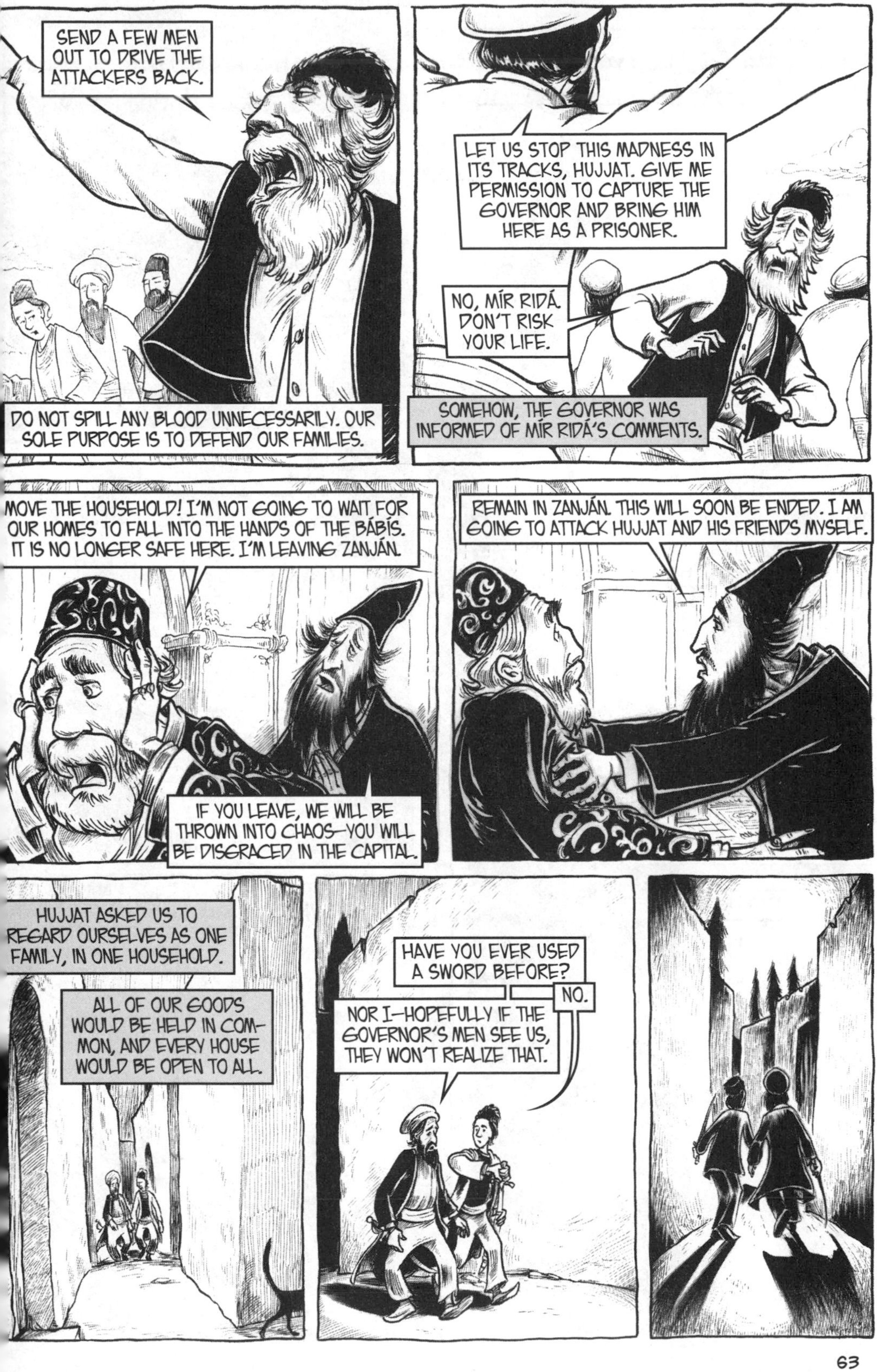
SEND A FEW MEN OUT TO DRIVE THE ATTACKERS BACK.
DO NOT SPILL ANY BLOOD UNNECESSARILY. OUR SOLE PURPOSE IS TO DEFEND OUR FAMILIES.
LET US STOP THIS MADNESS IN ITS TRACKS, HUJJAT. GIVE ME PERMISSION TO CAPTURE THE GOVERNOR AND BRING HIM HERE AS A PRISONER.
NO, MÍR RIDÁ. DON'T RISK YOUR LIFE.
SOMEHOW, THE GOVERNOR WAS INFORMED OF MÍR RIDÁ'S COMMENTS.
MOVE THE HOUSEHOLD! I'M NOT GOING TO WAIT FOR OUR HOMES TO FALL INTO THE HANDS OF THE BÁBÍS. IT IS NO LONGER SAFE HERE. I'M LEAVING ZANJÁN.
IF YOU LEAVE, WE WILL BE THROWN INTO CHAOS—YOU WILL BE DISGRACED IN THE CAPITAL.
REMAIN IN ZANJÁN. THIS WILL SOON BE ENDED. I AM GOING TO ATTACK HUJJAT AND HIS FRIENDS MYSELF.
HUJJAT ASKED US TO REGARD OURSELVES AS ONE FAMILY, IN ONE HOUSEHOLD.
ALL OF OUR GOODS WOULD BE HELD IN COMMON, AND EVERY HOUSE WOULD BE OPEN TO ALL.
HAVE YOU EVER USED A SWORD BEFORE?
NO.
NOR I—HOPEFULLY IF THE GOVERNOR'S MEN SEE US, THEY WON'T REALIZE THAT.

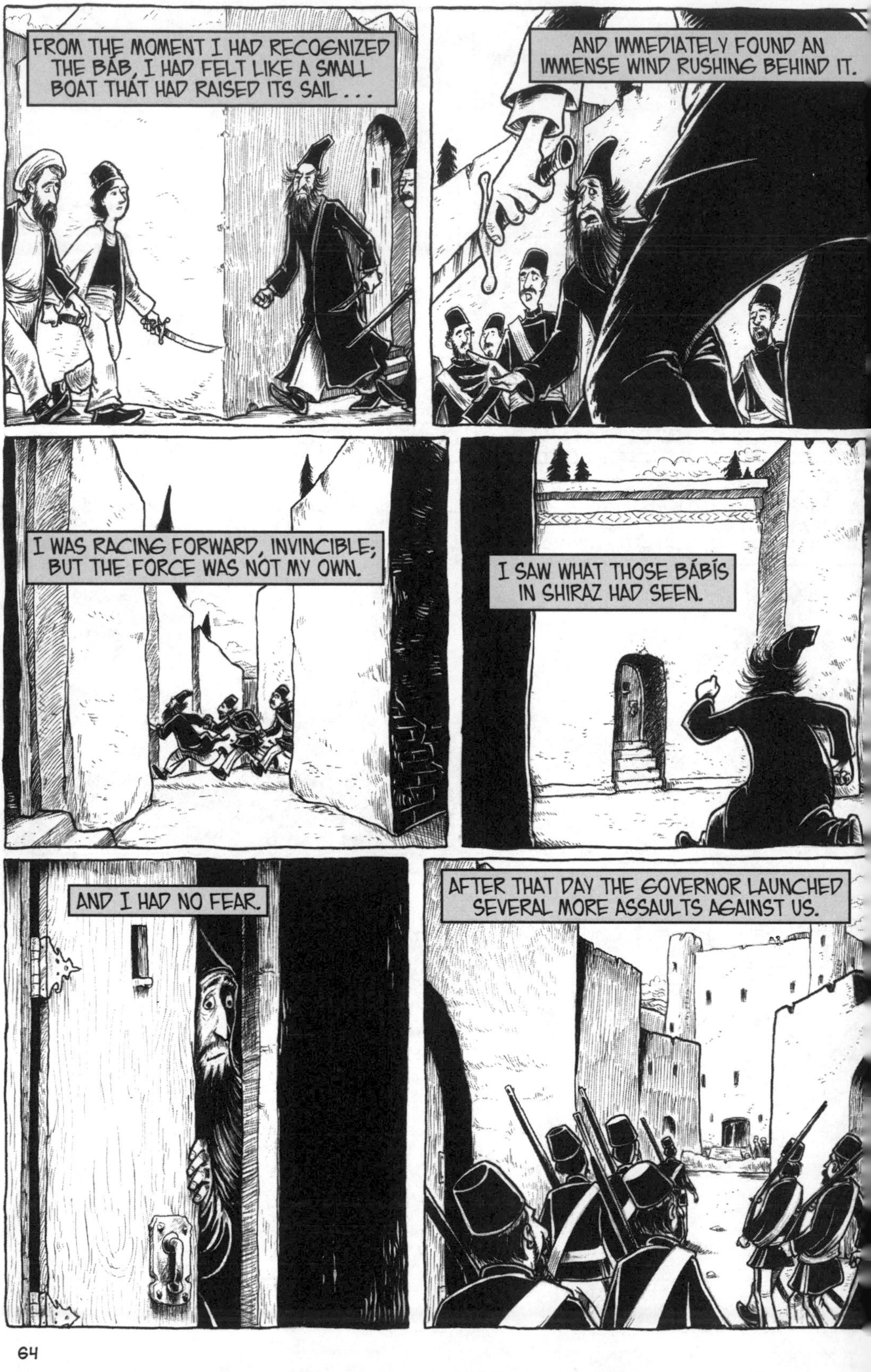
FROM THE MOMENT I HAD RECOGNIZED THE BÁB, I HAD FELT LIKE A SMALL BOAT THAT HAD RAISED ITS SAIL . . .
AND IMMEDIATELY FOUND AN IMMENSE WIND RUSHING BEHIND IT.
I WAS RACING FORWARD, INVINCIBLE; BUT THE FORCE WAS NOT MY OWN.
I SAW WHAT THOSE BÁBÍS IN SHIRAZ HAD SEEN.
AND I HAD NO FEAR.
AFTER THAT DAY THE GOVERNOR LAUNCHED SEVERAL MORE ASSAULTS AGAINST US.

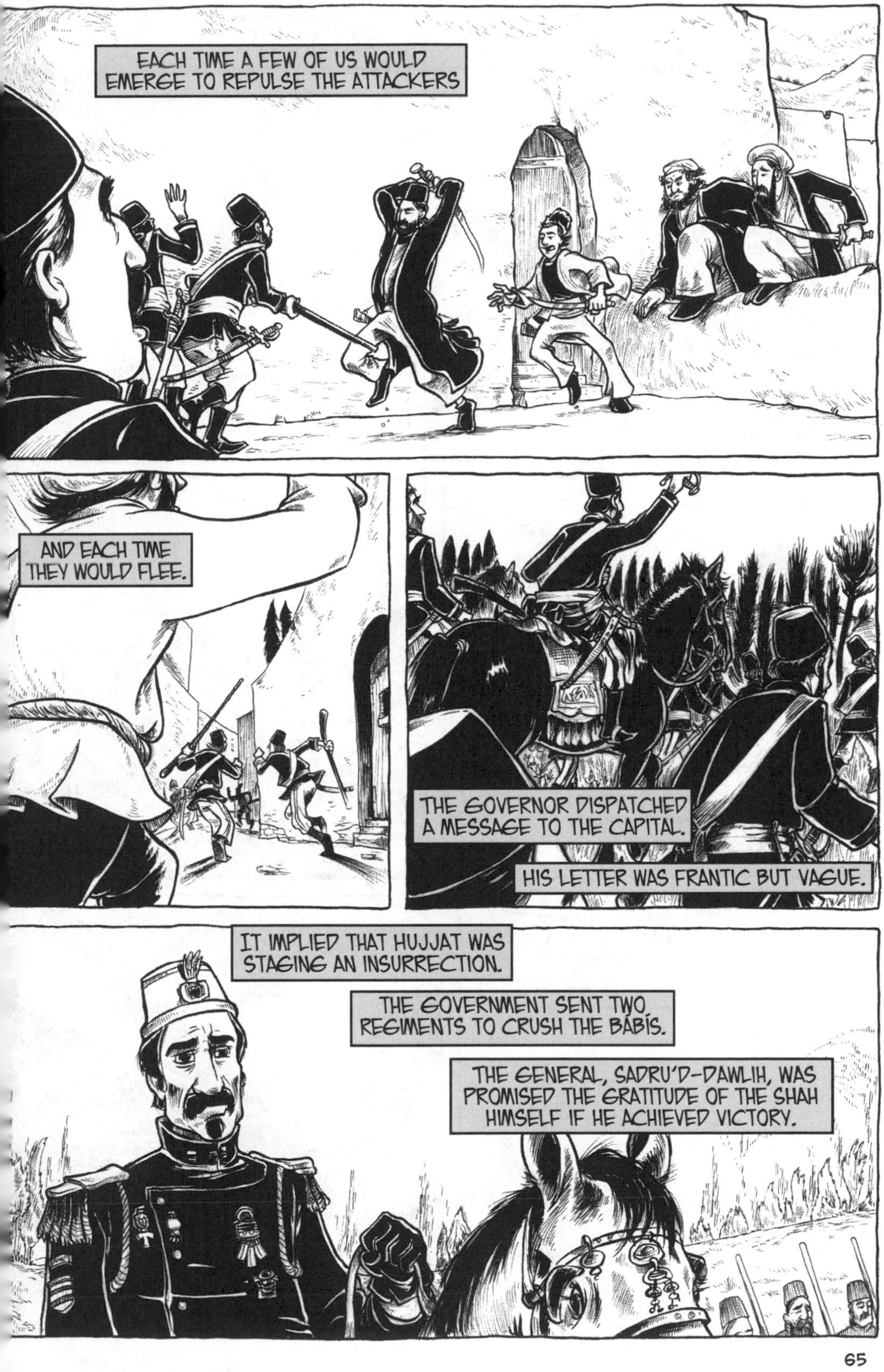
EACH TIME A FEW OF US WOULD EMERGE TO REPULSE THE ATTACKERS
AND EACH TIME THEY WOULD FLEE.
THE GOVERNOR DISPATCHED A MESSAGE TO THE CAPITAL.
HIS LETTER WAS FRANTIC BUT VAGUE.
IT IMPLIED THAT HUJJAT WAS STAGING AN INSURRECTION.
THE GOVERNMENT SENT TWO REGIMENTS TO CRUSH THE BÁBÍS.
THE GENERAL, SADRU'D-DAWLIH, WAS PROMISED THE GRATITUDE OF THE SHAH HIMSELF IF HE ACHIEVED VICTORY.

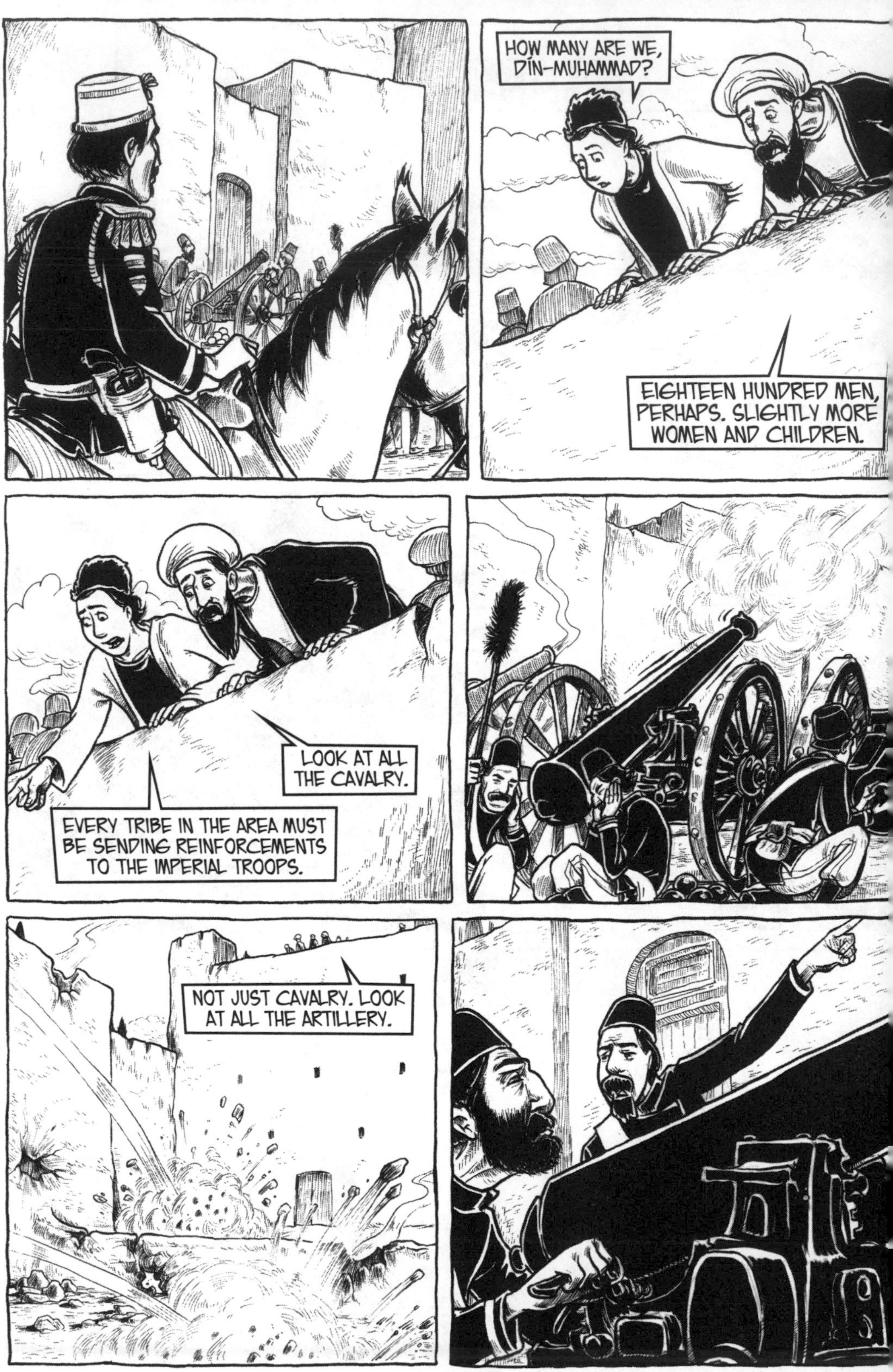
HOW MANY ARE WE, DĪN-MUHAMMAD?
EIGHTEEN HUNDRED MEN, PERHAPS. SLIGHTLY MORE WOMEN AND CHILDREN.
LOOK AT ALL THE CAVALRY.
EVERY TRIBE IN THE AREA MUST BE SENDING REINFORCEMENTS TO THE IMPERIAL TROOPS.
NOT JUST CAVALRY. LOOK AT ALL THE ARTILLERY.

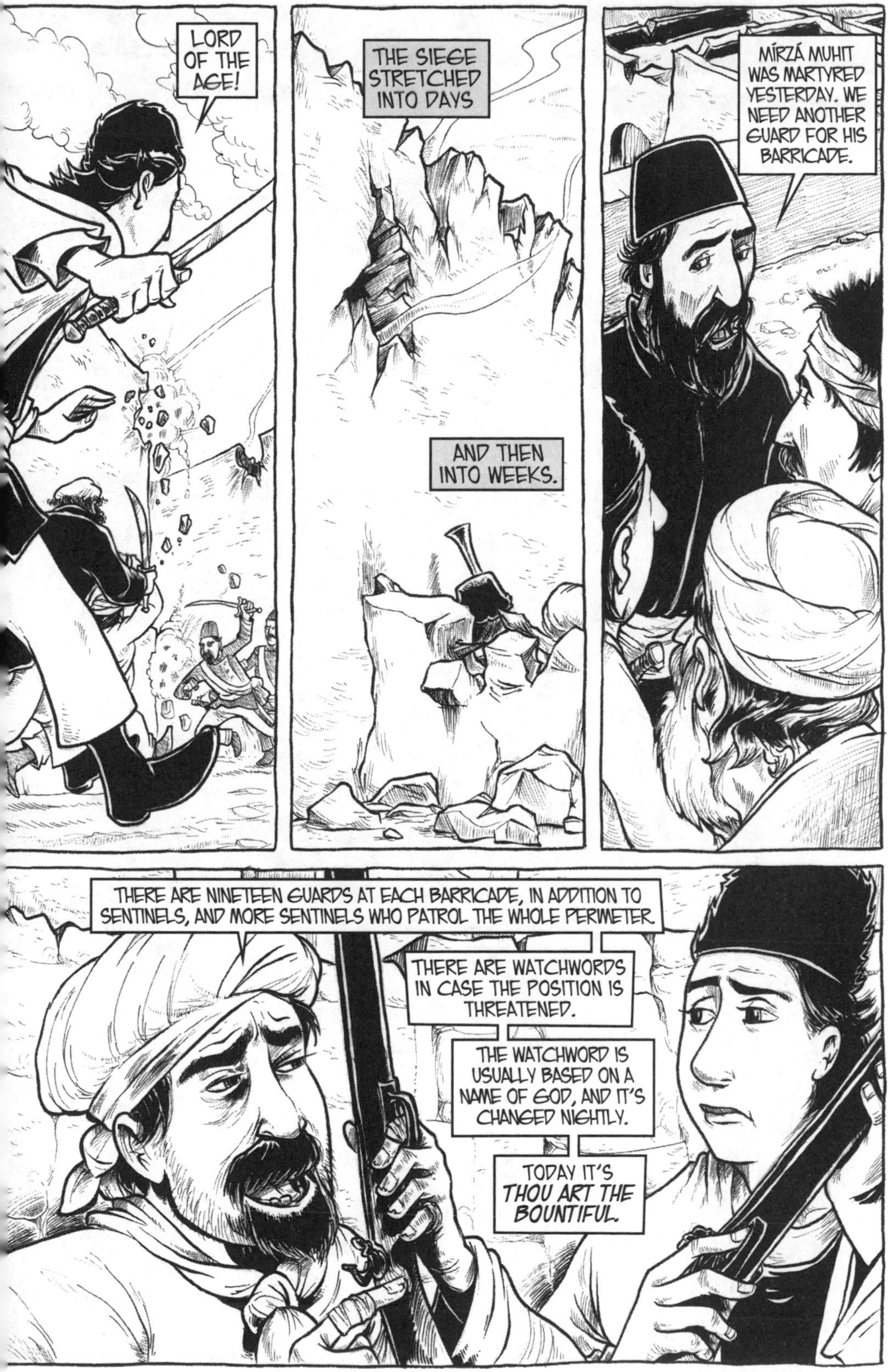
LORD OF THE AGE!
THE SIEGE STRETCHED INTO DAYS
AND THEN INTO WEEKS.
MÍRZÁ MUHIT WAS MARTYRED YESTERDAY. WE NEED ANOTHER GUARD FOR HIS BARRICADE.
THERE ARE NINETEEN GUARDS AT EACH BARRICADE, IN ADDITION TO SENTINELS, AND MORE SENTINELS WHO PATROL THE WHOLE PERIMETER.
THERE ARE WATCHWORDS IN CASE THE POSITION IS THREATENED.
THE WATCHWORD IS USUALLY BASED ON A NAME OF GOD, AND IT'S CHANGED NIGHTLY.
TODAY IT'S *THOU ART THE BOUNTIFUL.*

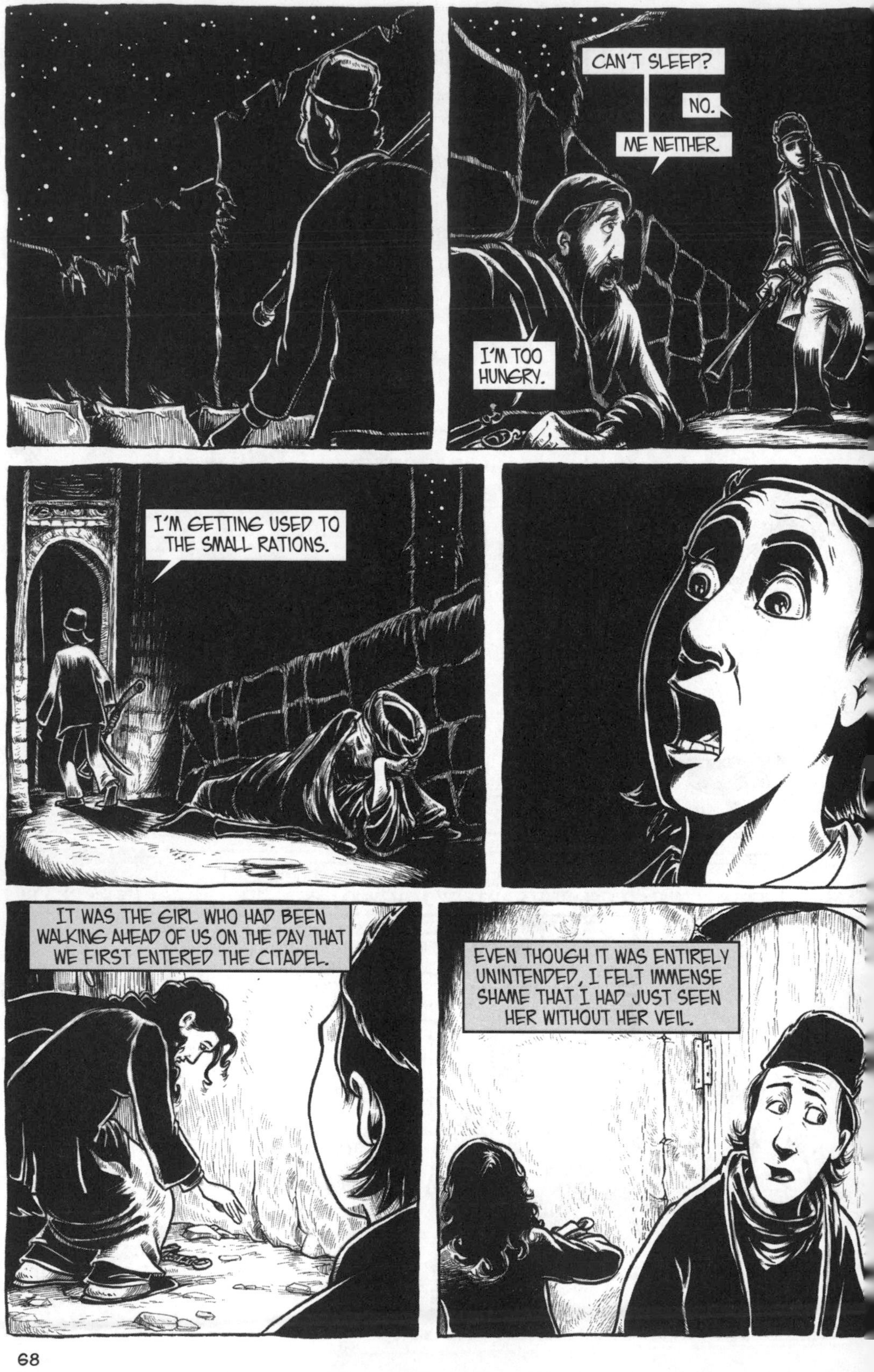
CAN'T SLEEP?
NO.
ME NEITHER.
I'M TOO HUNGRY.
I'M GETTING USED TO THE SMALL RATIONS.
IT WAS THE GIRL WHO HAD BEEN WALKING AHEAD OF US ON THE DAY THAT WE FIRST ENTERED THE CITADEL.
EVEN THOUGH IT WAS ENTIRELY UNINTENDED, I FELT IMMENSE SHAME THAT I HAD JUST SEEN HER WITHOUT HER VEIL.

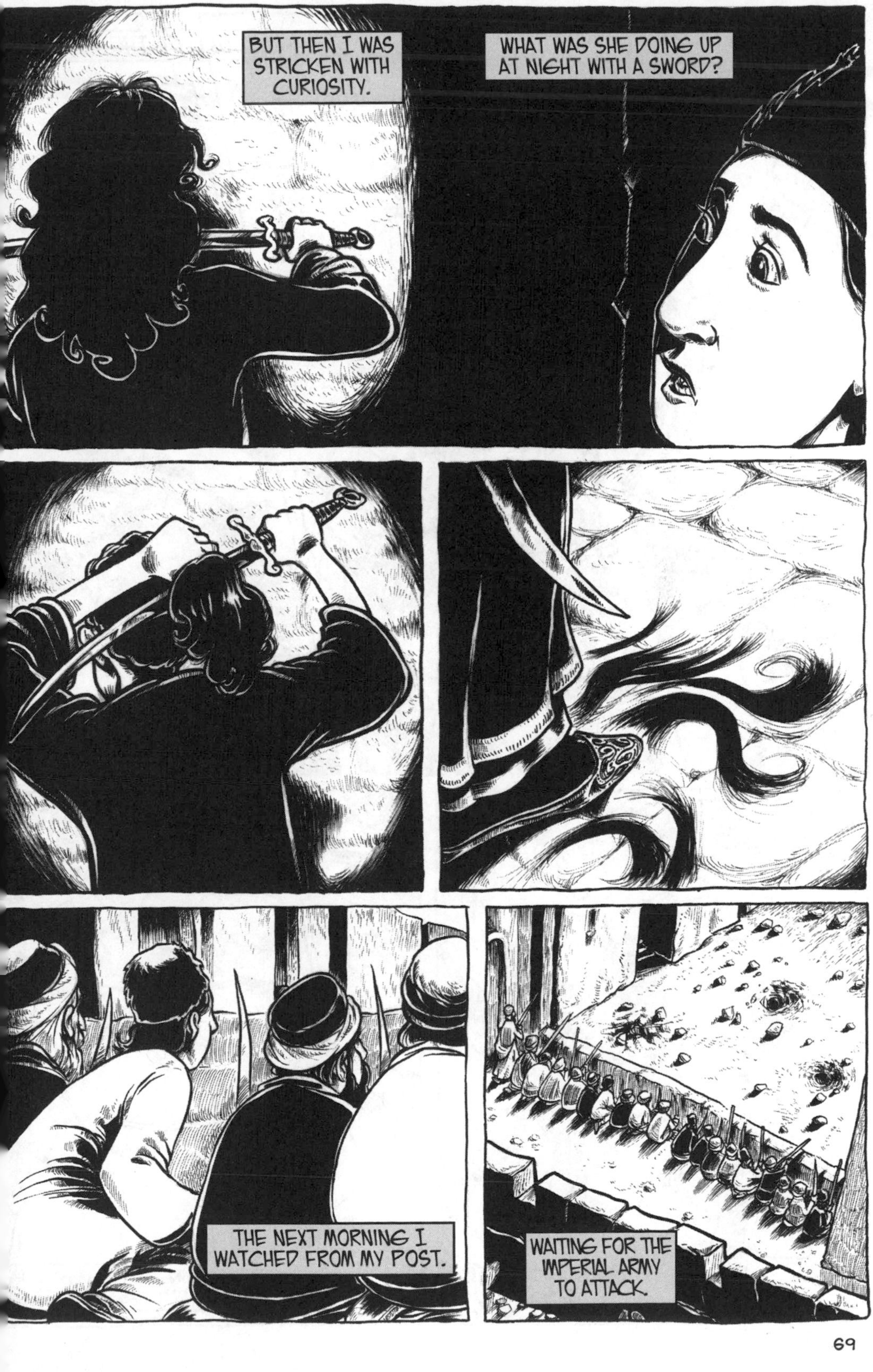
BUT THEN I WAS STRICKEN WITH CURIOSITY.
WHAT WAS SHE DOING UP AT NIGHT WITH A SWORD?
THE NEXT MORNING I WATCHED FROM MY POST.
WAITING FOR THE IMPERIAL ARMY TO ATTACK.

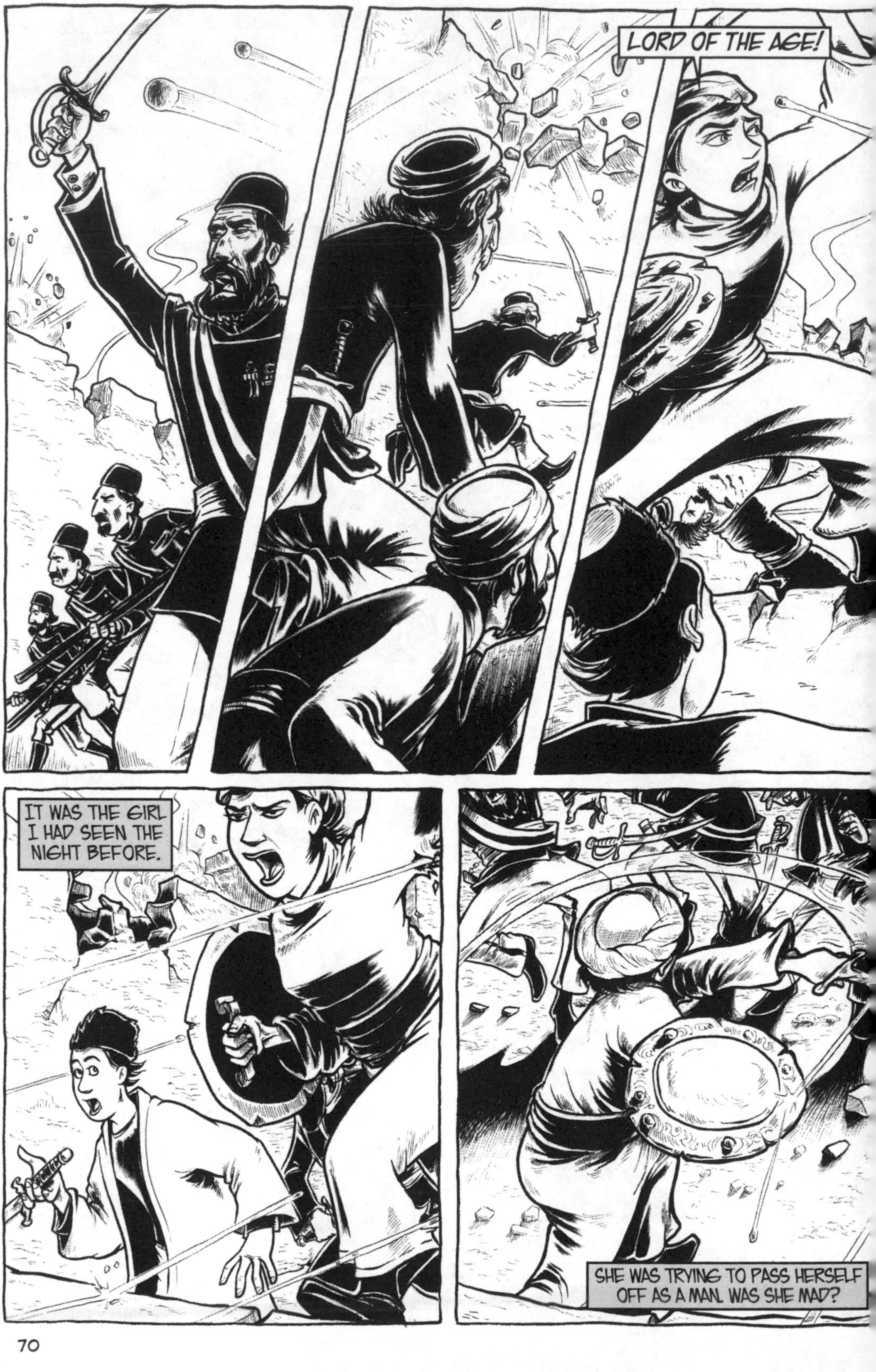
LORD OF THE AGE!
IT WAS THE GIRL I HAD SEEN THE NIGHT BEFORE.
SHE WAS TRYING TO PASS HERSELF OFF AS A MAN. WAS SHE MAD?

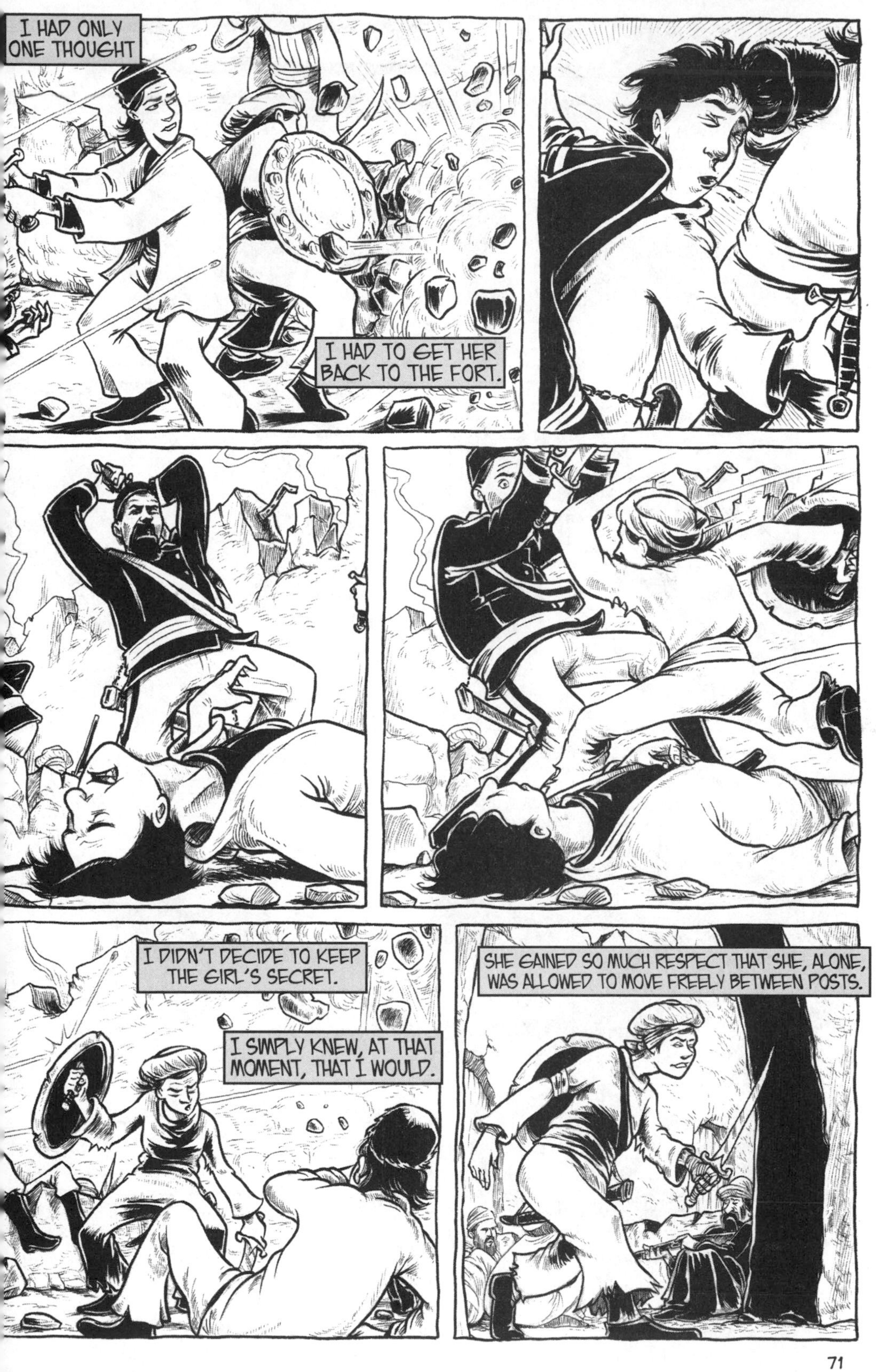
I HAD ONLY ONE THOUGHT
I HAD TO GET HER BACK TO THE FORT.
I DIDN'T DECIDE TO KEEP THE GIRL'S SECRET.
I SIMPLY KNEW, AT THAT MOMENT, THAT I WOULD.
SHE GAINED SO MUCH RESPECT THAT SHE, ALONE, WAS ALLOWED TO MOVE FREELY BETWEEN POSTS.

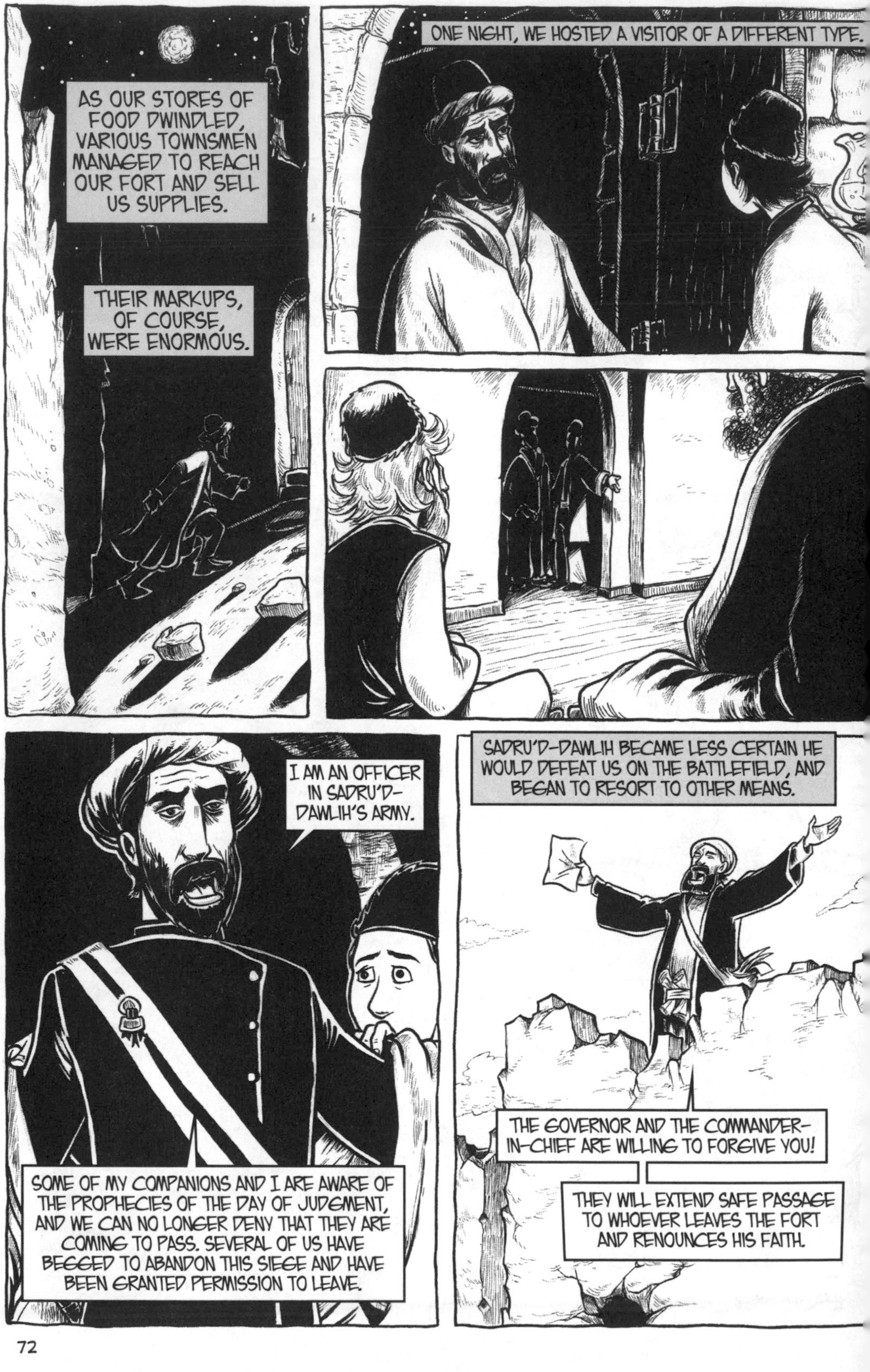
AS OUR STORES OF FOOD DWINDLED, VARIOUS TOWNSMEN MANAGED TO REACH OUR FORT AND SELL US SUPPLIES.
THEIR MARKUPS, OF COURSE, WERE ENORMOUS.
ONE NIGHT, WE HOSTED A VISITOR OF A DIFFERENT TYPE.
I AM AN OFFICER IN SADRU'D-DAWLIH'S ARMY.
SOME OF MY COMPANIONS AND I ARE AWARE OF THE PROPHECIES OF THE DAY OF JUDGMENT, AND WE CAN NO LONGER DENY THAT THEY ARE COMING TO PASS. SEVERAL OF US HAVE BEGGED TO ABANDON THIS SIEGE AND HAVE BEEN GRANTED PERMISSION TO LEAVE.
SADRU'D-DAWLIH BECAME LESS CERTAIN HE WOULD DEFEAT US ON THE BATTLEFIELD, AND BEGAN TO RESORT TO OTHER MEANS.
THE GOVERNOR AND THE COMMANDER-IN-CHIEF ARE WILLING TO FORGIVE YOU!
THEY WILL EXTEND SAFE PASSAGE TO WHOEVER LEAVES THE FORT AND RENOUNCES HIS FAITH.

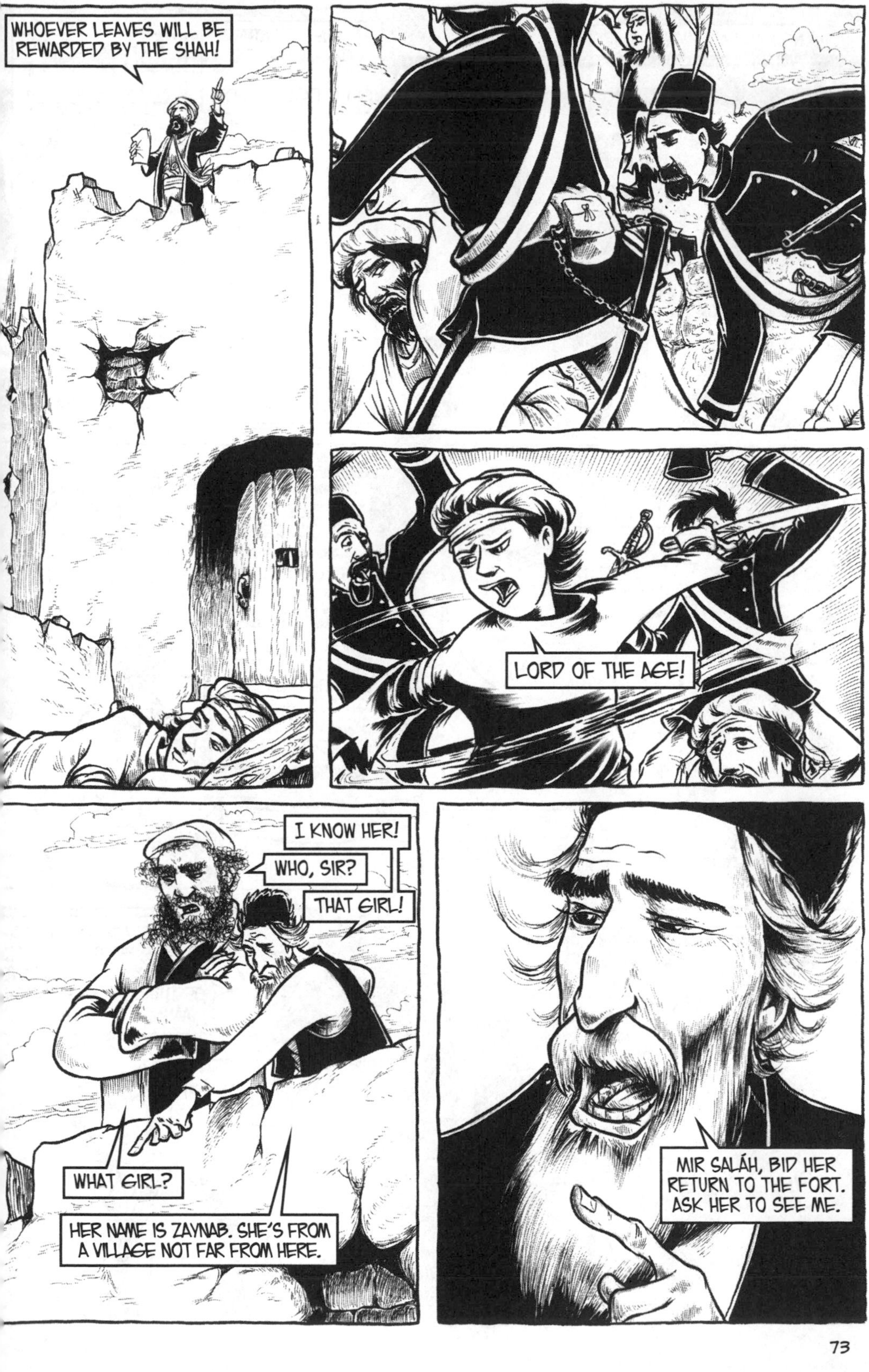

WHOEVER LEAVES WILL BE REWARDED BY THE SHAH!
LORD OF THE AGE!
I KNOW HER!
WHO, SIR?
THAT GIRL!
WHAT GIRL?
HER NAME IS ZAYNAB. SHE'S FROM A VILLAGE NOT FAR FROM HERE.
MIR SALÁH, BID HER RETURN TO THE FORT. ASK HER TO SEE ME.

NO MAN HAS SHOWN YOUR VITALITY AND COURAGE.

WHAT HAS IMPELLED YOU TO TAKE UP MUSKET AND SWORD?

I HAVE NO FATHER OR BROTHER TO FIGHT THE HOLY WAR IN THE PATH OF GOD.

MY HEART ACHED WHEN I BEHELD THE SUFFERINGS OF MY FELLOW-DISCIPLES.

BUT I WAS AFRAID LEST YOU WOULD DENY ME T[H]E PRIVILEGE OF THROWING IN MY LOT WITH THE ME[N]

YOU ARE SURELY ZAYNAB, THE SISTER OF SHAH-SANAM, FROM THE VILLAGE OF FÍRÚZ-KÚH?

I AM.

I ASSURE YOU THAT YOU ALONE HAVE RECOGNIZED ME. I BEG OF YOU, BY THE BÁB, DO NOT EXPOSE ME.

DO NOT WITHHOLD FROM ME THE PRIVILEGE OF MARTYRDOM, THE ONE DESIRE OF MY LIFE.

WAR IS PROHIBITED FOR WOMEN.

IN THIS DISPENSATION THE ILLUSIONS AND VEILS OF THE PAST ARE TORN ASUNDER. ISSUE YOUR JUDG-MENT ACCORDINGLY!

THIS IS THE DAY PROMISED BY THE QUR'ÁN WHEN "ALL SECRETS SHALL BE SEARCHED OUT."

GOD JUDGES HIS CREA-TURES, BE THEY MEN OR WOMEN, BY THE CHARACTE[R] OF THEIR BELIEFS AND TH[E] MANNER OF THEIR LIVES.

YOUR NATURE HAS ALREADY BEEN REVEALED. WHAT ELSE IS THERE TO EXPOSE?

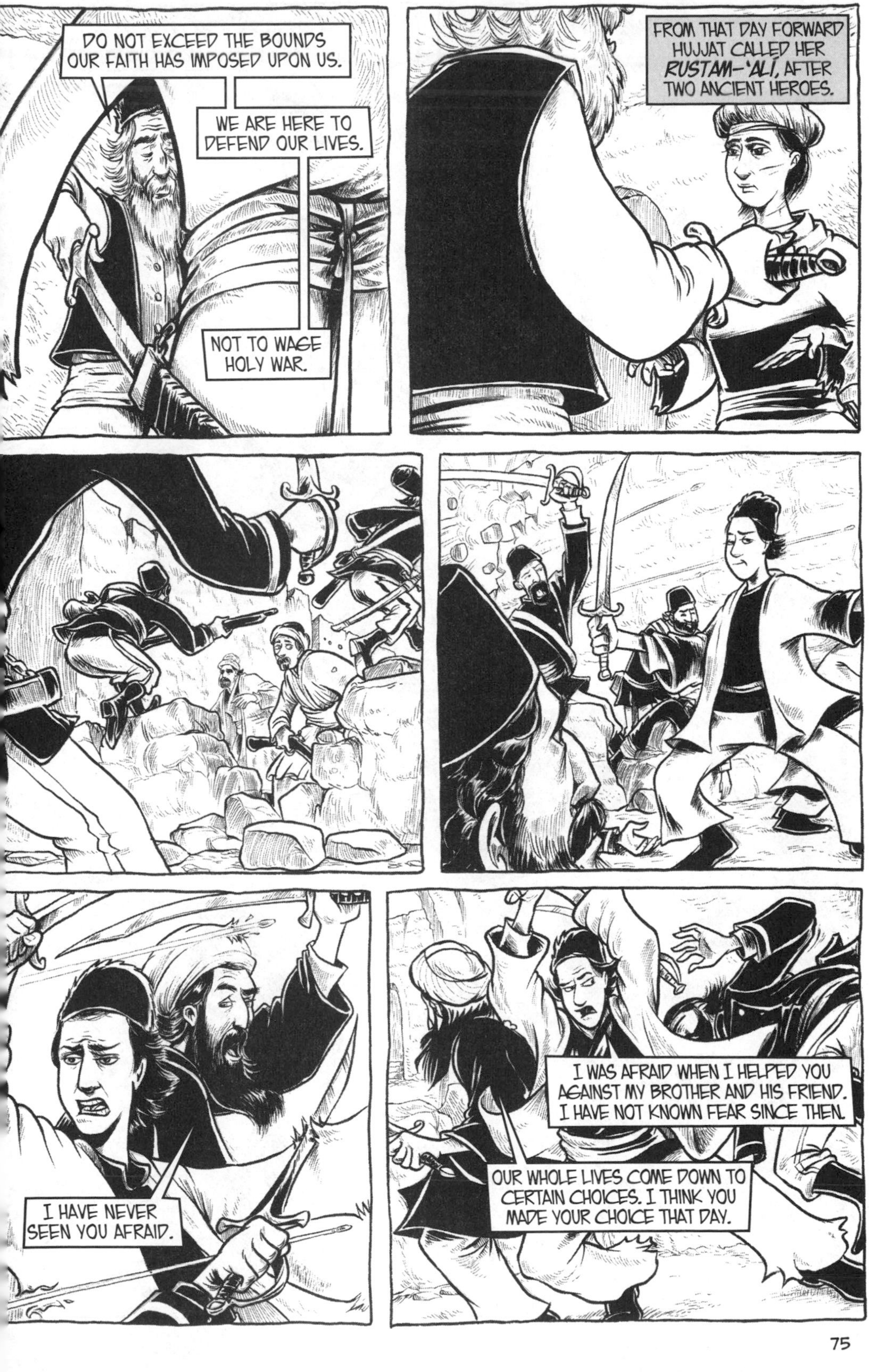
DO NOT EXCEED THE BOUNDS OUR FAITH HAS IMPOSED UPON US.
WE ARE HERE TO DEFEND OUR LIVES.
NOT TO WAGE HOLY WAR.
FROM THAT DAY FORWARD HUJJAT CALLED HER *RUSTAM-'ALÍ*, AFTER TWO ANCIENT HEROES.
I HAVE NEVER SEEN YOU AFRAID.
I WAS AFRAID WHEN I HELPED YOU AGAINST MY BROTHER AND HIS FRIEND. I HAVE NOT KNOWN FEAR SINCE THEN.
OUR WHOLE LIVES COME DOWN TO CERTAIN CHOICES. I THINK YOU MADE YOUR CHOICE THAT DAY.

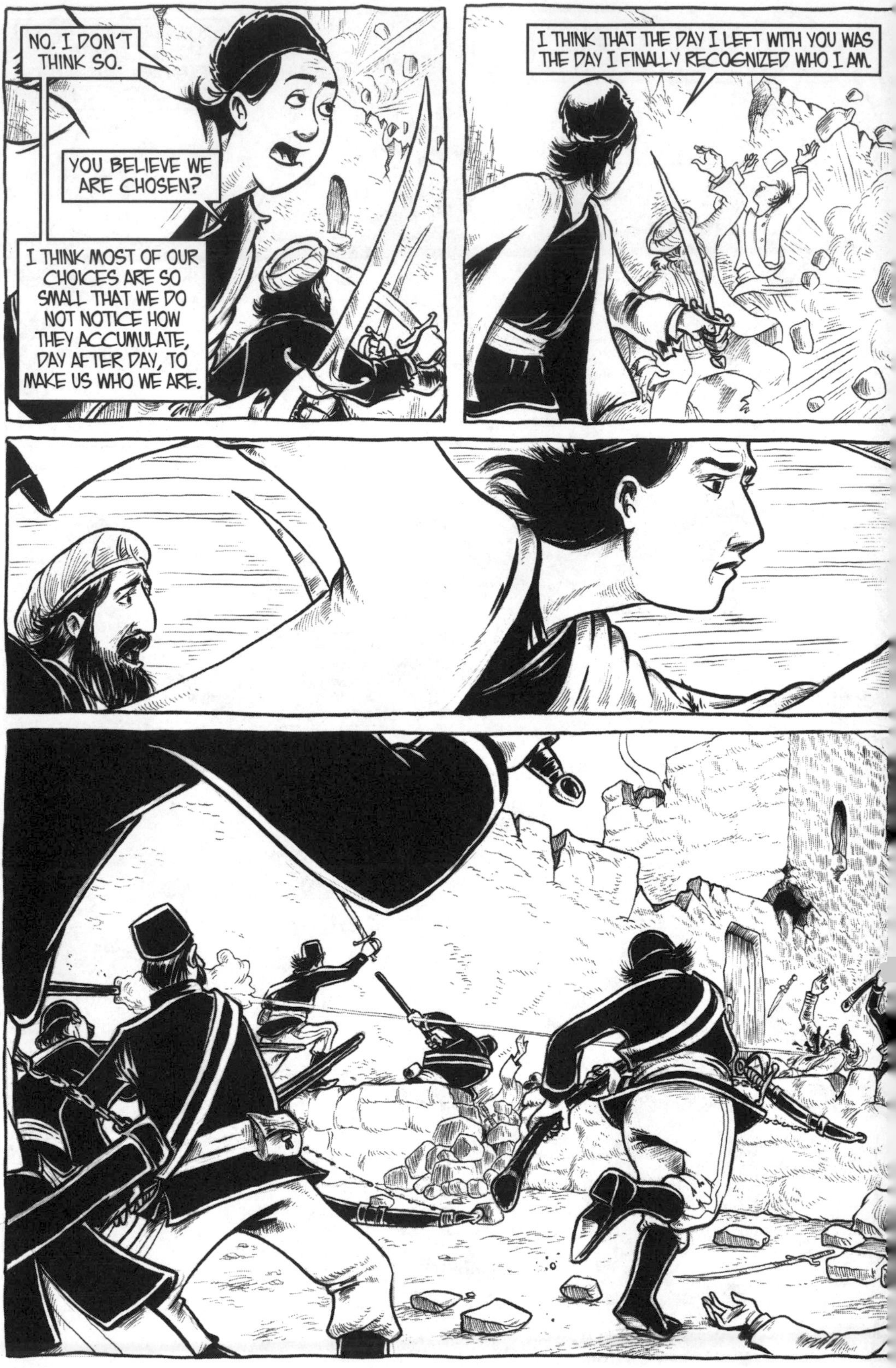
NO. I DON'T THINK SO.
YOU BELIEVE WE ARE CHOSEN?
I THINK MOST OF OUR CHOICES ARE SO SMALL THAT WE DO NOT NOTICE HOW THEY ACCUMULATE, DAY AFTER DAY, TO MAKE US WHO WE ARE.
I THINK THAT THE DAY I LEFT WITH YOU WAS THE DAY I FINALLY RECOGNIZED WHO I AM.

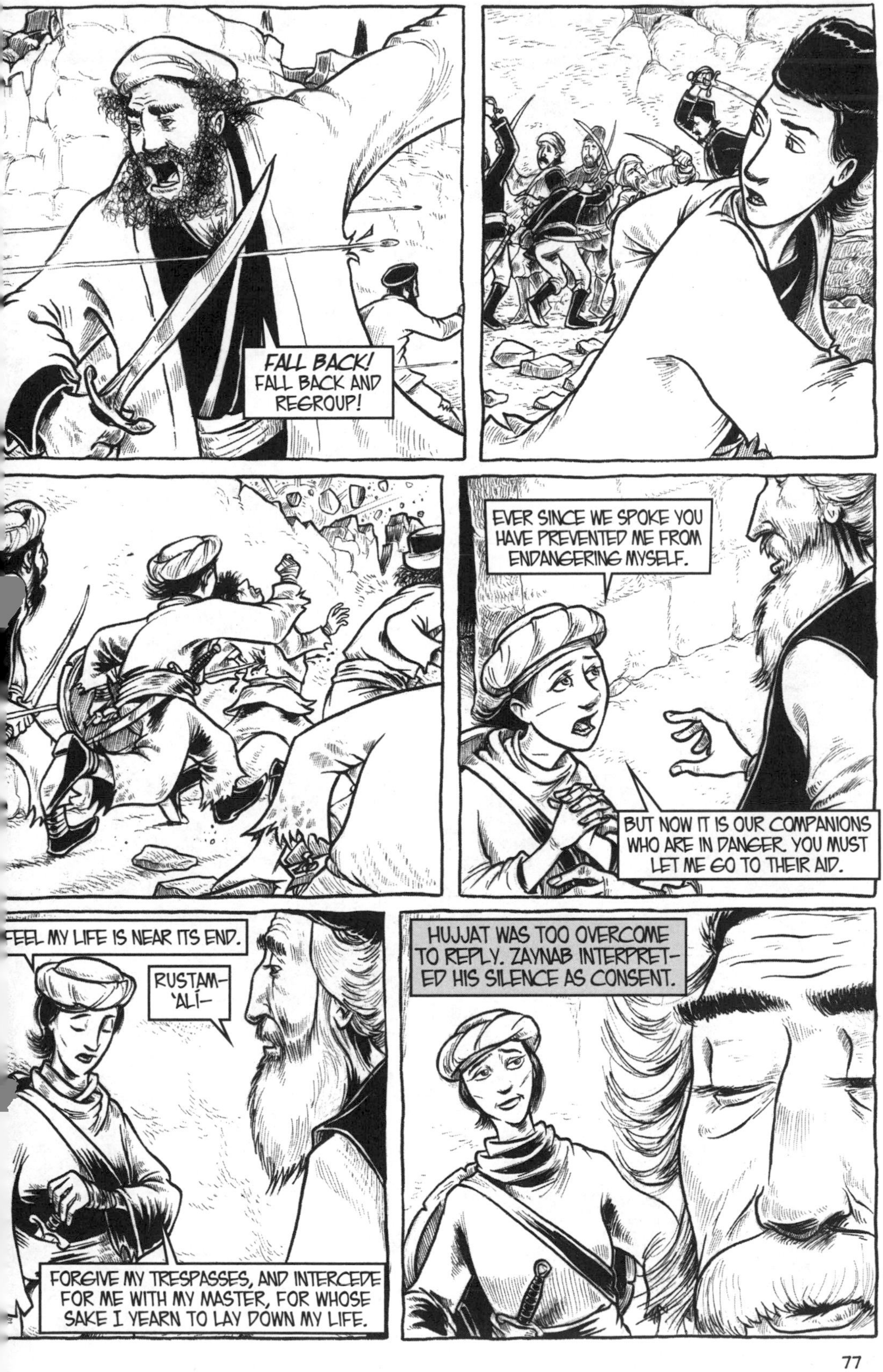
FALL BACK! FALL BACK AND REGROUP!
EVER SINCE WE SPOKE YOU HAVE PREVENTED ME FROM ENDANGERING MYSELF.
BUT NOW IT IS OUR COMPANIONS WHO ARE IN DANGER. YOU MUST LET ME GO TO THEIR AID.
FEEL MY LIFE IS NEAR ITS END.
RUSTAM-'ALÍ-
FORGIVE MY TRESPASSES, AND INTERCEDE FOR ME WITH MY MASTER, FOR WHOSE SAKE I YEARN TO LAY DOWN MY LIFE.
HUJJAT WAS TOO OVERCOME TO REPLY. ZAYNAB INTERPRETED HIS SILENCE AS CONSENT.

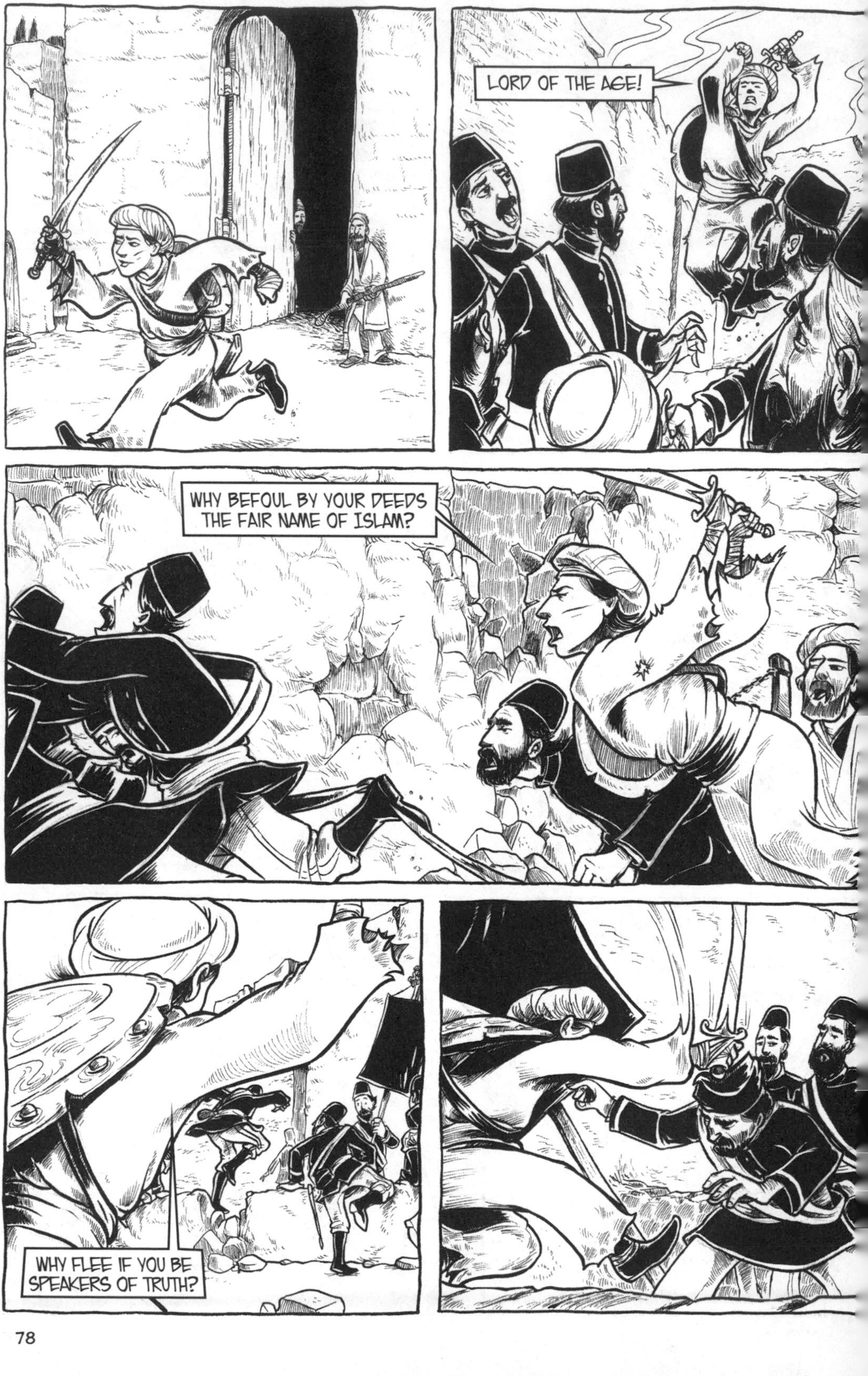
LORD OF THE AGE!
WHY BEFOUL BY YOUR DEEDS THE FAIR NAME OF ISLAM?
WHY FLEE IF YOU BE SPEAKERS OF TRUTH?

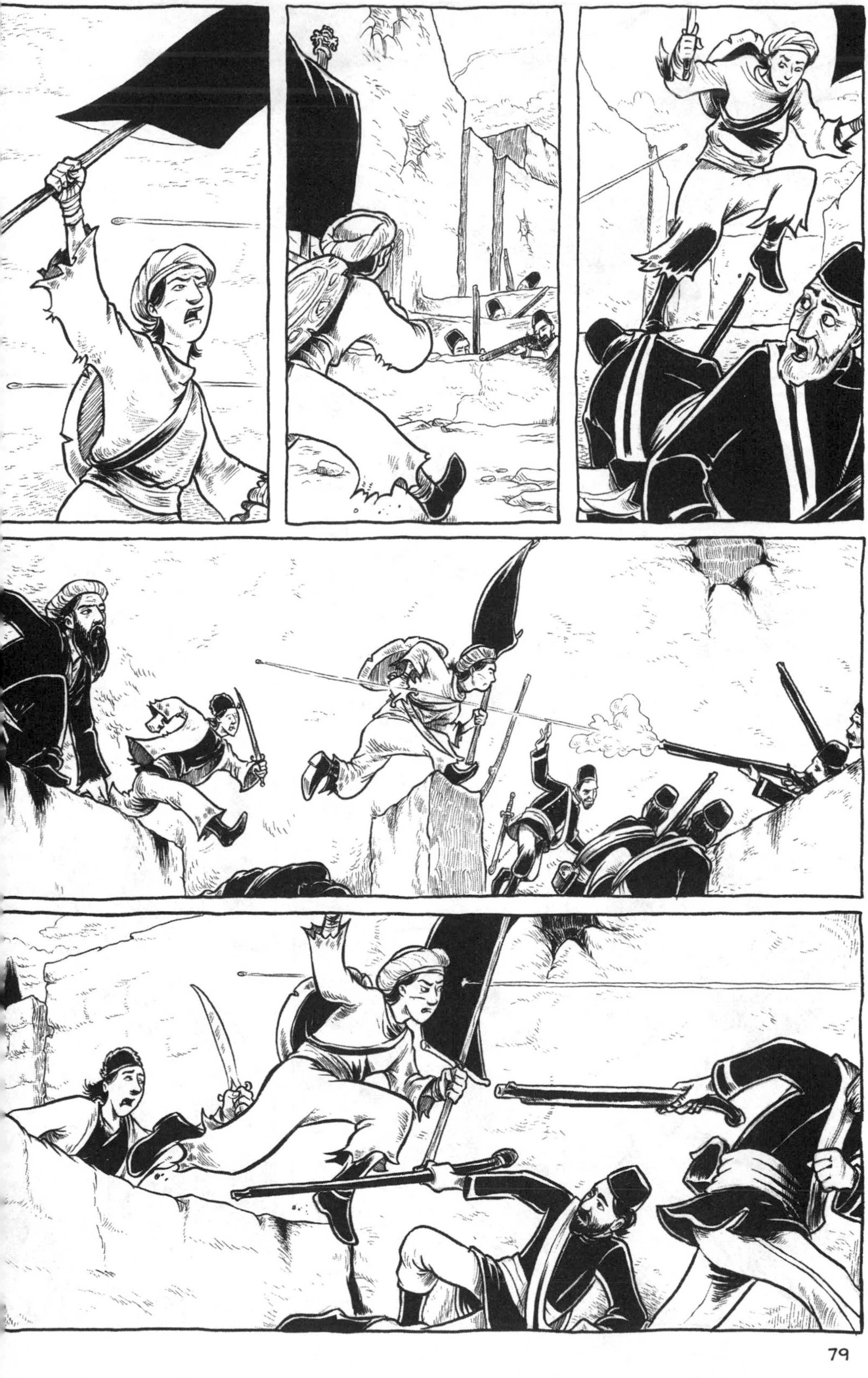

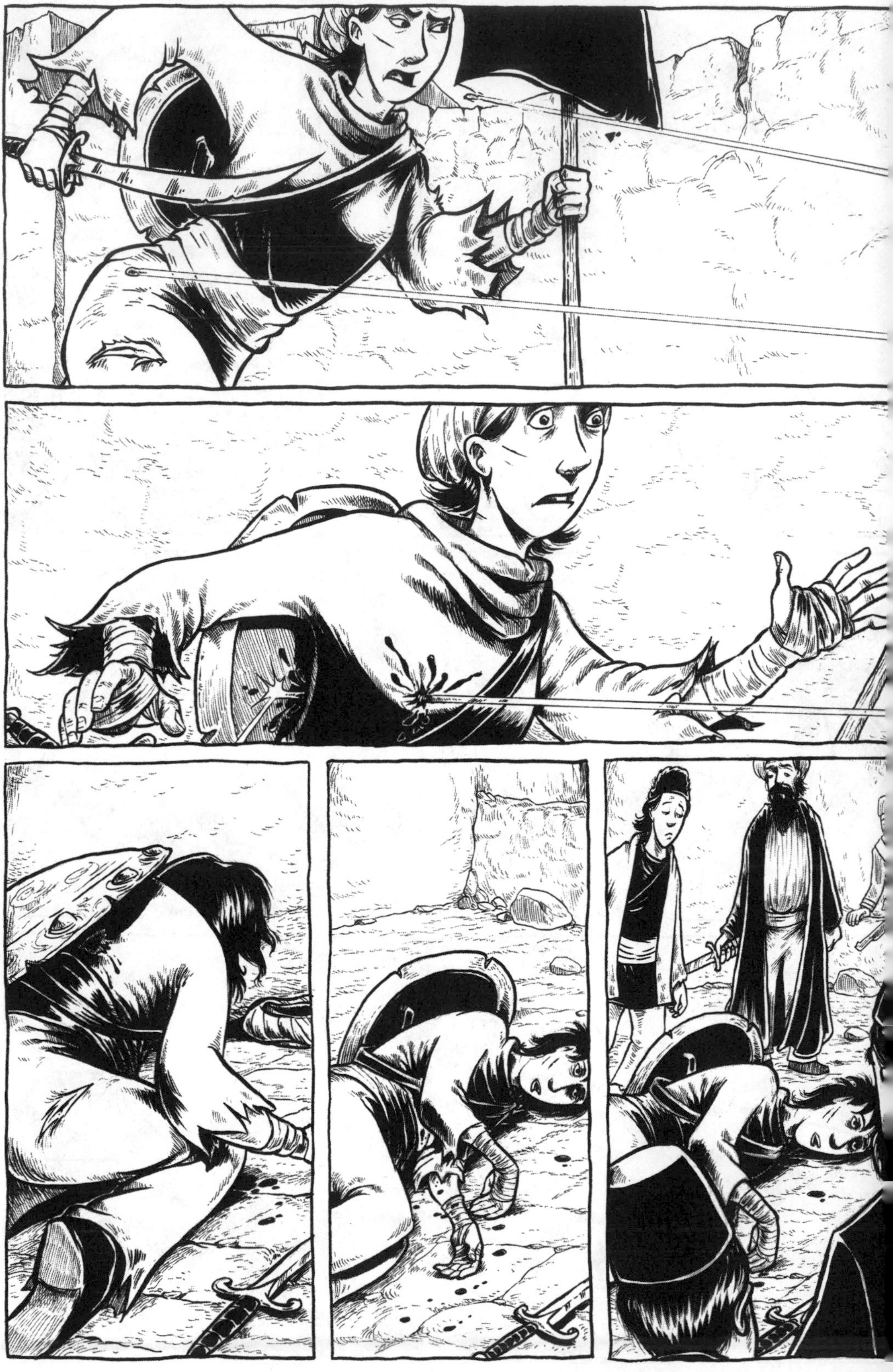

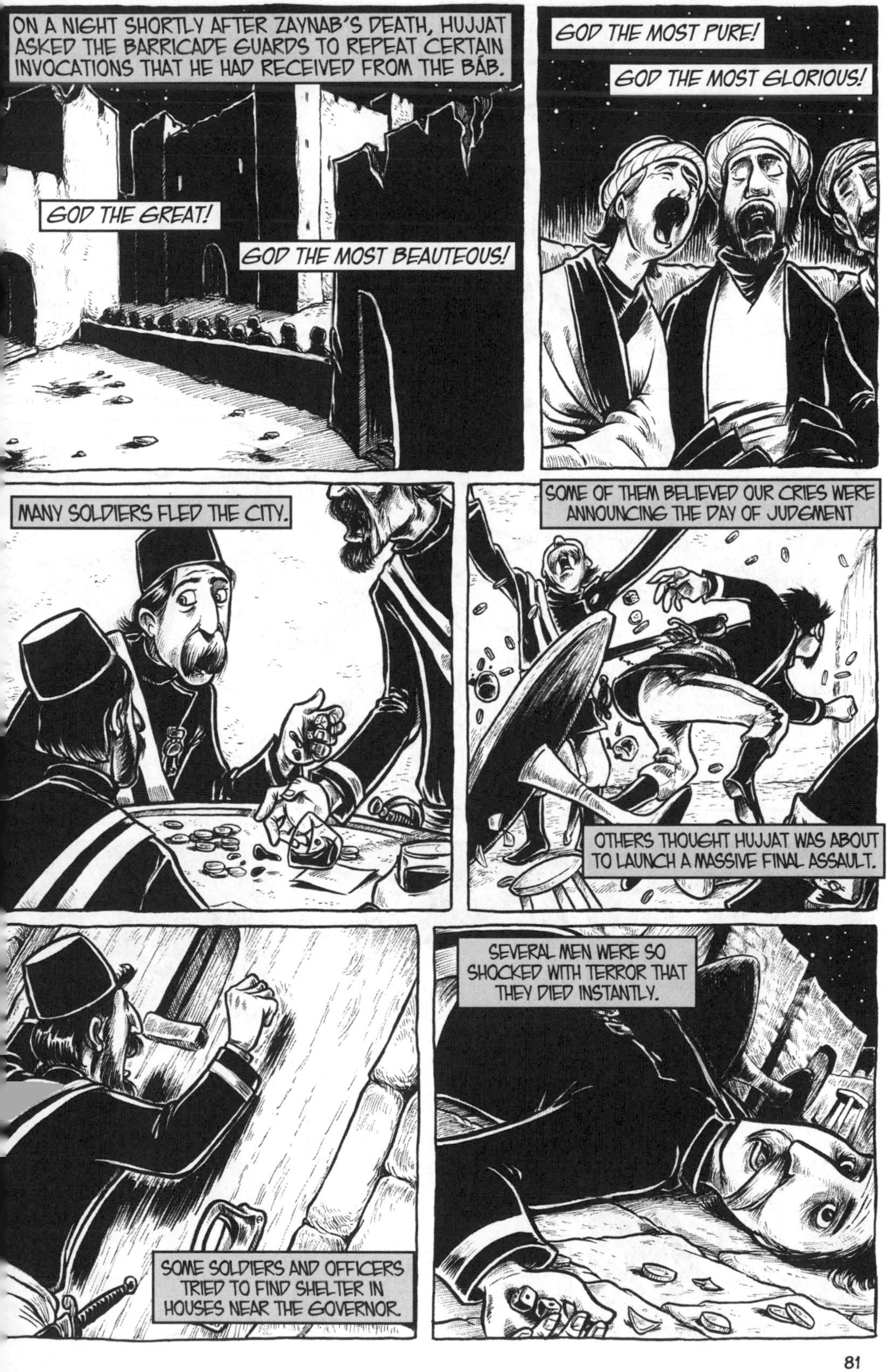
ON A NIGHT SHORTLY AFTER ZAYNAB'S DEATH, HUJJAT ASKED THE BARRICADE GUARDS TO REPEAT CERTAIN INVOCATIONS THAT HE HAD RECEIVED FROM THE BÁB.
GOD THE GREAT!
GOD THE MOST BEAUTEOUS!
GOD THE MOST PURE!
GOD THE MOST GLORIOUS!
MANY SOLDIERS FLED THE CITY.
SOME OF THEM BELIEVED OUR CRIES WERE ANNOUNCING THE DAY OF JUDGEMENT
OTHERS THOUGHT HUJJAT WAS ABOUT TO LAUNCH A MASSIVE FINAL ASSAULT.
SOME SOLDIERS AND OFFICERS TRIED TO FIND SHELTER IN HOUSES NEAR THE GOVERNOR.
SEVERAL MEN WERE SO SHOCKED WITH TERROR THAT THEY DIED INSTANTLY.

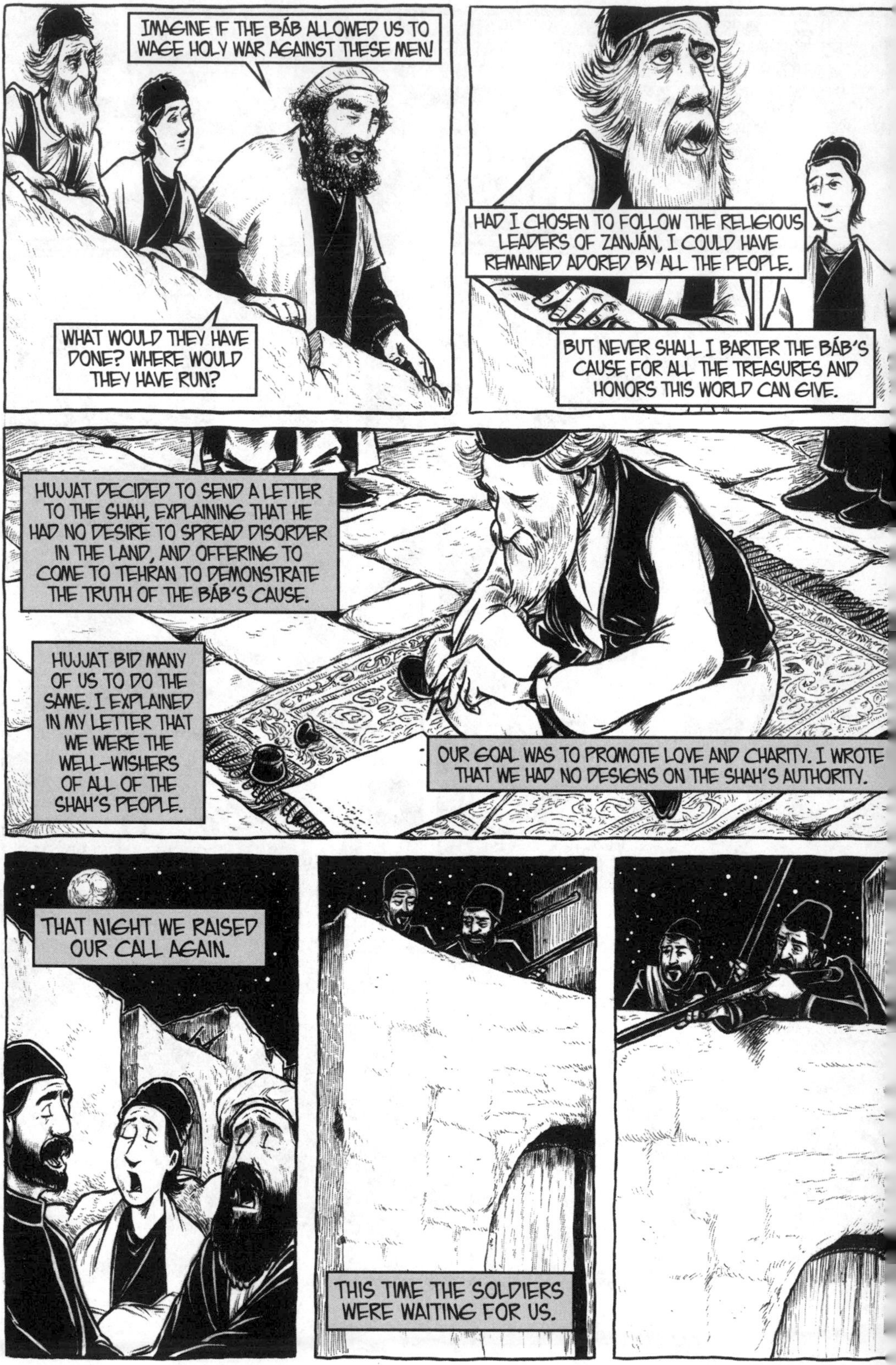
IMAGINE IF THE BÁB ALLOWED US TO WAGE HOLY WAR AGAINST THESE MEN!
WHAT WOULD THEY HAVE DONE? WHERE WOULD THEY HAVE RUN?
HAD I CHOSEN TO FOLLOW THE RELIGIOUS LEADERS OF ZANJÁN, I COULD HAVE REMAINED ADORED BY ALL THE PEOPLE.
BUT NEVER SHALL I BARTER THE BÁB'S CAUSE FOR ALL THE TREASURES AND HONORS THIS WORLD CAN GIVE.
HUJJAT DECIDED TO SEND A LETTER TO THE SHAH, EXPLAINING THAT HE HAD NO DESIRE TO SPREAD DISORDER IN THE LAND, AND OFFERING TO COME TO TEHRAN TO DEMONSTRATE THE TRUTH OF THE BÁB'S CAUSE.
HUJJAT BID MANY OF US TO DO THE SAME. I EXPLAINED IN MY LETTER THAT WE WERE THE WELL-WISHERS OF ALL OF THE SHAH'S PEOPLE.
OUR GOAL WAS TO PROMOTE LOVE AND CHARITY. I WROTE THAT WE HAD NO DESIGNS ON THE SHAH'S AUTHORITY.
THAT NIGHT WE RAISED OUR CALL AGAIN.
THIS TIME THE SOLDIERS WERE WAITING FOR US.

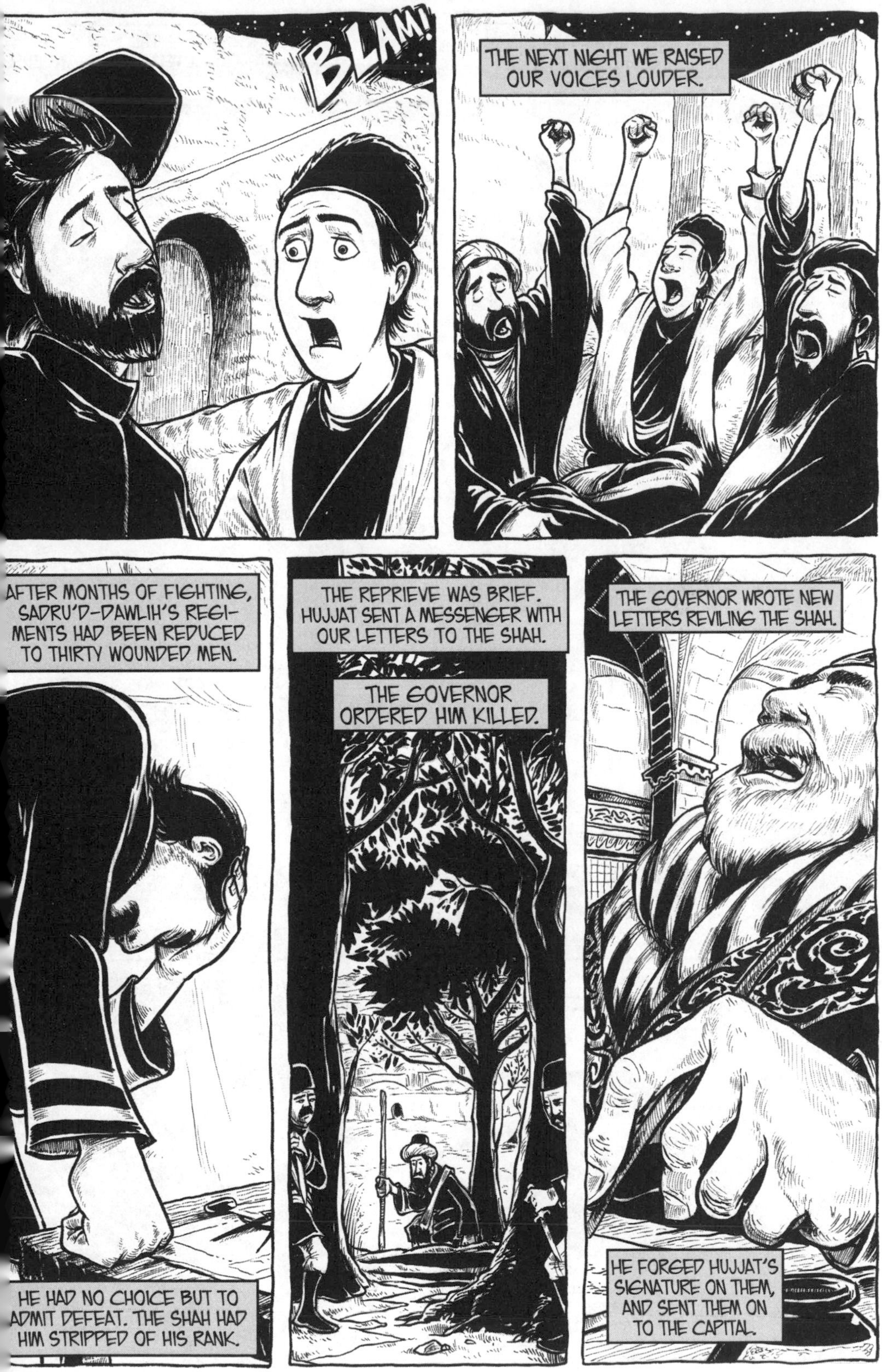
BLAM!
THE NEXT NIGHT WE RAISED OUR VOICES LOUDER.
AFTER MONTHS OF FIGHTING, SADRU'D-DAWLIH'S REGIMENTS HAD BEEN REDUCED TO THIRTY WOUNDED MEN.
HE HAD NO CHOICE BUT TO ADMIT DEFEAT. THE SHAH HAD HIM STRIPPED OF HIS RANK.
THE REPRIEVE WAS BRIEF. HUJJAT SENT A MESSENGER WITH OUR LETTERS TO THE SHAH.
THE GOVERNOR ORDERED HIM KILLED.
THE GOVERNOR WROTE NEW LETTERS REVILING THE SHAH.
HE FORGED HUJJAT'S SIGNATURE ON THEM, AND SENT THEM ON TO THE CAPITAL.

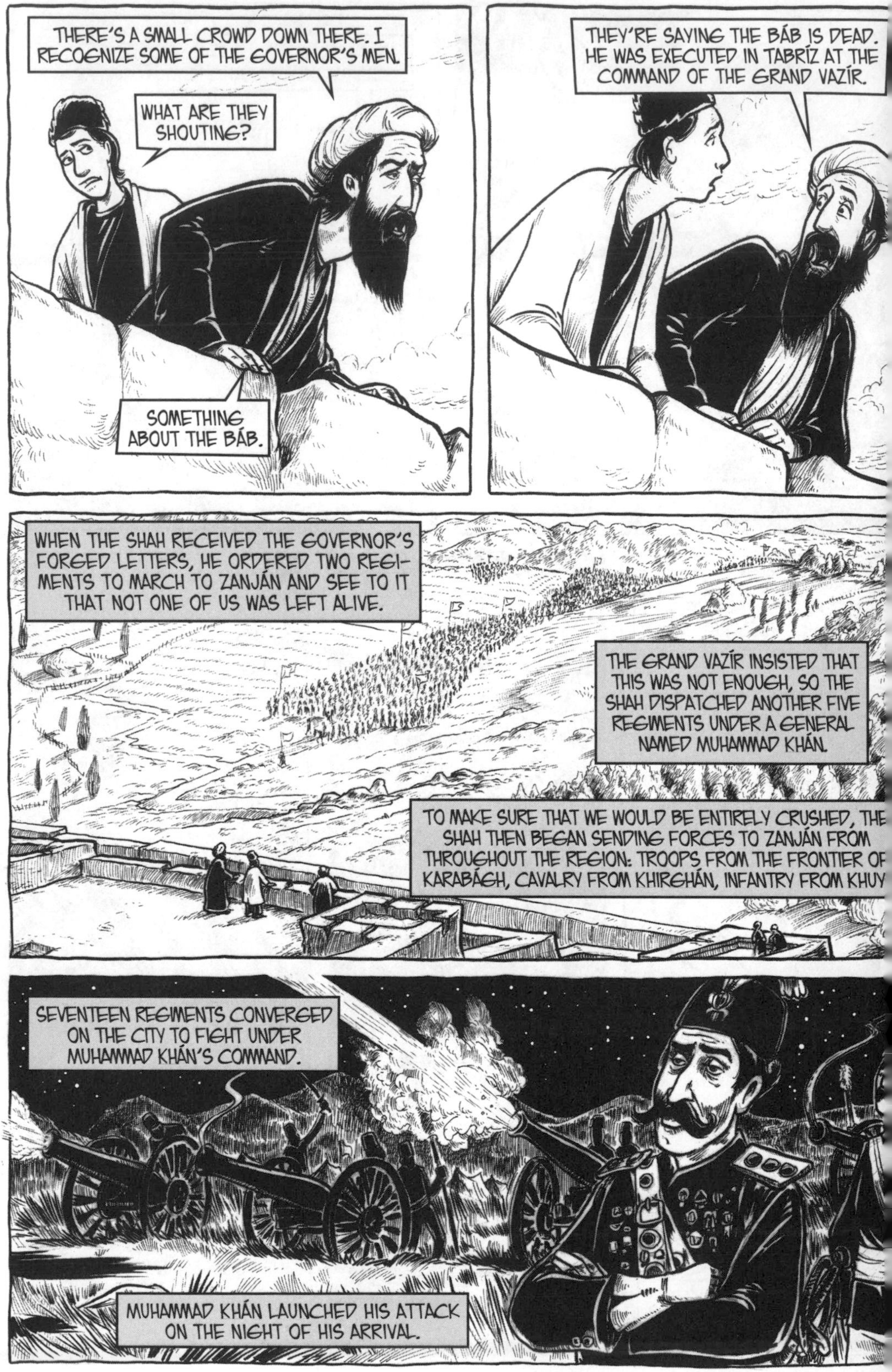
THERE'S A SMALL CROWD DOWN THERE. I RECOGNIZE SOME OF THE GOVERNOR'S MEN.
WHAT ARE THEY SHOUTING?
SOMETHING ABOUT THE BÁB.
THEY'RE SAYING THE BÁB IS DEAD. HE WAS EXECUTED IN TABRÍZ AT THE COMMAND OF THE GRAND VAZÍR.
WHEN THE SHAH RECEIVED THE GOVERNOR'S FORGED LETTERS, HE ORDERED TWO REGI-MENTS TO MARCH TO ZANJÁN AND SEE TO IT THAT NOT ONE OF US WAS LEFT ALIVE.
THE GRAND VAZÍR INSISTED THAT THIS WAS NOT ENOUGH, SO THE SHAH DISPATCHED ANOTHER FIVE REGIMENTS UNDER A GENERAL NAMED MUHAMMAD KHÁN.
TO MAKE SURE THAT WE WOULD BE ENTIRELY CRUSHED, THE SHAH THEN BEGAN SENDING FORCES TO ZANJÁN FROM THROUGHOUT THE REGION: TROOPS FROM THE FRONTIER OF KARABÁGH, CAVALRY FROM KHIRGHÁN, INFANTRY FROM KHUY
SEVENTEEN REGIMENTS CONVERGED ON THE CITY TO FIGHT UNDER MUHAMMAD KHÁN'S COMMAND.
MUHAMMAD KHÁN LAUNCHED HIS ATTACK ON THE NIGHT OF HIS ARRIVAL.

THE CITADEL WAS FILLED WITH PRAYER.

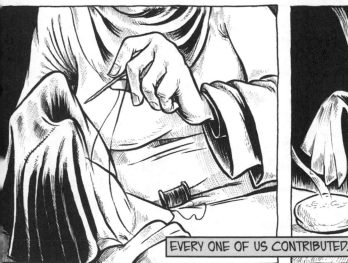

EVERY ONE OF US CONTRIBUTED.

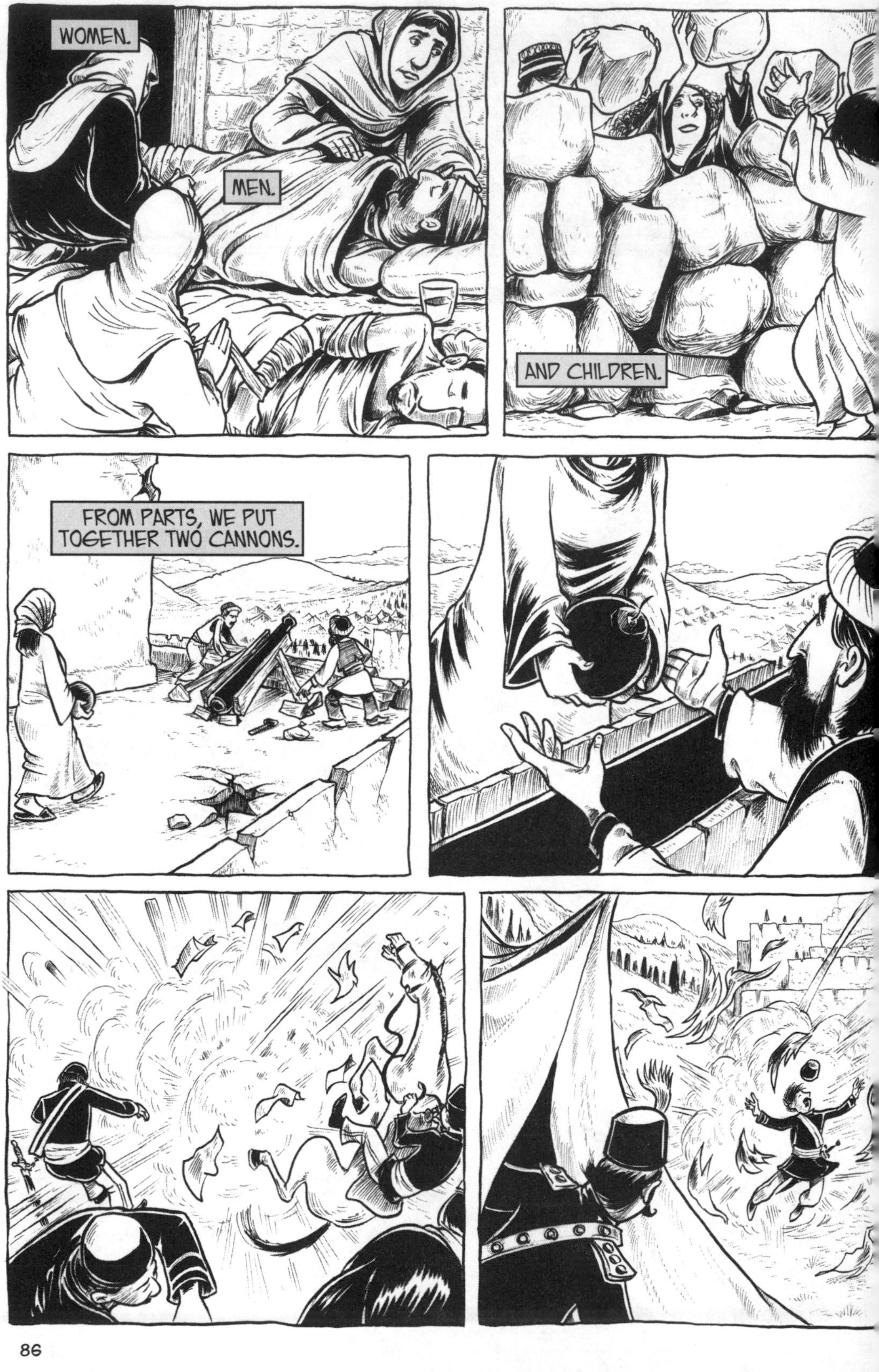
WOMEN.
MEN.
AND CHILDREN.
FROM PARTS, WE PUT TOGETHER TWO CANNONS.

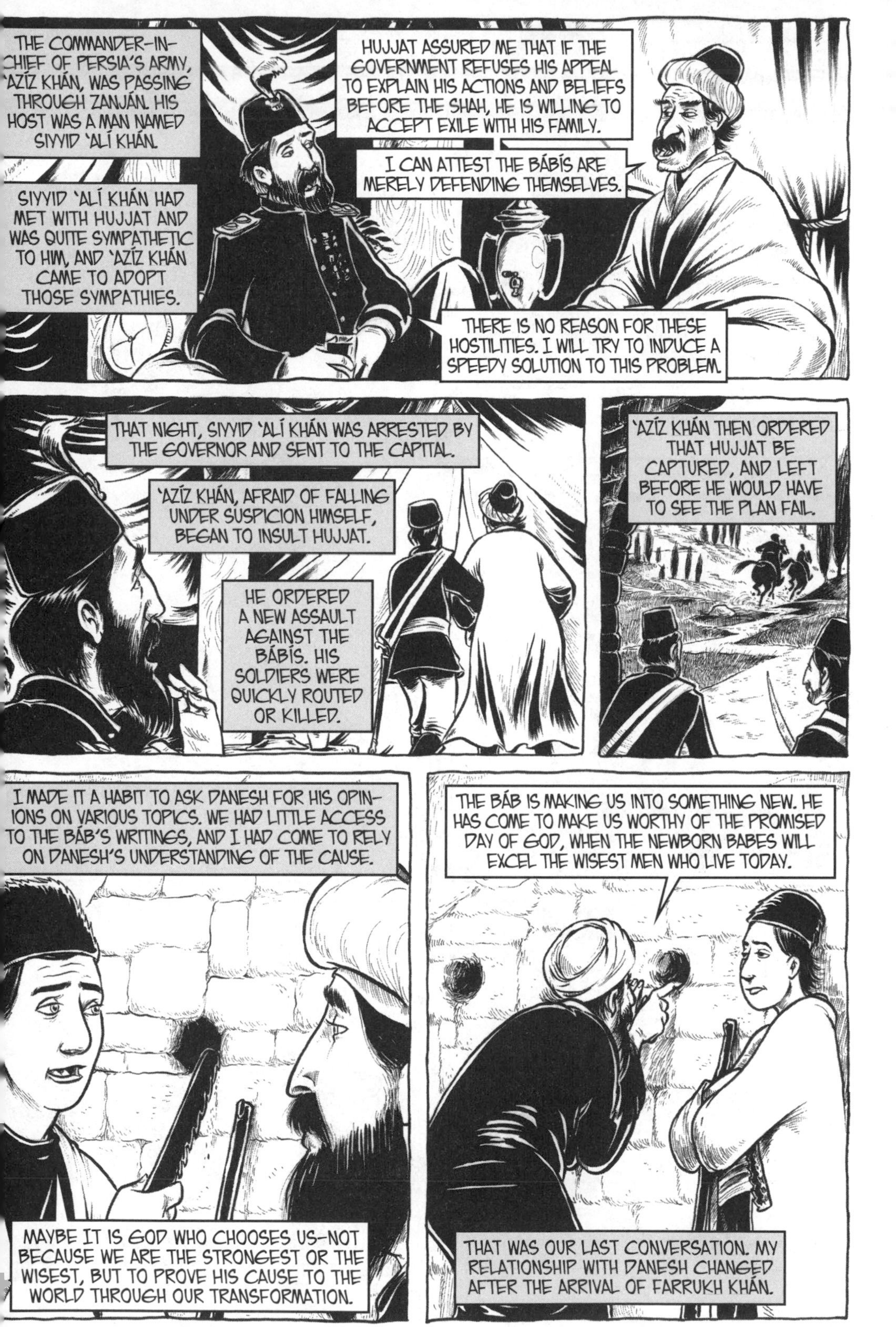
THE COMMANDER-IN-CHIEF OF PERSIA'S ARMY, 'AZÍZ KHÁN, WAS PASSING THROUGH ZANJÁN. HIS HOST WAS A MAN NAMED SIYYID 'ALÍ KHÁN.
SIYYID 'ALÍ KHÁN HAD MET WITH HUJJAT AND WAS QUITE SYMPATHETIC TO HIM, AND 'AZÍZ KHÁN CAME TO ADOPT THOSE SYMPATHIES.
HUJJAT ASSURED ME THAT IF THE GOVERNMENT REFUSES HIS APPEAL TO EXPLAIN HIS ACTIONS AND BELIEFS BEFORE THE SHAH, HE IS WILLING TO ACCEPT EXILE WITH HIS FAMILY.
I CAN ATTEST THE BÁBÍS ARE MERELY DEFENDING THEMSELVES.
THERE IS NO REASON FOR THESE HOSTILITIES. I WILL TRY TO INDUCE A SPEEDY SOLUTION TO THIS PROBLEM.
THAT NIGHT, SIYYID 'ALÍ KHÁN WAS ARRESTED BY THE GOVERNOR AND SENT TO THE CAPITAL.
'AZÍZ KHÁN, AFRAID OF FALLING UNDER SUSPICION HIMSELF, BEGAN TO INSULT HUJJAT.
HE ORDERED A NEW ASSAULT AGAINST THE BÁBÍS. HIS SOLDIERS WERE QUICKLY ROUTED OR KILLED.
'AZÍZ KHÁN THEN ORDERED THAT HUJJAT BE CAPTURED, AND LEFT BEFORE HE WOULD HAVE TO SEE THE PLAN FAIL.
I MADE IT A HABIT TO ASK DANESH FOR HIS OPINIONS ON VARIOUS TOPICS. WE HAD LITTLE ACCESS TO THE BÁB'S WRITINGS, AND I HAD COME TO RELY ON DANESH'S UNDERSTANDING OF THE CAUSE.
MAYBE IT IS GOD WHO CHOOSES US—NOT BECAUSE WE ARE THE STRONGEST OR THE WISEST, BUT TO PROVE HIS CAUSE TO THE WORLD THROUGH OUR TRANSFORMATION.
THE BÁB IS MAKING US INTO SOMETHING NEW. HE HAS COME TO MAKE US WORTHY OF THE PROMISED DAY OF GOD, WHEN THE NEWBORN BABES WILL EXCEL THE WISEST MEN WHO LIVE TODAY.
THAT WAS OUR LAST CONVERSATION. MY RELATIONSHIP WITH DANESH CHANGED AFTER THE ARRIVAL OF FARRUKH KHÁN.

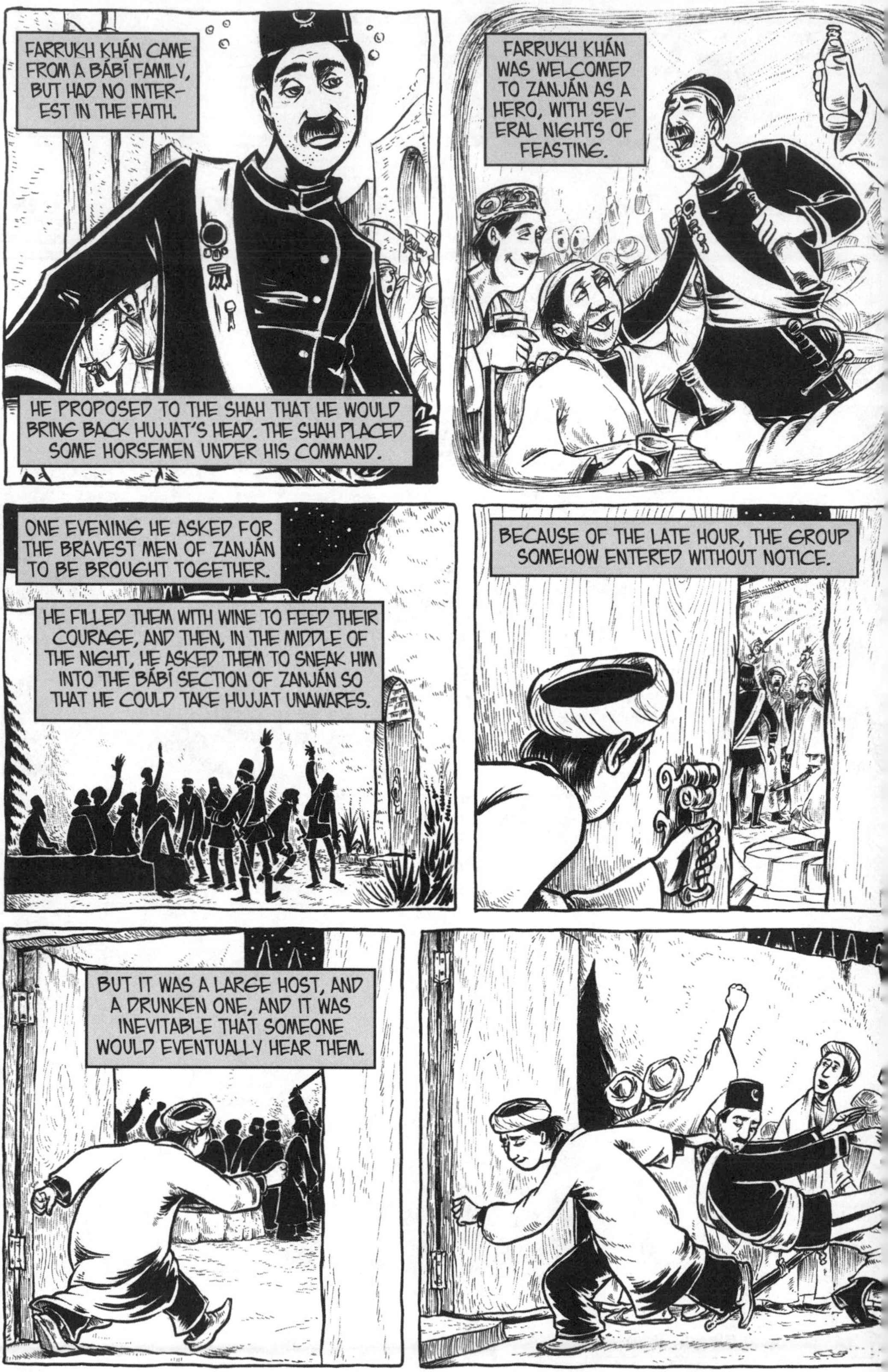
FARRUKH KHÁN CAME FROM A BÁBÍ FAMILY, BUT HAD NO INTEREST IN THE FAITH.
HE PROPOSED TO THE SHAH THAT HE WOULD BRING BACK HUJJAT'S HEAD. THE SHAH PLACED SOME HORSEMEN UNDER HIS COMMAND.
FARRUKH KHÁN WAS WELCOMED TO ZANJÁN AS A HERO, WITH SEVERAL NIGHTS OF FEASTING.
ONE EVENING HE ASKED FOR THE BRAVEST MEN OF ZANJÁN TO BE BROUGHT TOGETHER.
HE FILLED THEM WITH WINE TO FEED THEIR COURAGE, AND THEN, IN THE MIDDLE OF THE NIGHT, HE ASKED THEM TO SNEAK HIM INTO THE BÁBÍ SECTION OF ZANJÁN SO THAT HE COULD TAKE HUJJAT UNAWARES.
BECAUSE OF THE LATE HOUR, THE GROUP SOMEHOW ENTERED WITHOUT NOTICE.
BUT IT WAS A LARGE HOST, AND A DRUNKEN ONE, AND IT WAS INEVITABLE THAT SOMEONE WOULD EVENTUALLY HEAR THEM.

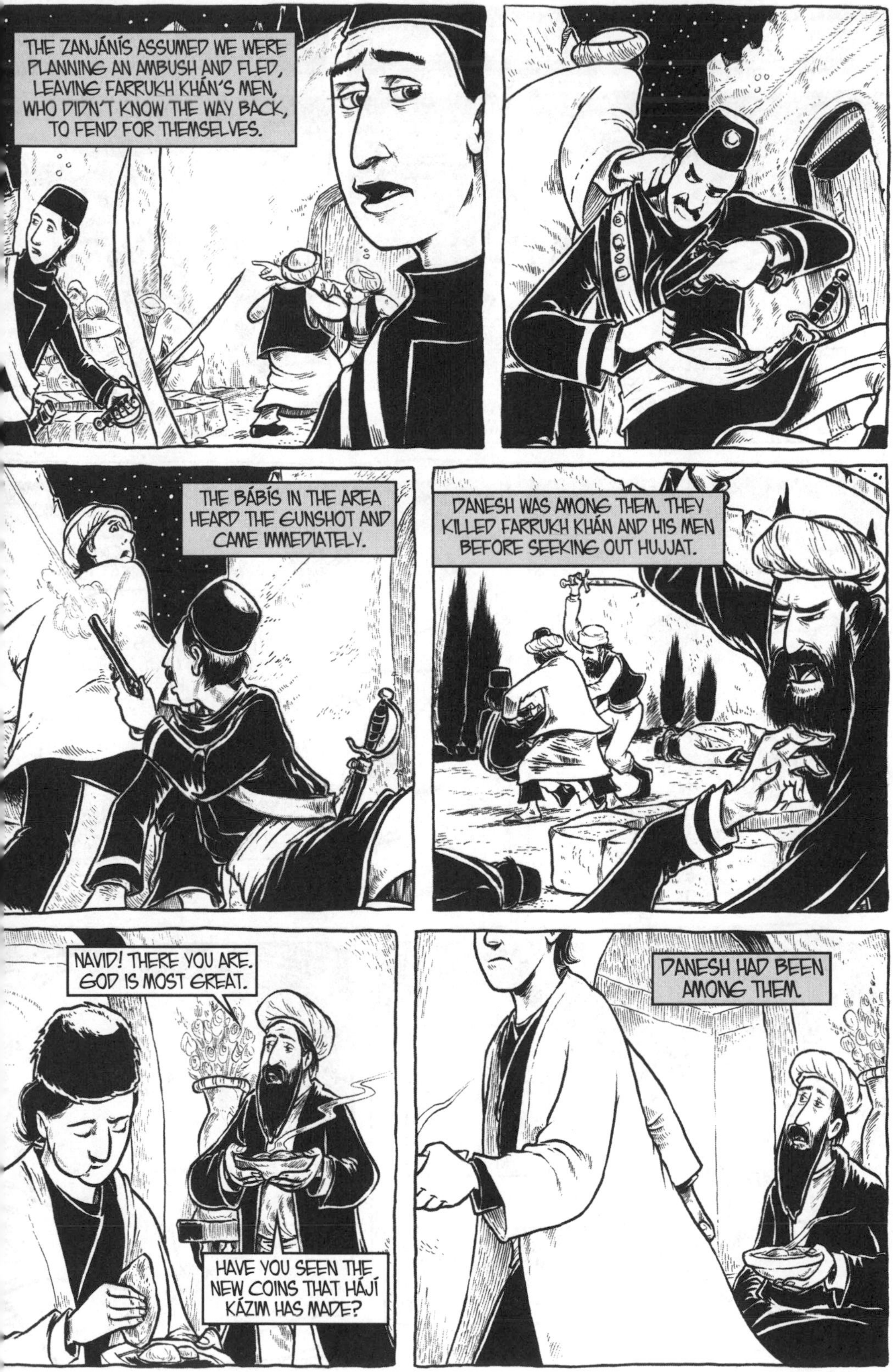
THE ZANJÁNÍS ASSUMED WE WERE PLANNING AN AMBUSH AND FLED, LEAVING FARRUKH KHÁN'S MEN, WHO DIDN'T KNOW THE WAY BACK, TO FEND FOR THEMSELVES.
THE BÁBÍS IN THE AREA HEARD THE GUNSHOT AND CAME IMMEDIATELY.
DANESH WAS AMONG THEM. THEY KILLED FARRUKH KHÁN AND HIS MEN BEFORE SEEKING OUT HUJJAT.
NAVID! THERE YOU ARE. GOD IS MOST GREAT.
HAVE YOU SEEN THE NEW COINS THAT HÁJÍ KÁZIM HAS MADE?
DANESH HAD BEEN AMONG THEM.

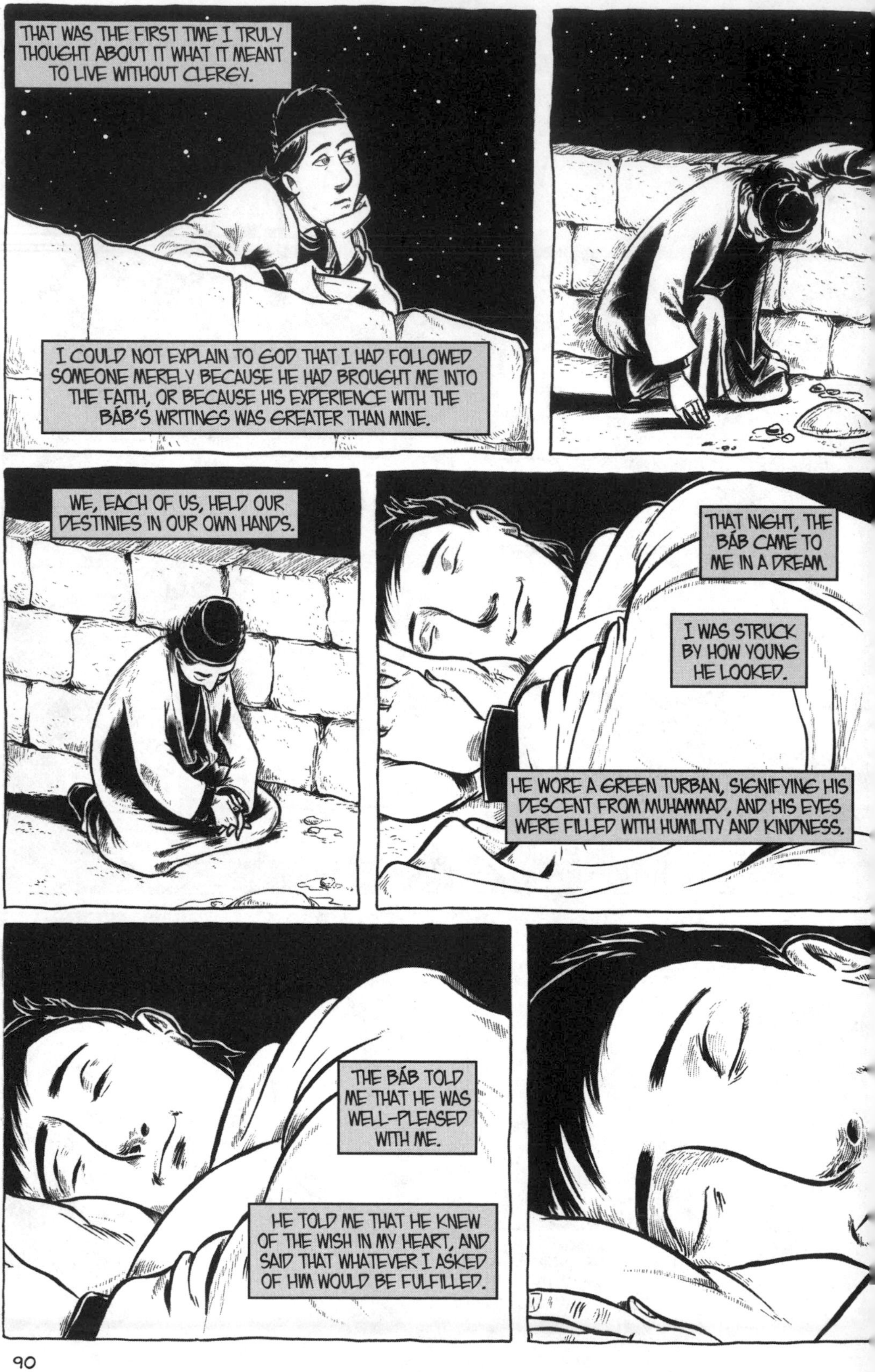
THAT WAS THE FIRST TIME I TRULY THOUGHT ABOUT IT WHAT IT MEANT TO LIVE WITHOUT CLERGY.
I COULD NOT EXPLAIN TO GOD THAT I HAD FOLLOWED SOMEONE MERELY BECAUSE HE HAD BROUGHT ME INTO THE FAITH, OR BECAUSE HIS EXPERIENCE WITH THE BÁB'S WRITINGS WAS GREATER THAN MINE.
WE, EACH OF US, HELD OUR DESTINIES IN OUR OWN HANDS.
THAT NIGHT, THE BÁB CAME TO ME IN A DREAM.
I WAS STRUCK BY HOW YOUNG HE LOOKED.
HE WORE A GREEN TURBAN, SIGNIFYING HIS DESCENT FROM MUHAMMAD, AND HIS EYES WERE FILLED WITH HUMILITY AND KINDNESS.
THE BÁB TOLD ME THAT HE WAS WELL-PLEASED WITH ME.
HE TOLD ME THAT HE KNEW OF THE WISH IN MY HEART, AND SAID THAT WHATEVER I ASKED OF HIM WOULD BE FULFILLED.

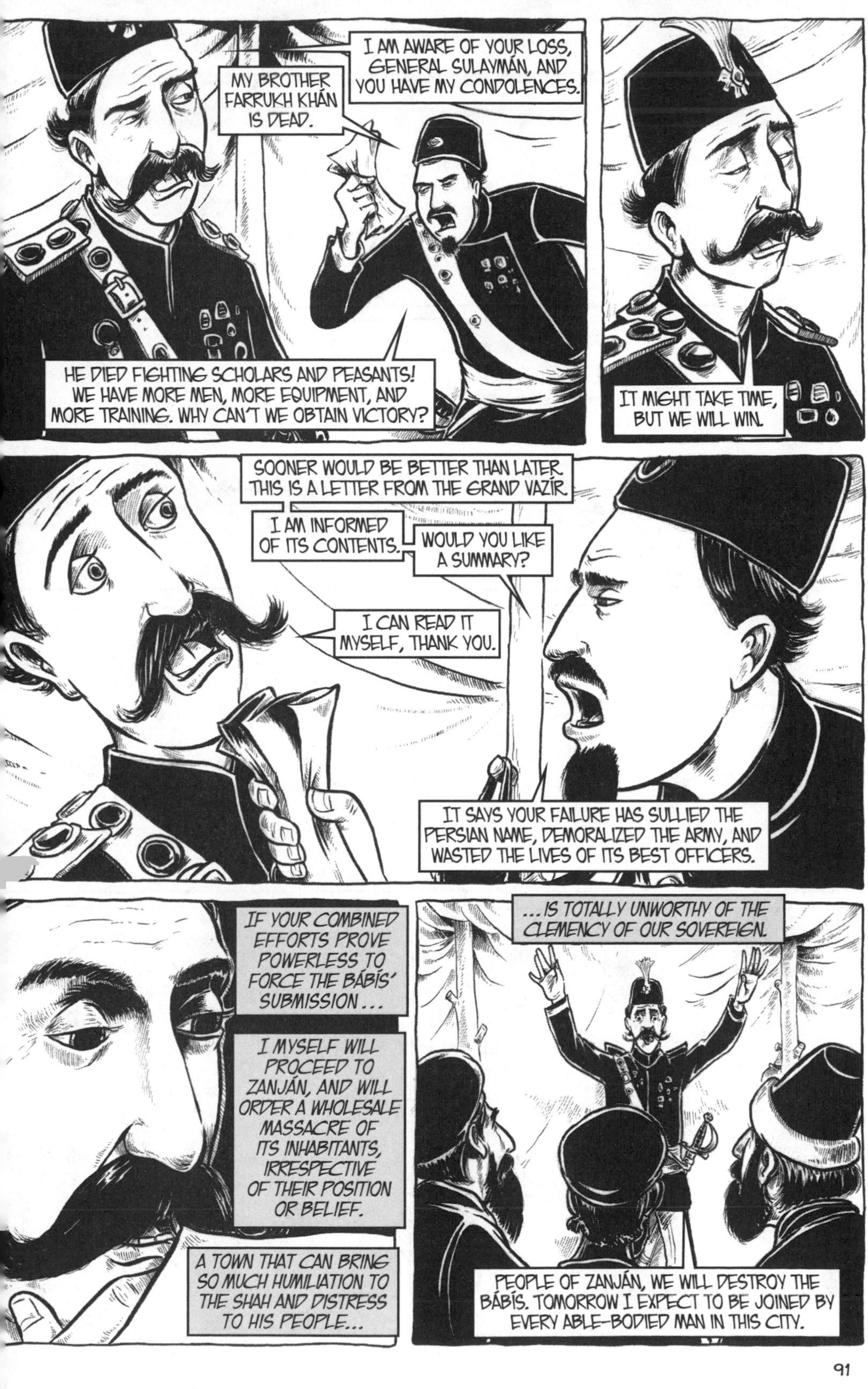

MY BROTHER FARRUKH KHÁN IS DEAD.
I AM AWARE OF YOUR LOSS, GENERAL SULAYMÁN, AND YOU HAVE MY CONDOLENCES.
HE DIED FIGHTING SCHOLARS AND PEASANTS! WE HAVE MORE MEN, MORE EQUIPMENT, AND MORE TRAINING. WHY CAN'T WE OBTAIN VICTORY?
IT MIGHT TAKE TIME, BUT WE WILL WIN.
SOONER WOULD BE BETTER THAN LATER. THIS IS A LETTER FROM THE GRAND VAZÍR.
I AM INFORMED OF ITS CONTENTS.
WOULD YOU LIKE A SUMMARY?
I CAN READ IT MYSELF, THANK YOU.
IT SAYS YOUR FAILURE HAS SULLIED THE PERSIAN NAME, DEMORALIZED THE ARMY, AND WASTED THE LIVES OF ITS BEST OFFICERS.
IF YOUR COMBINED EFFORTS PROVE POWERLESS TO FORCE THE BÁBÍS' SUBMISSION...
I MYSELF WILL PROCEED TO ZANJÁN, AND WILL ORDER A WHOLESALE MASSACRE OF ITS INHABITANTS, IRRESPECTIVE OF THEIR POSITION OR BELIEF.
A TOWN THAT CAN BRING SO MUCH HUMILIATION TO THE SHAH AND DISTRESS TO HIS PEOPLE...
...IS TOTALLY UNWORTHY OF THE CLEMENCY OF OUR SOVEREIGN.
PEOPLE OF ZANJÁN, WE WILL DESTROY THE BÁBÍS. TOMORROW I EXPECT TO BE JOINED BY EVERY ABLE-BODIED MAN IN THIS CITY.

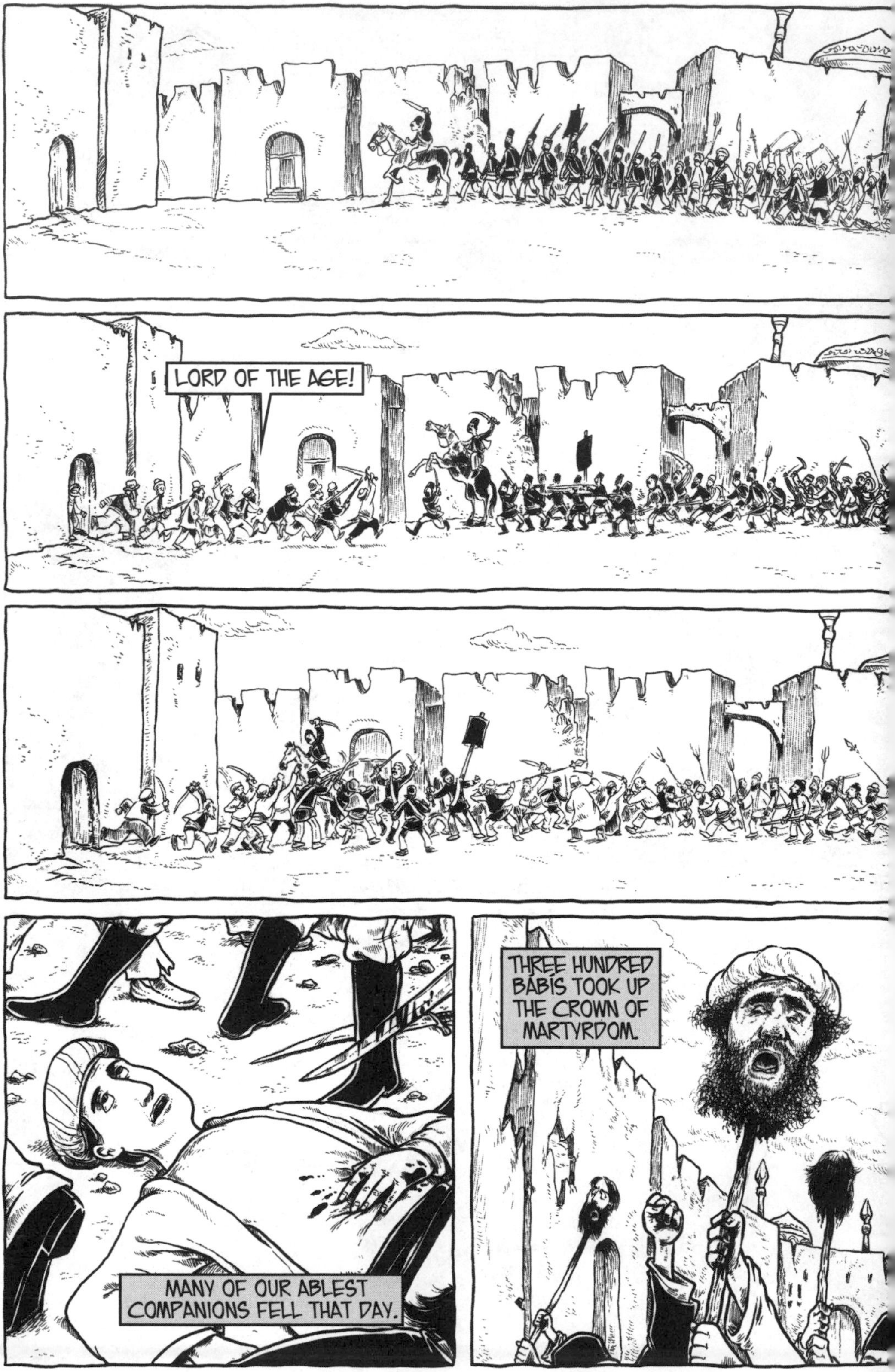

LORD OF THE AGE!
MANY OF OUR ABLEST COMPANIONS FELL THAT DAY.
THREE HUNDRED BÁBÍS TOOK UP THE CROWN OF MARTYRDOM.

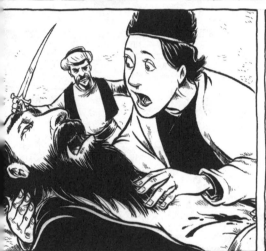

I AM CERTAIN WE ACHIEVED VICTORY THAT DAY BECAUSE OF THE WOMEN.

REMEMBERING ZAYNAB, SEVERAL WOMEN SEIZED SWORDS AND JOINED US.

THEIR VOICES, EXHORTING US ONWARD, RENEWED OUR SPIRITS.

OTHERS BROUGHT US WATER AND TENDED TO THE WOUNDED.

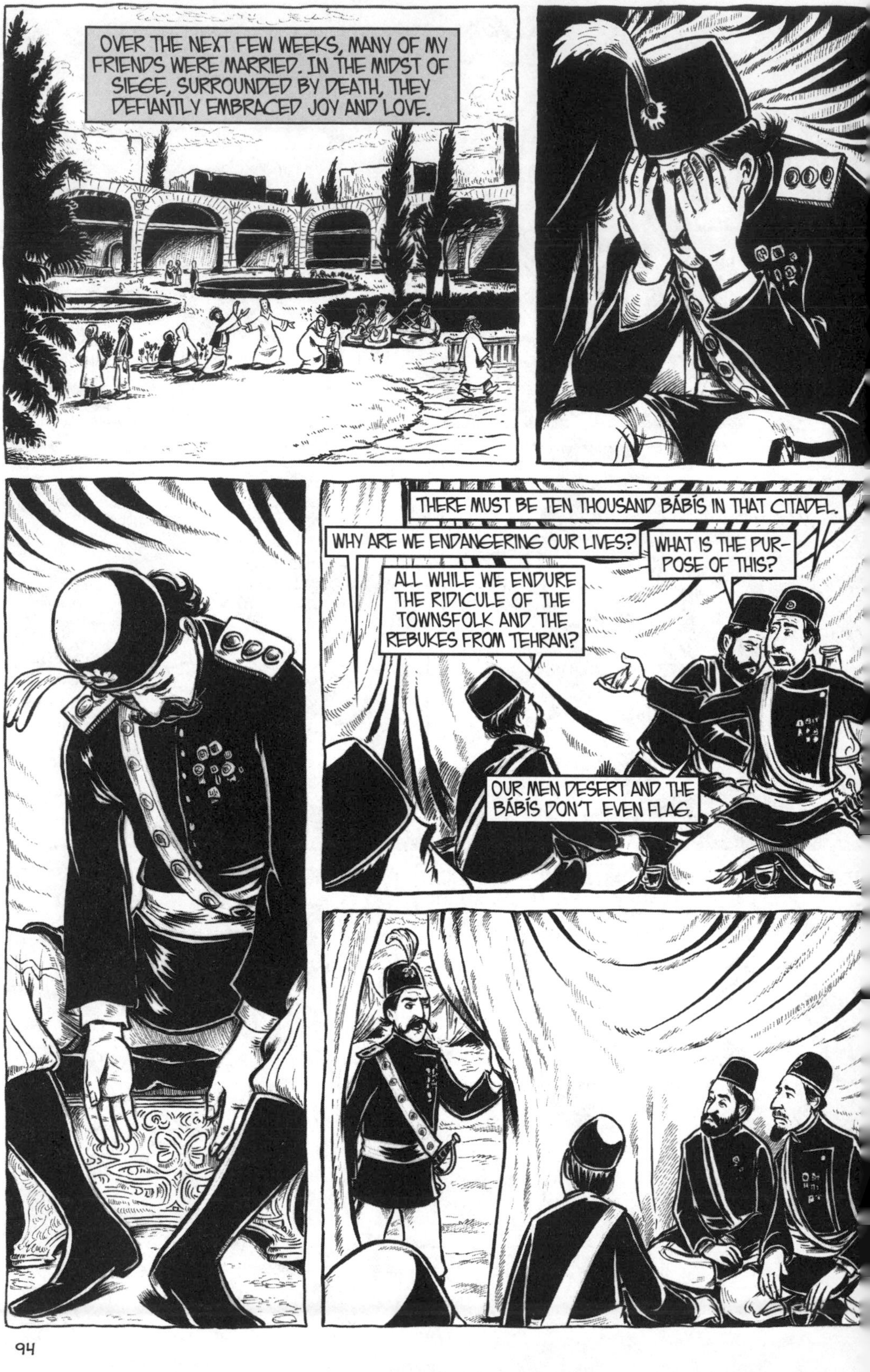
OVER THE NEXT FEW WEEKS, MANY OF MY FRIENDS WERE MARRIED. IN THE MIDST OF SIEGE, SURROUNDED BY DEATH, THEY DEFIANTLY EMBRACED JOY AND LOVE.
THERE MUST BE TEN THOUSAND BÁBÍS IN THAT CITADEL.
WHY ARE WE ENDANGERING OUR LIVES?
WHAT IS THE PURPOSE OF THIS?
ALL WHILE WE ENDURE THE RIDICULE OF THE TOWNSFOLK AND THE REBUKES FROM TEHRAN?
OUR MEN DESERT AND THE BÁBÍS DON'T EVEN FLAG.

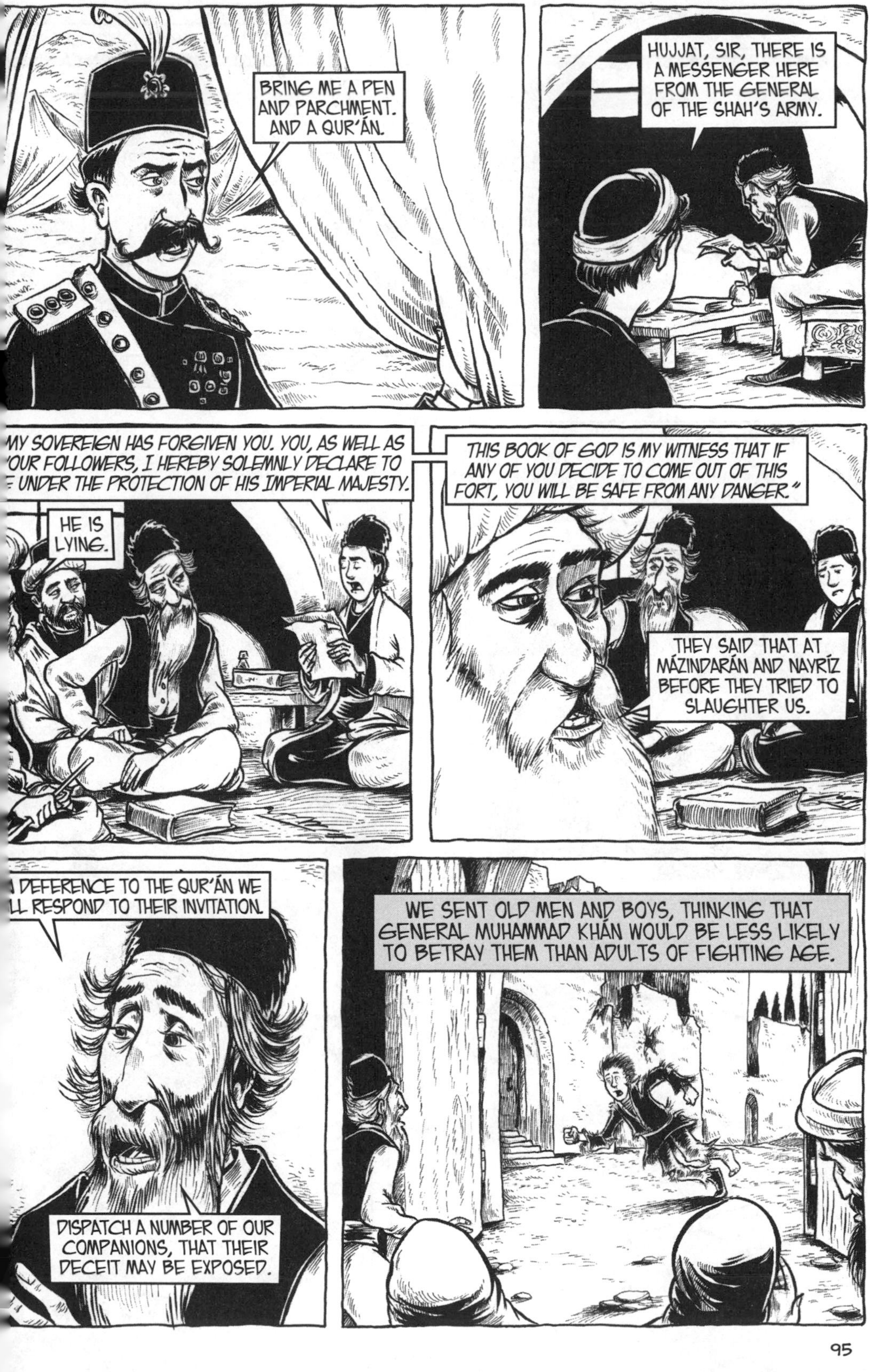
BRING ME A PEN AND PARCHMENT. AND A QUR'ÁN.
HUJJAT, SIR, THERE IS A MESSENGER HERE FROM THE GENERAL OF THE SHAH'S ARMY.
MY SOVEREIGN HAS FORGIVEN YOU. YOU, AS WELL AS OUR FOLLOWERS, I HEREBY SOLEMNLY DECLARE TO UNDER THE PROTECTION OF HIS IMPERIAL MAJESTY.
THIS BOOK OF GOD IS MY WITNESS THAT IF ANY OF YOU DECIDE TO COME OUT OF THIS FORT, YOU WILL BE SAFE FROM ANY DANGER."
HE IS LYING.
THEY SAID THAT AT MÁZINDARÁN AND NAYRÍZ BEFORE THEY TRIED TO SLAUGHTER US.
DEFERENCE TO THE QUR'ÁN WE LL RESPOND TO THEIR INVITATION.
DISPATCH A NUMBER OF OUR COMPANIONS, THAT THEIR DECEIT MAY BE EXPOSED.
WE SENT OLD MEN AND BOYS, THINKING THAT GENERAL MUHAMMAD KHÁN WOULD BE LESS LIKELY TO BETRAY THEM THAN ADULTS OF FIGHTING AGE.

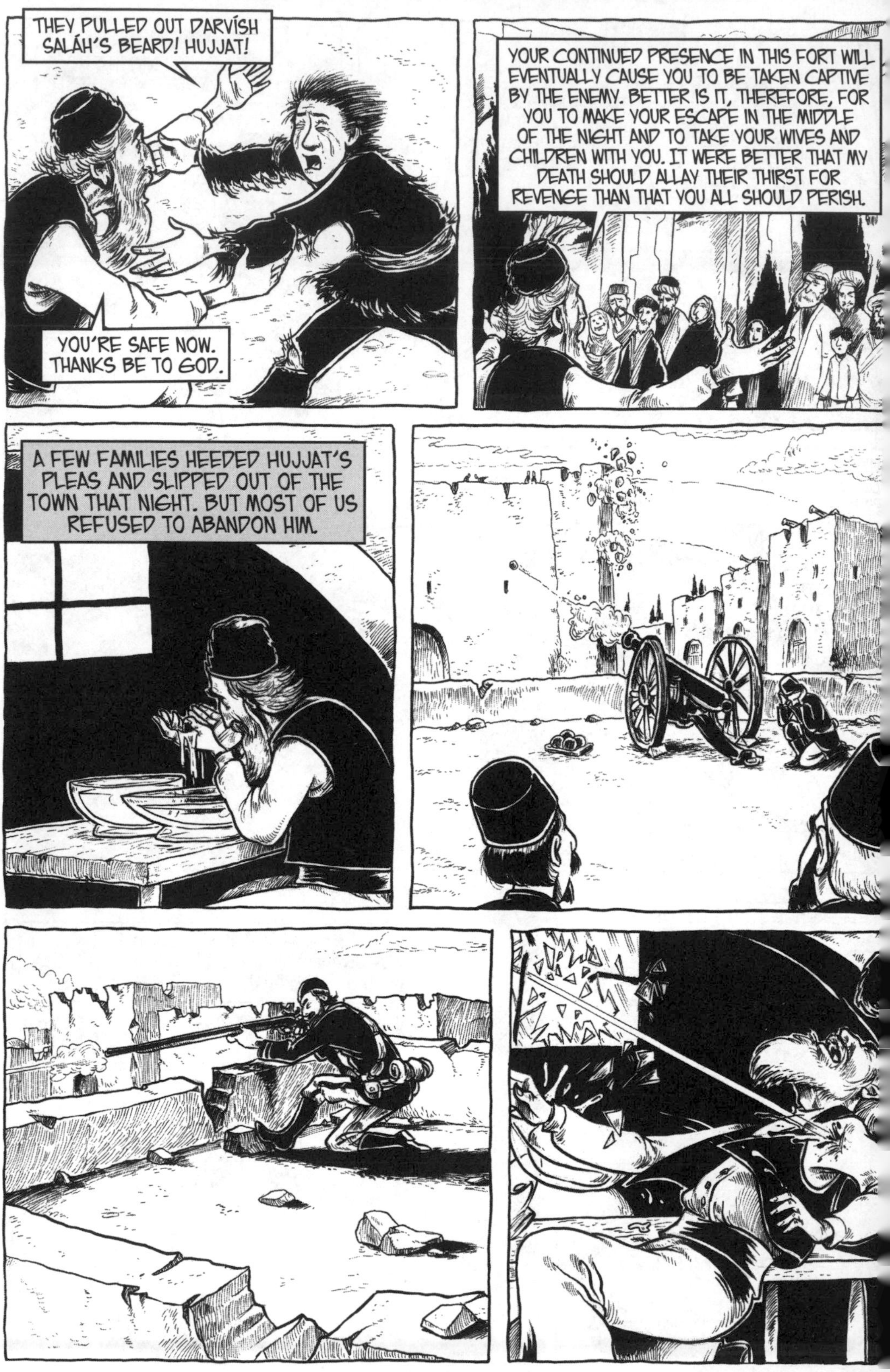
THEY PULLED OUT DARVÍSH SALÁH'S BEARD! HUJJAT!
YOU'RE SAFE NOW. THANKS BE TO GOD.
YOUR CONTINUED PRESENCE IN THIS FORT WILL EVENTUALLY CAUSE YOU TO BE TAKEN CAPTIVE BY THE ENEMY. BETTER IS IT, THEREFORE, FOR YOU TO MAKE YOUR ESCAPE IN THE MIDDLE OF THE NIGHT AND TO TAKE YOUR WIVES AND CHILDREN WITH YOU. IT WERE BETTER THAT MY DEATH SHOULD ALLAY THEIR THIRST FOR REVENGE THAN THAT YOU ALL SHOULD PERISH.
A FEW FAMILIES HEEDED HUJJAT'S PLEAS AND SLIPPED OUT OF THE TOWN THAT NIGHT. BUT MOST OF US REFUSED TO ABANDON HIM.

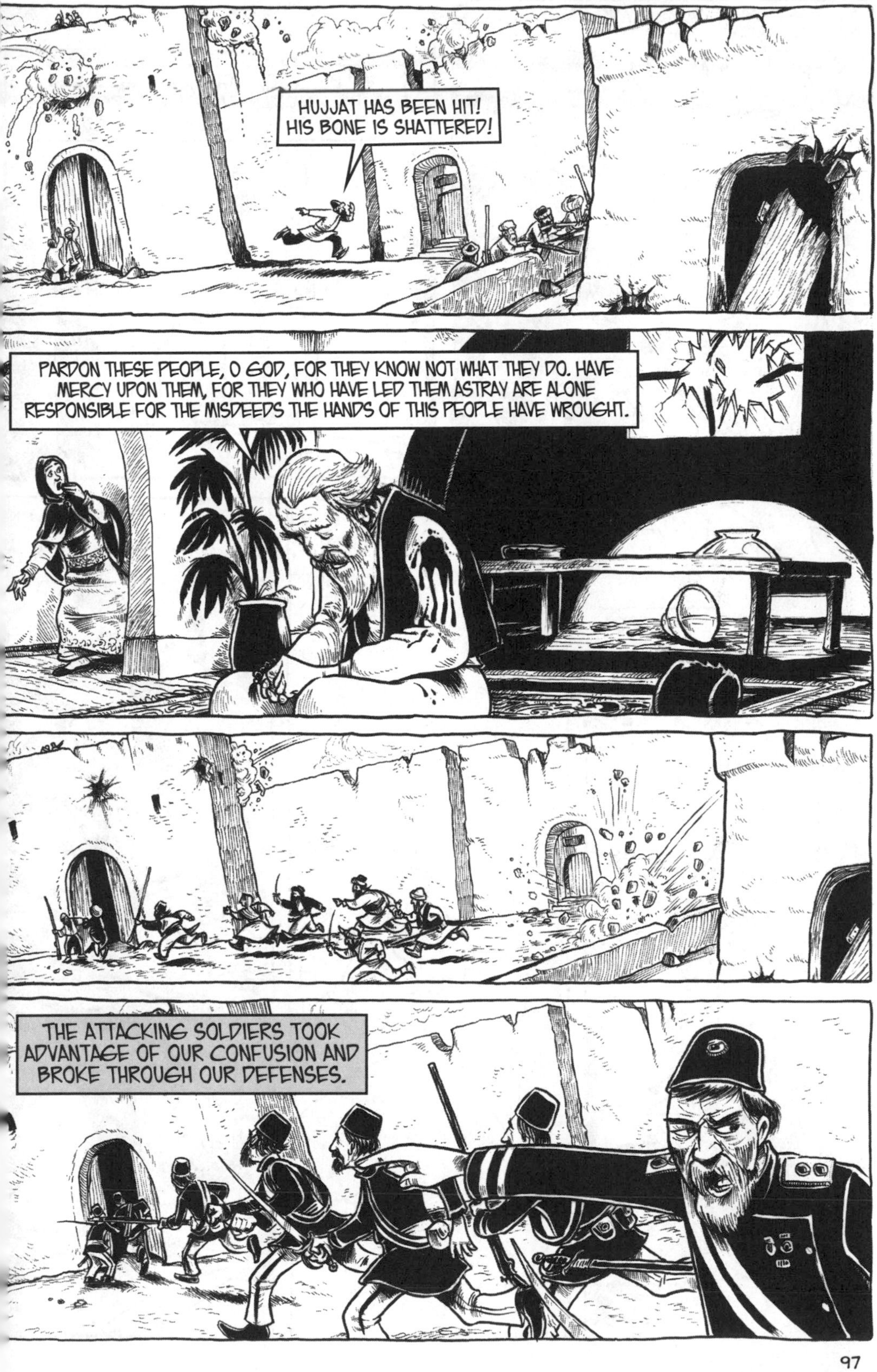

HUJJAT HAS BEEN HIT! HIS BONE IS SHATTERED!
PARDON THESE PEOPLE, O GOD, FOR THEY KNOW NOT WHAT THEY DO. HAVE MERCY UPON THEM, FOR THEY WHO HAVE LED THEM ASTRAY ARE ALONE RESPONSIBLE FOR THE MISDEEDS THE HANDS OF THIS PEOPLE HAVE WROUGHT.
THE ATTACKING SOLDIERS TOOK ADVANTAGE OF OUR CONFUSION AND BROKE THROUGH OUR DEFENSES.

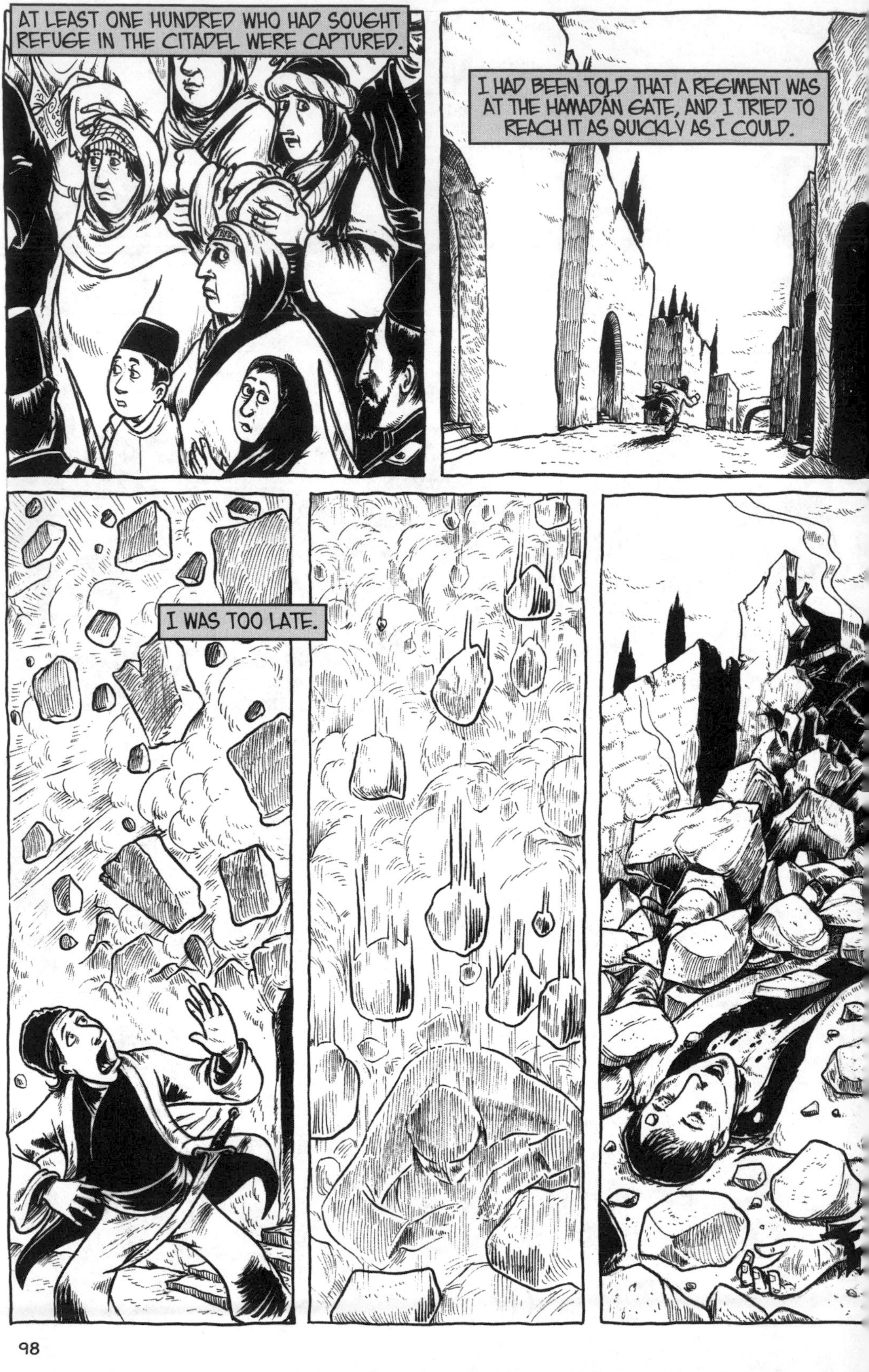
AT LEAST ONE HUNDRED WHO HAD SOUGHT REFUGE IN THE CITADEL WERE CAPTURED.
I HAD BEEN TOLD THAT A REGIMENT WAS AT THE HAMADÁN GATE, AND I TRIED TO REACH IT AS QUICKLY AS I COULD.
I WAS TOO LATE.

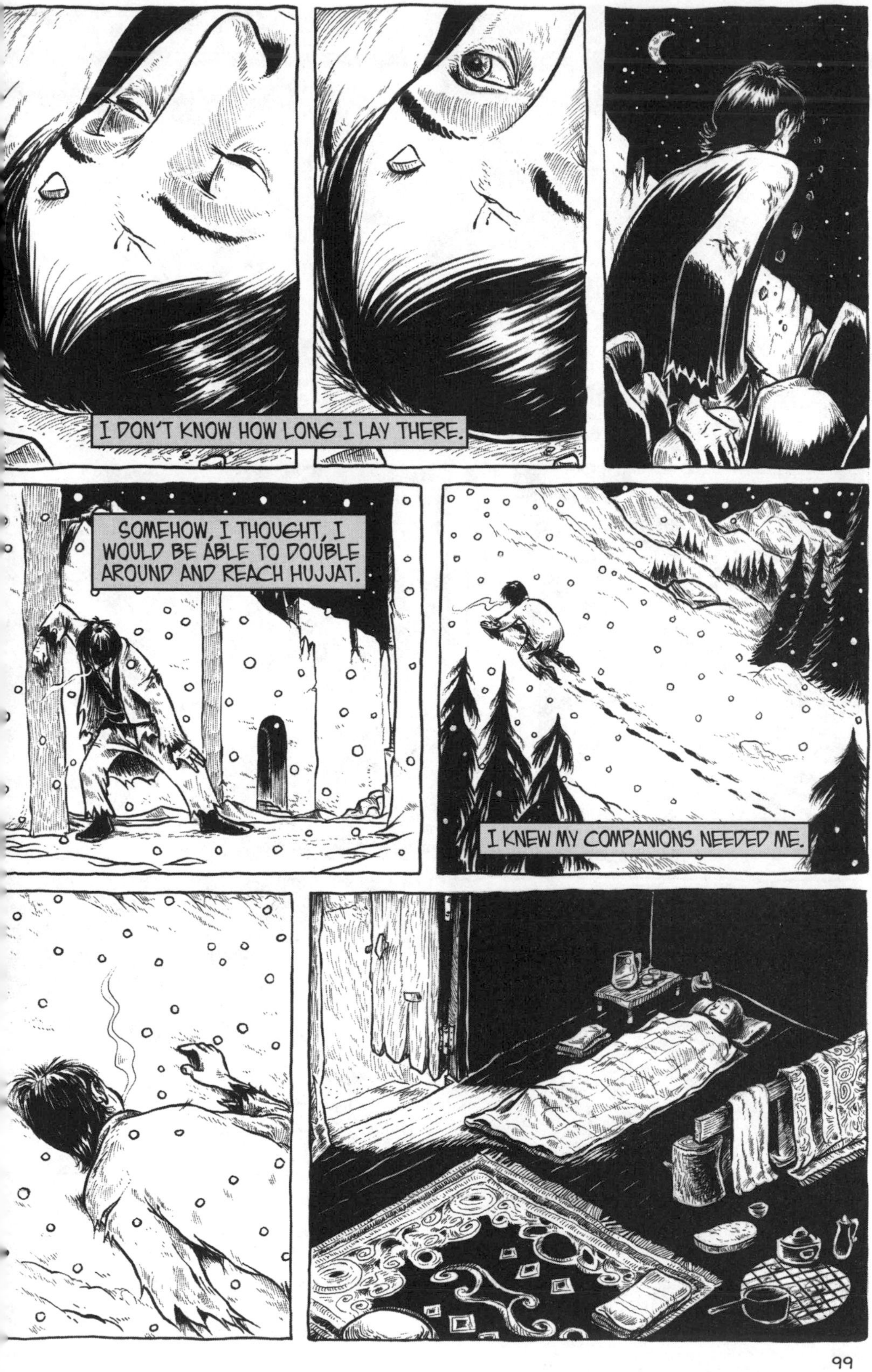
I DON'T KNOW HOW LONG I LAY THERE.
SOMEHOW, I THOUGHT, I WOULD BE ABLE TO DOUBLE AROUND AND REACH HUJJAT.
I KNEW MY COMPANIONS NEEDED ME.

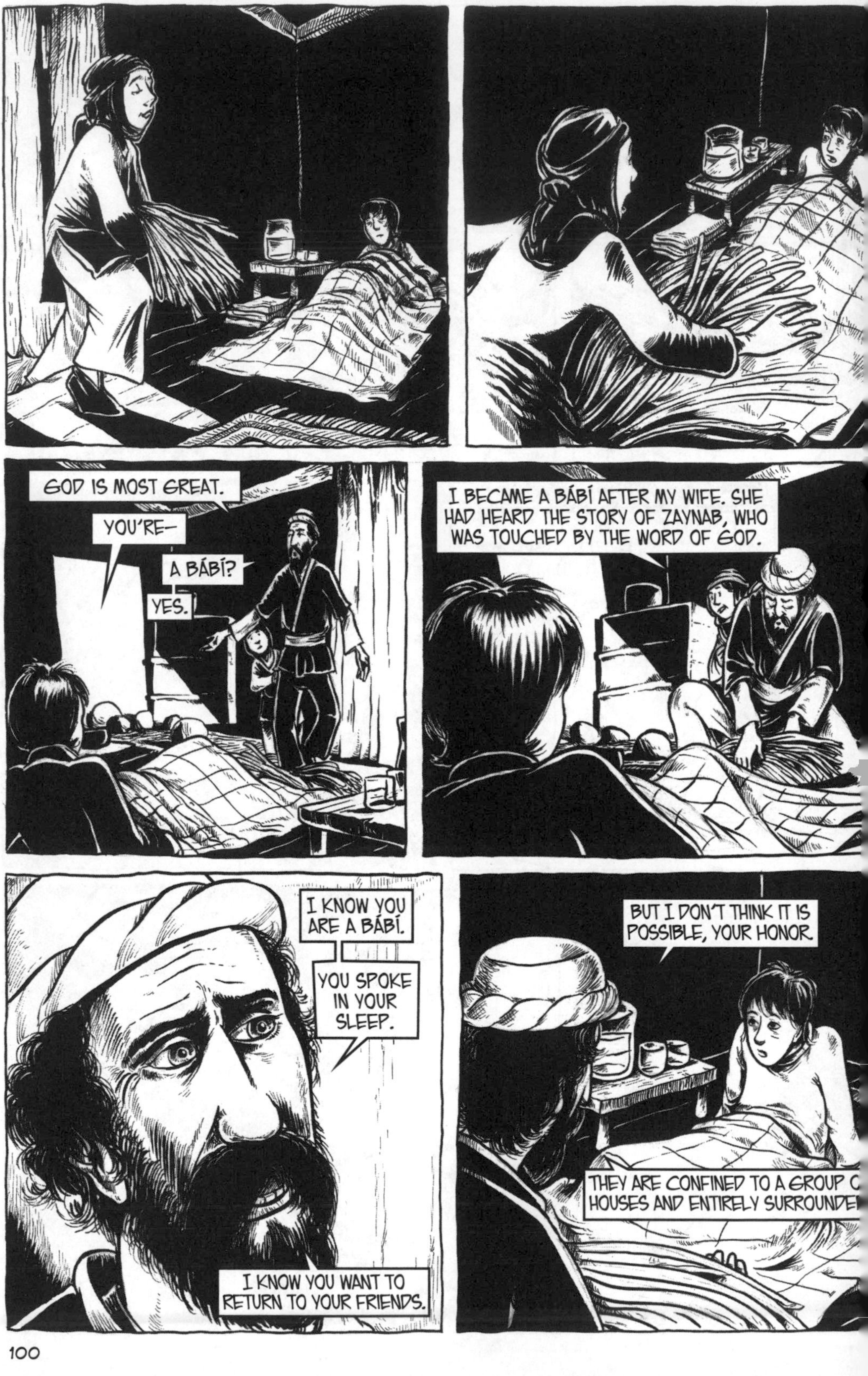
GOD IS MOST GREAT.
YOU'RE–
A BÁBÍ?
YES.
I BECAME A BÁBÍ AFTER MY WIFE. SHE HAD HEARD THE STORY OF ZAYNAB, WHO WAS TOUCHED BY THE WORD OF GOD.
I KNOW YOU ARE A BÁBÍ.
YOU SPOKE IN YOUR SLEEP.
I KNOW YOU WANT TO RETURN TO YOUR FRIENDS.
BUT I DON'T THINK IT IS POSSIBLE, YOUR HONOR.
THEY ARE CONFINED TO A GROUP O
HOUSES AND ENTIRELY SURROUNDE

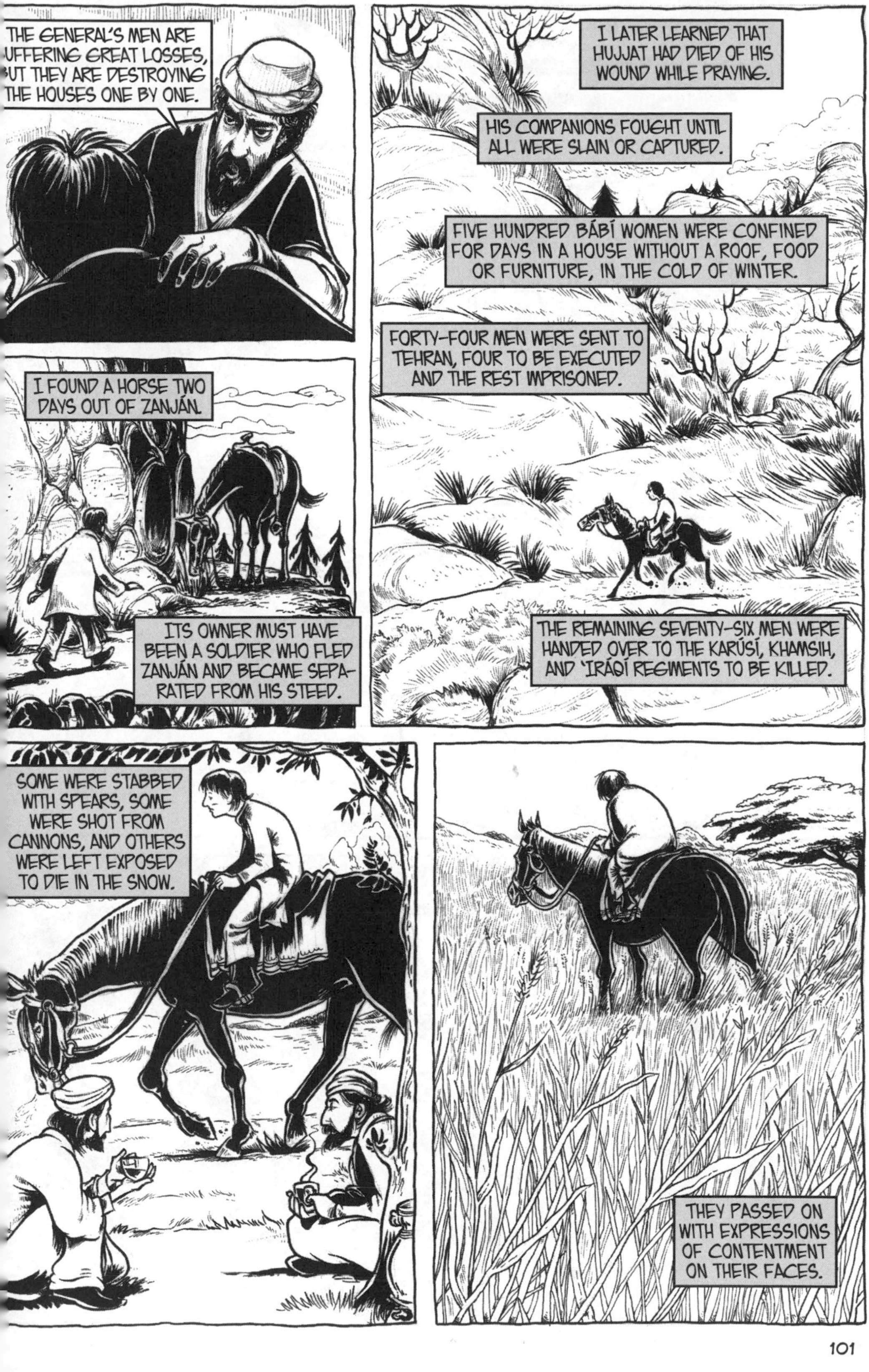
THE GENERAL'S MEN ARE SUFFERING GREAT LOSSES, BUT THEY ARE DESTROYING THE HOUSES ONE BY ONE.
I LATER LEARNED THAT HUJJAT HAD DIED OF HIS WOUND WHILE PRAYING.
HIS COMPANIONS FOUGHT UNTIL ALL WERE SLAIN OR CAPTURED.
FIVE HUNDRED BÁBÍ WOMEN WERE CONFINED FOR DAYS IN A HOUSE WITHOUT A ROOF, FOOD OR FURNITURE, IN THE COLD OF WINTER.
FORTY-FOUR MEN WERE SENT TO TEHRAN, FOUR TO BE EXECUTED AND THE REST IMPRISONED.
I FOUND A HORSE TWO DAYS OUT OF ZANJÁN.
ITS OWNER MUST HAVE BEEN A SOLDIER WHO FLED ZANJÁN AND BECAME SEPA-RATED FROM HIS STEED.
THE REMAINING SEVENTY-SIX MEN WERE HANDED OVER TO THE KARÚSÍ, KHAMSIH, AND 'IRÁQÍ REGIMENTS TO BE KILLED.
SOME WERE STABBED WITH SPEARS, SOME WERE SHOT FROM CANNONS, AND OTHERS WERE LEFT EXPOSED TO DIE IN THE SNOW.
THEY PASSED ON WITH EXPRESSIONS OF CONTENTMENT ON THEIR FACES.

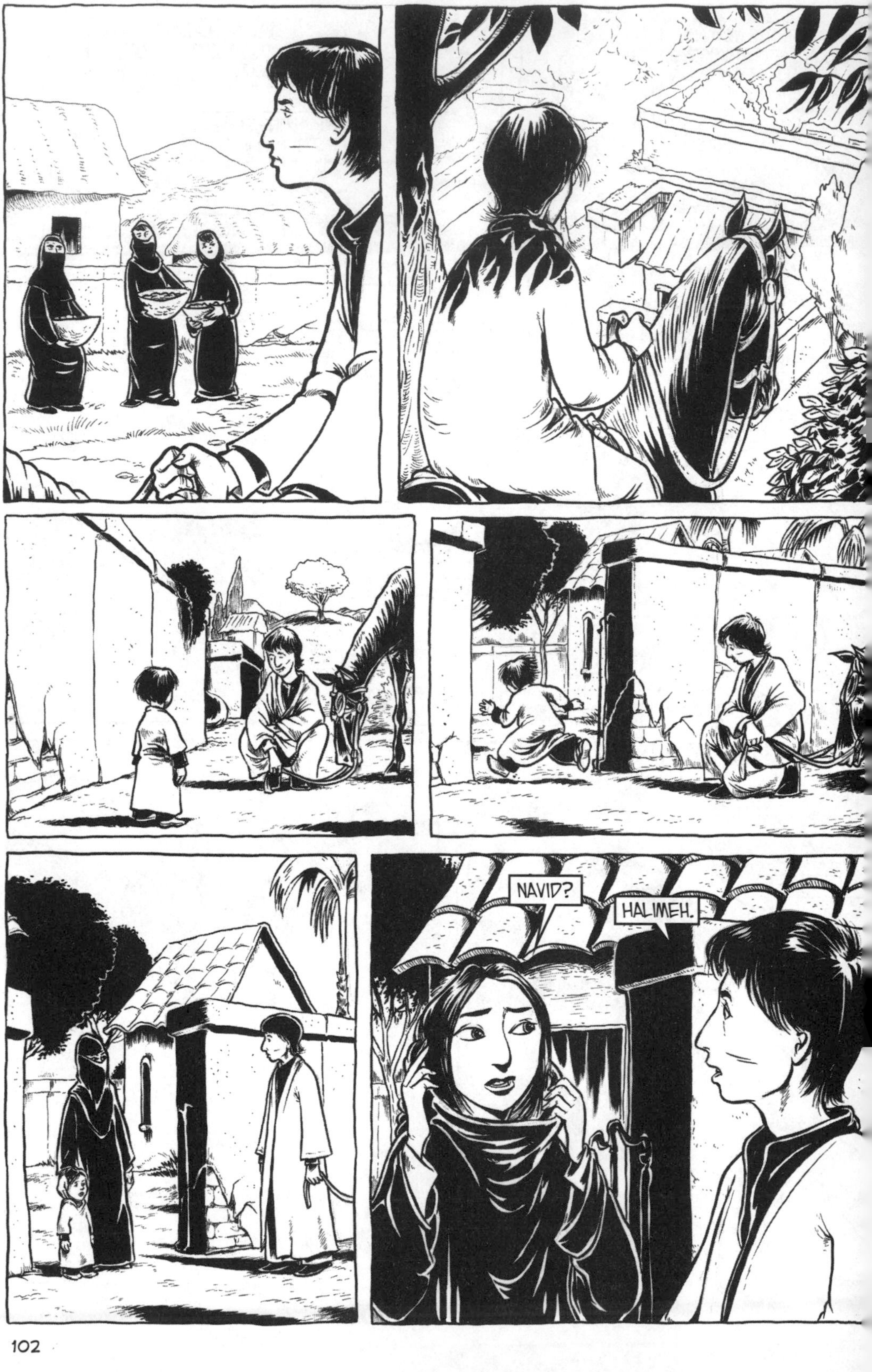
NAVID?
HALIMEH.

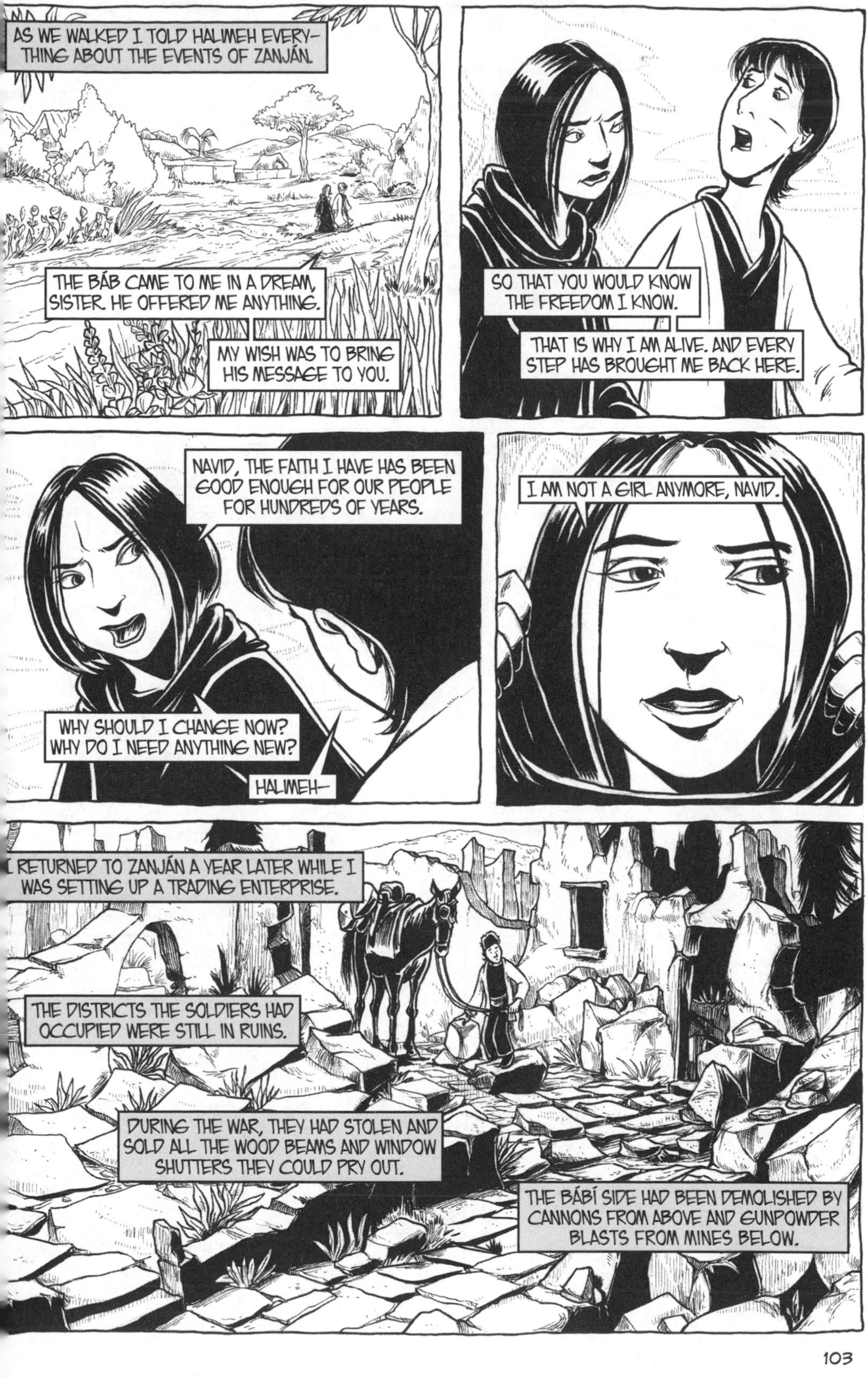
AS WE WALKED I TOLD HALIMEH EVERYTHING ABOUT THE EVENTS OF ZANJÁN.
THE BÁB CAME TO ME IN A DREAM, SISTER. HE OFFERED ME ANYTHING.
MY WISH WAS TO BRING HIS MESSAGE TO YOU.
SO THAT YOU WOULD KNOW THE FREEDOM I KNOW.
THAT IS WHY I AM ALIVE. AND EVERY STEP HAS BROUGHT ME BACK HERE.
NAVID, THE FAITH I HAVE HAS BEEN GOOD ENOUGH FOR OUR PEOPLE FOR HUNDREDS OF YEARS.
WHY SHOULD I CHANGE NOW? WHY DO I NEED ANYTHING NEW?
HALIMEH-
I AM NOT A GIRL ANYMORE, NAVID.
I RETURNED TO ZANJÁN A YEAR LATER WHILE I WAS SETTING UP A TRADING ENTERPRISE.
THE DISTRICTS THE SOLDIERS HAD OCCUPIED WERE STILL IN RUINS.
DURING THE WAR, THEY HAD STOLEN AND SOLD ALL THE WOOD BEAMS AND WINDOW SHUTTERS THEY COULD PRY OUT.
THE BÁBÍ SIDE HAD BEEN DEMOLISHED BY CANNONS FROM ABOVE AND GUNPOWDER BLASTS FROM MINES BELOW.

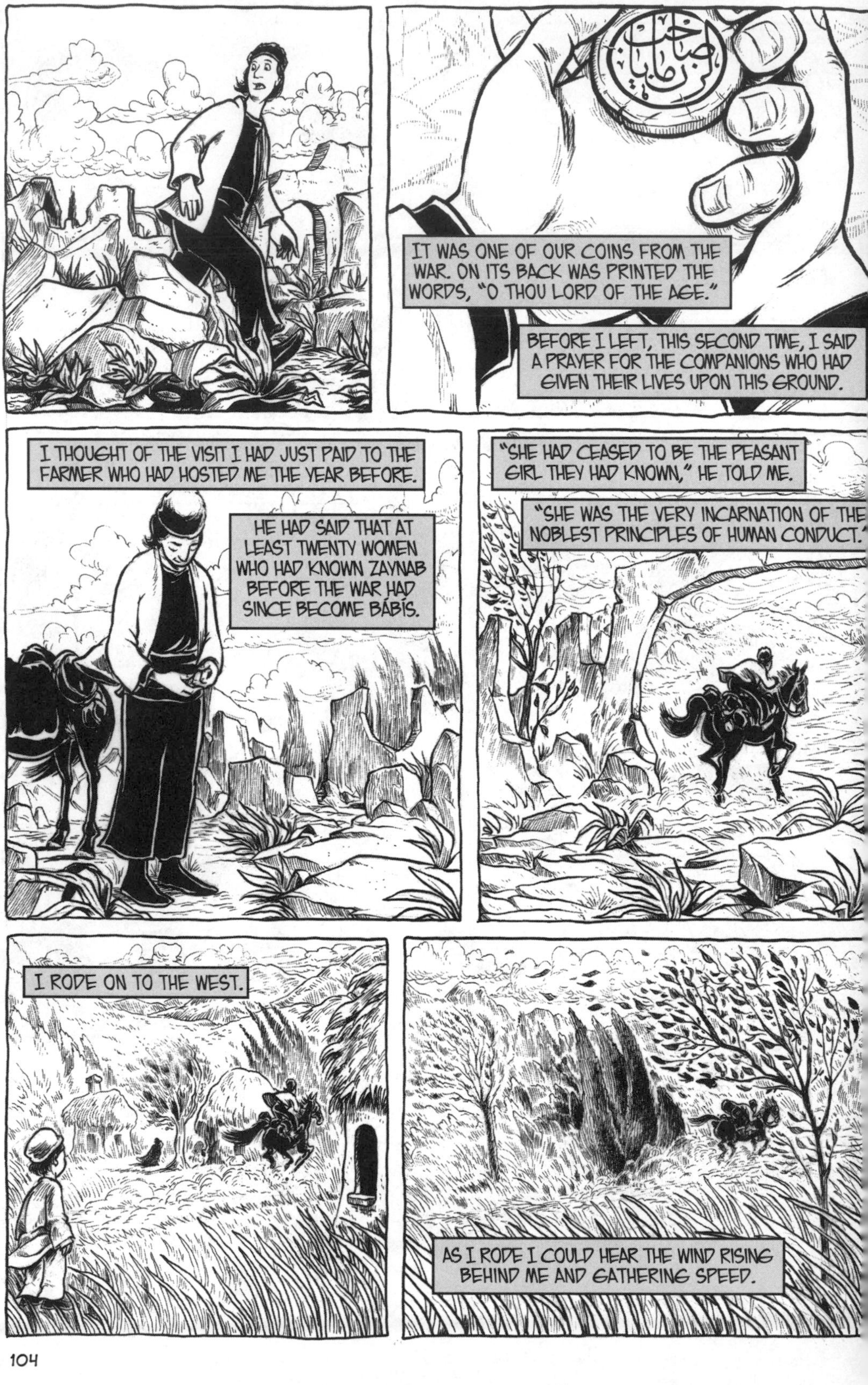
IT WAS ONE OF OUR COINS FROM THE WAR. ON ITS BACK WAS PRINTED THE WORDS, "O THOU LORD OF THE AGE."
BEFORE I LEFT, THIS SECOND TIME, I SAID A PRAYER FOR THE COMPANIONS WHO HAD GIVEN THEIR LIVES UPON THIS GROUND.
I THOUGHT OF THE VISIT I HAD JUST PAID TO THE FARMER WHO HAD HOSTED ME THE YEAR BEFORE.
HE HAD SAID THAT AT LEAST TWENTY WOMEN WHO HAD KNOWN ZAYNAB BEFORE THE WAR HAD SINCE BECOME BÁBÍS.
"SHE HAD CEASED TO BE THE PEASANT GIRL THEY HAD KNOWN," HE TOLD ME.
"SHE WAS THE VERY INCARNATION OF THE NOBLEST PRINCIPLES OF HUMAN CONDUCT."
I RODE ON TO THE WEST.
AS I RODE I COULD HEAR THE WIND RISING BEHIND ME AND GATHERING SPEED.

END

Aaron Emmel has edited and written for books, magazines, newspapers, and websites. He lives with his wife in Maryland, where he oversees U.S. advocacy and policy for a global health and development organization. Formerly, he ran an internationally distributed record label, served as the assistant director of the U.S. Bahá'í Refugee Office, and represented the U.S. Bahá'í Office of External Affairs as human rights officer. He is the author of *Taking Action in a Changing World*, a handbook for positive social change. Visit him online at www.aaronemmel.com.

C. Aaron Kreader is a member of the Bahá'í Faith. He works as a staff illustrator and graphic designer for the *Brilliant Star* magazine. He has received numerous awards for his illustration and design in magazines, picture books, and games. He and his wife live in Illinois and run Studio 9 Inc. To view Aaron's work, visit www.studio9inc.com.

Bahá'í
PUBLISHING

Bahá'í Publishing produces books based on the teachings of the Bahá'í Faith. Founded over 160 years ago, the Bahá'í Faith is among the fastest growing world religions. It has spread to some 235 nations and territories and is now accepted by more than five million people. Bahá'ís believe that there is essentially only one religion and that all the Messengers of God—such as Abraham, Zoroaster, Moses, Krishna, Buddha, Jesus, and Muhammad—have progressively revealed its nature. Bahá'í Publishing is the principle source of trade paper books in the U.S. about the Bahá'í Faith and its teachings, history, and perspectives on a broad range of social and economic issues.

Recommended Reading on Bahá'í History

Release the Sun by William Sears • Trade Paper
ISBN 978-1-931847-09-4
A captivating account of the emergence of the Bábí Faith
in mid-nineteenth century Persia.

**The Story of Bahá'u'lláh: Promised One of All
Religions** by Druzelle Cederquist • Trade Paper
ISBN 978-1-931847-13-1
Brings to life in rich detail the compelling story of the
Prophet and Founder of the Bahá'í Faith.

**God Speaks Again: An Introduction to the Bahá'í
Faith** by Kenneth E. Bowers • Trade Paper
ISBN 978-1-931847-12-4
A comprehensive introduction to the Bahá'í Faith that
places the life of its Founder at its center.

Rejoice in My Gladness: The Life of Táhirih
by Janet Ruhe-Schoen • Trade Paper
ISBN 978-1-931847-84-1
The definitive biography of the renowned nineteenth-
century poetess and early heroine of the Bábí Faith.